ADOPTION BEYOND BORDERS

We were the people who were not in the papers. We lived in the blank white spaces at the edges of print. It gave us more freedom. We lived in the gaps between the stories.
—Margaret Atwood, *The Handmaid's Tale*[1]

Some people meet the way the sky meets the earth, inevitably, and there is no stopping or holding back their love.
—Louise Erdrich, *Tales of Burning Love*[2]

Adoption Beyond Borders

*How International Adoption
Benefits Children*

Rebecca J. Compton

OXFORD
UNIVERSITY PRESS

OXFORD

UNIVERSITY PRESS

Oxford University Press is a department of the University of Oxford. It furthers
the University's objective of excellence in research, scholarship, and education
by publishing worldwide. Oxford is a registered trade mark of Oxford University
Press in the UK and certain other countries.

Published in the United States of America by Oxford University Press
198 Madison Avenue, New York, NY 10016, United States of America.

© Oxford University Press 2016

First Edition published in 2016

First issued as an Oxford University Press paperback, 2018

Library of Congress Cataloging-in-Publication Data
Compton, Rebecca J. (Rebecca Jean), author.
Adoption beyond borders : how international adoption benefits children/
Rebecca J. Compton
   pages cm
Includes index.
ISBN 978-0-19-024779-9 (hardcover); 978-0-19-091481-3 (paperback)
1. Intercountry adoption.   I. Title.
HV875.5.C636 2016
362.734—dc23
2015031415

For Nurbolat and all the others still there

CONTENTS ■

ACKNOWLEDGMENTS ▪

My deepest gratitude extends to many people for their roles in making this book possible. For believing in the worth of the project and getting the book into print, I am most deeply indebted to editor Joan Bossert and her team at Oxford. I also gratefully appreciate the matchmaking assistance of agent Cecelia Cancellaro at Idea Architects.

I am thankful for research assistance from Bryn Bissey, Hanaan Bing-Canar, Ellen Reinhart, Sharoda Worby-Selim, and Rob Haley and the Haverford interlibrary loan office. For scholarly support, advice, and accommodation, I humbly thank Haverford College then-provost Kim Benston and faculty colleagues Jen Lilgendahl, Ben Le, Marilyn Boltz, Shu-wen Wang, Wendy Sternberg, Doug Davis, and Sid Perloe. Debra Zeifman and Matthew Budman both supported the project when it was just a twinkle in my eye. Diane Kunz provided helpful comments on the entire manuscript and words of encouragement at just the right moments.

For inspiration and camaraderie during the long, dark days, I am extraordinarily grateful to Mary Colasurdo, Fil Casacalenda, Jean-François Lefier, Anick Maranda, Wendy and Shane Sterk, Marcia and Randy Newton, Nathalie Marquis, Christoph Trachsel, Eric Desjardins, Annie Chao Ying Chen, Amber and Zach Watt, Nathalie Szpak, and Ernie and Katrin Jöhnk. For their love of Kazakhstan and work on behalf of marginalized people there, as well as to their kindness to me, I thank Victoria Charbonneau, Beth Turnock, and their local partners. For nurturing children in Umit and other baby houses throughout Kazakhstan, I thank Nazira, Gulmira, Lyazzat, Aziza, Dariga, Gulnara, Balzhan, and many others. I am deeply grateful to Suzanne Bilyeu for allowing me to share Altynai's story. I thank Clifford Levy for believing that our story was worth telling.

For friendship without borders, I am thankful to Indira Tulebayeva, Eser Yeniceri, Damira Argymbayeva, and Shirina Pulatova, as well as Maryam Nureliyeva and Renat Bekbolatov, who helped prepare me for Kazakhstan. For local assistance, I thank Janetta Jumagulova, Vera Abbassi, and Medetbek Baimenov. Without Oleg Semykin's combination of pessimism, grit, and savvy, our family might never have come to be.

I am grateful for the team of professionals who helped me learn about adoption and navigate its processes and consequences, including Lisa Dillard, Freida Myers, Leonette Boiarski, and Amy Drurie (Pearl S. Buck Welcome House); Wenonah Nelson (Bryn Mawr Pediatrics); Amy Lynch and Rachel Hachen (International Adoption Clinic at Children's Hospital of Philadelphia); and Abigail Janney (University of Delaware Infant Caregiver Project).

I owe an enormous debt of gratitude to Noah Aldanysh's grandparents—Judy and Richard Ellis, David and Cindy Compton, Ellen and Robert Meyer—who each in their own ways made this possible by teaching their children compassion, humility, and stubbornness in the face of injustice. Mom and Dad both read entire drafts of the manuscript and offered suggestions and encouragement. This book could not have been written without the unwavering support of my primary advisors on all matters, my first readers, and my closest confidantes, my husband Jeremy Meyer and my sister Gwendolyn Compton-Engle.

And finally, to the woman and man who brought our son into the world and changed our lives forever, I am eternally grateful and indebted in ways that words cannot begin to express.

PART 1

The Adopted Child: Patterns of Loss and Gain

1 ■
Introduction

Adoption is an ancient practice, both historically and evo-
lutionarily, one that continues to generate fervent debate
and controversy. It involves the most essential of human
relationships, the relationship between parent and child.
What does it mean to be a parent? In what kinds of settings
can or should children be raised, and who should decide?
International adoption in particular is controversial
because it raises complex issues of culture and privilege. It
calls attention to the abysmal circumstances in which
many of the world's people live, circumstances that can
include deep poverty, lack of medical care and social services, unaccountable governments, malnutrition, fractured
families, alcoholism and drug addiction, and even abuse
and neglect. Adoption is controversial because it compels
us to consider our moral obligations to children born into
these circumstances.

Two tragic cases, one highly publicized and one not,
illustrate some of the profound dilemmas surrounding

international adoption. Notoriously, in April 2010, a Tennessee woman put her adopted 7-year-old Russian boy, Artyom, alone on a plane to Moscow, with a note saying that she was unable to handle him and was sending him back to Russia. The incident generated high-profile stories in international news outlets.[1] People on all sides of the adoption debate wondered why the woman was allowed to adopt a child, whether the Russian orphanage had been honest about the status of the boy's medical and psychological condition, whether years of institutionalization had created a child who was difficult to parent, whether the adoptive mother received needed support from local social services, and, most importantly, whether American parents could be trusted to care for needy children adopted from around the world.

On the other side of the world, an equally tragic story unfolded, in the Central Asian country of Kyrgyzstan. This story received virtually no media attention.[2] An orphaned girl there, Altynai, died a preventable death, what we might call "death by bureaucracy." Altynai was matched for adoption by an American family, who met her in July 2008 when she was 3 months old. The prospective adoptive mother was a pediatrician. While awaiting completion of the adoption amidst unexplained bureaucratic delays, she and her husband became concerned over signs that Altynai had developed hydrocephalus, a potentially fatal brain condition. Before the adoption could be completed, Kyrgyzstan abruptly closed its international adoption program, under allegations of corruption. Altynai and 64 other orphans, all of whom had been matched with American families, were stranded in impoverished orphanages while the Kyrgyzstani government struggled to formulate a new system for determining the fate of its unparented children. In April 2010, the government of Kyrgyzstan was toppled and a new government was installed; issues surrounding the international adoption program remained unresolved. In

August 2010, Altynai died at the age of 29 months from a condition that would have been treatable in the United States. She had spent her entire short life in an orphanage and was buried near it.

The implications of Artyom's and Altynai's stories merge together in both conflicting and converging ways. Artyom's story seems a condemnation of international adoption: How could an adoptive parent be so callous as to treat a child as "damaged goods" that could be sent back? Altynai's story seems an indictment of the structures and systems that prevent adoptions: How could bureaucrats be so heartless as to halt an international adoptive placement that would have saved an orphaned child's life? Whatever their differences in circumstance and implication, both stories center on innocent children who were tragically and repeatedly wronged by adults who should have been protecting their best interests.

These stories had special resonance for me because as they unfolded, in 2010, my husband and I were in Kazakhstan, the Central Asian country bordering Russia and Kyrgyzstan, to adopt our son, whose Kazakh name is Aldanysh. When we arrived in Kazakhstan in December 2009, we expected to be in-country for a maximum of 3 months to complete the adoption. Aldanysh was 9 months old at the time and was living in an orphanage, or what is commonly referred to in Kazakhstan as a "baby house."

After we completed a 2-week bonding period and fulfilled all requirements of U.S. and Kazakhstani law, a municipal Kazakhstani judge denied our adoption petition, as well as those of all other foreigners attempting to adopt within that municipality. The judge contended that the orphanage had not done enough to seek possible domestic placements for the children. A lengthy legal battle ensued over the next year, involving indescribably heartbreaking events. In the end, we successfully gained custody of Aldanysh and brought him to the United States in December 2010.[3] During that year, I visited the orphanage nearly every day, and as the months went by, my worldview was radically changed. I observed firsthand the deprivation inherent in even the best institutions for infants and young children, and I learned about the paradoxes, contradictions, and complications surrounding the adoption debate both in Kazakhstan and at home in the United States.

I learned that many people view international adoption with deep suspicion and mistrust. Within my own family and my husband's family, attitudes toward adoption are uniformly positive. Several members of our extended family have been adopted, either domestically or internationally, and others have worked professionally in child welfare or adoption law. For these reasons and others, I understood adoption to be a moral good, a joyous embracing of family regardless of blood connections. However, in the process of adopting my own son, I was to learn that not everyone views it that way. In Kazakhstan, many people believe that foreigners adopt children in order to harvest their organs.[4] Others believe that foreigners "steal" Kazakhstani babies who belong in Kazakhstan—despite the fact that Kazakhstani people resist adopting unrelated children themselves due to deep cultural stigmas associated with infertility, the essential importance of blood and clan ties, and fears about medical problems in a country with poor healthcare. As I read more literature about adoption, I learned that some influential Western intellectuals argue strenuously against international adoption and the people who engage in it—by seeking to adopt an unparented child from another country, I was supposedly enacting Western imperialism and all of the race-, class-, and gender-based violence that characterizes the privileged West's interactions with the developing world.[5]

I also learned that in Kazakhstan in particular, and I believe in other places in the world as well, scientific knowledge about child development plays little to no role in guiding policy about child welfare. Given my professional training as an academic psychologist and neuroscientist, I find this deeply troubling. I remember a telling moment with crystal clarity. A second Kazakhstani court had refused our adoption on appeal and I was consulting with our local adoption advisor about strategies for the next appeal. At that time, I had been visiting Aldanysh daily in the orphanage for approximately 6 months. He was 15 months old and had never experienced the possibility of a bond with a primary caregiver. I asked, "Can we bring in expert witnesses to testify about the importance of attachment for infants?" My Kazakh advisor smiled sadly at my naiveté. "There is no one here in Kazakhstan who is an expert on attachment," she said dismissively. "And even if there was, the judges would not care." I was taken aback. Anyone who has taken Psychology 101 in the last 40 years knows how essential the attachment process is in organizing an infant's world for normal and healthy development. This bedrock principle of developmental psychology was either unknown or completely disregarded in the adoption process in Kazakhstan, despite legal codes that supposedly uphold the "best interest of the child."[6]

My training as a researcher has taught me to examine questions about human well-being by looking at the evidence. For example, how should we evaluate whether particular policies or practices promote the "best interests" of a child? What is actually best for a child? The scientific method requires moving beyond anecdote, emotion, and rhetoric to examine systematic patterns of data. In this book, I have integrated my personal experience with evidence from decades of psychology and neuroscience research on the ways that effective nurturance can be provided to promote healthy development.

The first half of this book summarizes evidence pertaining to the well-being of an unparented child. What is known about the effects of institutionalization or other forms of parental deprivation on children's development? How can we relate such findings to knowledge about the developing brain? In what ways do adopted children still retain the capacity to catch up developmentally? Do they suffer long-term consequences of early deprivation? Are there long-term consequences of adoption itself?

The general picture painted in these chapters is a trajectory of gain following loss. At the time of adoption, internationally adopted children are usually developmentally delayed. They have lost ground. The delays are likely due to an unknown combination of factors such as genetics, poor prenatal nutrition, prenatal exposure to toxic substances, and environmental deprivation between birth and adoption. Delays can cut across the areas of physical growth, motor skills, cognitive skills, and social-emotional development. The extent can vary from child to child, depending on unique family circumstances, duration and severity of deprivation, and child welfare policies and practices in the country of origin.

These initial losses are followed by tremendous gains after adoption. Adopted children's developmental pathways ramp up steeply when they are transferred to settings with adequate nutrition, nurturing, and stimulation. In such settings, the children make up a substantial amount of lost ground. In other words, there is strong evidence that international adoption is a highly successful intervention for children without parental care. Post-adoption gains are particularly striking when children are placed in family homes as early in life as possible.

A pattern of loss and gain also describes the relationship between an internationally adopted child and cultural identity. Critics often accuse international adopters of taking children away from "their culture."[7] I will set aside the biological essentialism implied in this criticism (is culture transmitted via the sperm and egg?) and the romanticizing of cultures that may have poor records of caring for their unparented children. Others have addressed these points.[8] Instead, I focus on research on internationally adopted children. To what extent do they struggle to form cultural identities within their adopted homes and countries? Are their struggles with cultural identity different in nature or severity compared to those of non-adopted children raised in white families, in minority families within a dominant white culture, or in families with biracial or bicultural birth parents? Are the challenges of identity magnified when the adoptive parents are of a different race than that of the child? How can adoptive families best navigate issues of race and cultural identity?

I resist a simplistically rosy conclusion that adoption works because "love is all you need." A realistic look at development in internationally adopted children must acknowledge the losses these children have endured and the ensuing challenges they may carry forth in some way throughout their lives. If the world were fair and just, each newborn child would have the opportunity to thrive without tragedy in the birth family, and adoption would not be necessary. Unfortunately, that is not our world at present. To formulate rational policy, we must ask whether, given the origins and histories of unparented children, international adoption can promote the best interests of such children. Based on research evidence, I believe that the answer is a resounding "yes."

The second half of the book considers research on adoptive families. Both popular commentary and Western academic critiques of international adoption are full of caricatures of adoptive parents.[9] Their motivation is assumed to be a naïve and dangerous desire to "save" or "rescue" children,[10] or, alternatively, they are characterized as "consumers" in a "marketplace" of babies.[11] They are assumed to be culturally insensitive, motivated to deny the existence of the birth family, and uninterested in the welfare of people in the country from which they adopt.[12] They are accused of "outsourcing" the childbearing process to the Third World so that they can work in professional jobs.[13] They are sometimes assumed to choose international adoption because they can't easily get "white babies" in the United States;[14] yet most countries of origin for international adoption (such as China, South Korea, Guatemala, and Ethiopia) are populated primarily with non-white children.[15]

The profile of the adoptive parent in the public's imagination may be driven, unfortunately, by lurid stories presented in the media. We hear of adoptions in which celebrities with loads of money fly into Third-World villages and bring home a child.[16] Or, we hear of "adoptions gone wrong," such as the case of Artyom.[17] These stories paint a picture of adoptive parents as abnormal, not like regular parents. Tragically, a media story about an "adoption gone wrong" can even derail a country's adoption policies, denying a generation of children international family placement.[18]

In my experience, only one stereotype about adoptive parents holds true, and that is that they are tenacious fighters for the rights of "their" children. When they encounter obstacles, adoptive parents will organize, lobby politicians, and do whatever it takes to "bring their children home."[19] This motivation is sometimes misread as entitlement, but I view it as a powerful sense of moral imperative. As many adoptive parents will attest, once you have held a child in your arms, felt the child's vulnerability, and made an emotional commitment to parent that child, you cannot simply turn your back and walk away when obstacles arise. The strength of the adoptive parent's emotional bond with a biologically unrelated child, like the strength of a birth parent's bond with a child, itself raises intriguing questions about the biology and psychology of attachment and parenting.

So, in this section, I return to evidence: What does research tell us about adoptive parenting? Based on theories and evidence in evolutionary biology, is adoption a "natural" form of parenting? Where does the instinct or desire to parent come from? Does it come from having contributed a sperm or egg, does it come from gestating a child, does it come from exposure to a child, does it come from a sociocultural context that supports childrearing? In what ways do adoptive families differ from non-adoptive families? What evidence pertains to the suitability of "non-traditional" adoptive families, such as single people or gay and lesbian couples? This section of the book concludes with evidence about parenting interventions that may help adoptive parents (or any parents, for that matter) navigate the challenges of parenting in ways that best allow their children to thrive.

In the concluding chapter, I argue that research about adopted children and families must be part of the policy debate surrounding international adoption. At heart, the debate should be about what is best for children who have no parents to care for them. We must address this question empirically—that is, through evidence. An appreciation for the substantial evidence supporting the effectiveness of international adoption in promoting children's welfare should help to shift the language of the debate toward the positive benefits of adoption. Given this mass of evidence, I question why so many policy statements, from both governments and nongovernmental organizations, relegate international adoption to "last-resort" status.

Before delving into research on internationally adopted children and their families, it is important to acknowledge controversial issues related to the geographic and cultural origin of the children. When describing children available for international adoption, even basic vocabulary is hotly contested. What does the term *orphan* mean, and is it appropriate to use when discussing children available for adoption? Why are the children available for adoption, and how do the various countries of origin regulate and administer policies that affect children separated from their birth families?

Although it may seem merely a semantic dispute, critics and supporters of adoption have been at loggerheads over how to identify a child as an orphan and how many there are in the world.[20] The narrowest definition of the word *orphan* describes a child whose birth parents are both dead. However, most people working in adoption and child welfare understand that this narrow definition is too limiting, and it has never been the legal definition of *orphan*. For example, for purposes of immigration, the United States Citizenship and Immigration Service (USCIS) defines an orphan more broadly as

> a foreign-born child who does not have any parents because of the death or disappearance of, abandonment or desertion by, or separation or loss from, both parents, or has a sole or surviving parent who is unable to care for the child, consistent with the local standards of the foreign sending country, and who has, in writing, irrevocably released the child for emigration and adoption.[21]

By using this definition to identify children adopted abroad who are eligible for U.S. citizenship, the USCIS acknowledges the appropriateness, in certain circumstances, of adoption for children who may still have living parents elsewhere in the world.

Although estimates vary and data are questionable, it seems that most internationally adopted children are orphans by this broader definition rather than the narrower one.[22] Most are so-called social orphans—children who may have at least one parent living, but whose birth parents have either voluntarily relinquished the child or had their parental rights involuntarily terminated due to abandonment, abuse, or neglect. The children are functionally orphans, although their parents are not dead.[23]

Complicating this picture further, in many regions of the former Soviet Union (FSU) and elsewhere, struggling parents are encouraged to place children temporarily in baby houses (or children's homes for older children) to allow the state to care for the children until the parents are better able to take them back, an event that may happen in months, in years, or never.[24] A UNICEF study in 2010 reported over 600,000 children living in institutional care in FSU and former Soviet-bloc countries.[25] Many of these children are not orphans by either the narrow or the broad definition, because there has been neither a voluntary relinquishment nor a termination of parental rights. Reasons for the children's institutionalization, at least in the FSU and allied countries, are complex but typically include a combination of poverty and family breakdown.[26]

Most of the children in my son's baby house fell into this "limbo" category, living in an institution and yet legally ineligible for either domestic or international adoption because there was no legal relinquishment or termination of parental rights. Based on anecdotal experience, my Kazakhstani translator said that for most of these children, reunification will never happen, and the children will remain institutionalized for the duration of childhood. Supporting statistics are found in a UNICEF report summarizing the reasons for "outflow," or leaving institutional care, for several FSU countries.[27] Although the report did not present outflow data for Kazakhstan, in Russia in 2007, 44% of the children leaving institutions did so because they "aged out" by turning 18, while only 9% left institutions because of reunification with birth families and less than 5% left because they were adopted. The remainder left institutions for transfer to other forms of temporary care, such as another institution or foster care, or were unaccounted for.

Some writers believe that the rationale for international adoption is undermined by the fact that the major cause of orphanhood is not parental death but inability to fulfill parental obligations.[28] The implication, according to these critics, is that the very existence of living birth parents negates the need for adoption and points instead toward the need for reunification, regardless of the reason for the relinquishment or termination of rights. Some critics believe that even the term *unparented child*, while less fraught than the term *orphan*, is still suspect because every child "has parents" in the sense that he or she was created by biological parents.[29] These critiques notwithstanding, throughout this book I use the phrase "unparented children" to refer to those children whose birth parents are unable to offer nurturing caregiving on a permanent basis, regardless of the reason for that absence. In using the term *unparented*, I intentionally consider the term *parent* as a verb. The children who concern me are those who are "unparented" in the sense that no one is acting as a parent to them.

A final cautionary note concerns the tendency to make simplifying and generalizing assumptions about countries of origin of adopted children. Because these countries are generally poorer countries in the developing world, they are sometimes mistakenly assumed by Western writers to be essentially the same as one another. Countries from which international adoptions originate are sometimes collectively described as the "global south," as opposed to the "global north,"[30] which is simply academic jargon for "poor" versus "rich" countries. Besides being geographically confusing and inaccurate—anyone who has been in Russia in winter will attest that it is decidedly "north"— this simplification overlooks vast cultural, historical, political, and bureaucratic differences in countries as far-flung from one another as China, Ethiopia, and Guatemala, which are, of course, on entirely different continents. This can lead to logical errors, such as assuming that if kidnapping of children or coercion of birth parents is happening in one place (for example, Guatemala or Cambodia[31]), it must be characteristic of the "global south" generally, thereby tarring international adoption worldwide.[32]

Given the ever-changing landscape of international adoption, it can be challenging for either a supporter or critic of international adoption to fully appreciate the reality on the ground in all the countries of origin. Even a cursory consideration, however, makes clear that generalizations about countries of origin are problematic.[33] For example, the reasons for relinquishment of children in China, where the central government since 1979 promoted a one-child policy in order to limit population growth,[34] are different from those in Romania, where the Ceaușescu regime aimed to increase population growth by effectively forcing women to birth more children than they were able to nurture.[35] Countries in the FSU have a particular historical legacy that includes Soviet mentalities about state responsibility and entrenched bureaucratic and patronage interests in an existing system of institutions for children.[36] Many countries in sub-Saharan Africa face the scourge of AIDS mortality, which has challenged and burdened traditional kinship systems.[37] We should thus resist glib generalizations about the "global south" (or "global north") and the myriad reasons why children may be without parental care in different countries around the world. Ultimately, promoting effective policy will require detailed understanding of specific cultural contexts.

One important way that countries differ is in their systems of care for unparented children. These differences have implications for the children's well-being. Some governments in certain historical periods, such as Romania in the 1980s and 1990s, placed unparented children in institutions that were notoriously appalling.[38] Researchers often describe such institutions as "globally depriving," because children were deprived of even the most basic necessities of adequate food and hygiene. Other institutional settings for children, such as many of those that currently exist in the FSU and elsewhere, may provide adequate warmth, food, and protection from disease, but lack provision of social-emotional experiences that are known to be essential for human development. Even within a country that relies on institutionalization for unparented children, such as Russia, institutional settings may differ widely in quality from region to region, or they may differ for generally healthy children in contrast to those for disabled children. Still other countries have a child welfare system that includes pre-adoptive fostering rather than institutionalization, as in South Korea, or a system that includes a combination of fostering and institutional care, as in some places in China. Thus, in research that examines the effect of early adversity on development in internationally adopted children, we must recognize that the degree and nature of adversity vary tremendously across children depending on the historical time and geographical place of their birth.

While my own direct experience was in Kazakhstan, in this book I review research conducted on children adopted from many different countries of origin. Although I did not originally intend to spend a year living in Kazakhstan, I've benefited from doing so. I have experienced the culture in positive ways, increasing my deep appreciation for all that Kazakhstani families do under hardscrabble economic conditions and a politically oppressive regime. I've been warmly welcomed into Kazakh homes and have listened to the aspirations and values of many people there. At the same time, a year's experience has given me a more realistic and less romantic view than I might have gleaned from a brief trip to tourist highlights and exposure to the national dishes and costumes. It is this more complex view that I will be able to transmit to my son and that informs his life story and my own.

In this book, I weave together my son's adoption story with research from psychology and neuroscience fully knowing that my own experience is particular, while the research, like all scientific endeavors, aims to extract general patterns and principles. The narrative of my son's adoption is tied to a specific historical place and time, a dusty Silk Road town in post-Soviet Central Asia in 2010. Yet it is this particular experience that led me to seek out a more generalized understanding of how deprivation of parental care can affect children and how adoption can be part of a solution that helps children thrive.

While debates about international adoption will continue to rage on, it is my hope that some measure of balance can be restored to the debate. In recent years, international adoptions to the United States have plunged, dropping more than 70% from 22,991 children in 2004 to 6,441 children in 2014.[39] While the reasons for the steep drop-off are not fully clear, it is not because there are fewer needy children or fewer parents willing to adopt them. Instead, sadly, rhetoric both in countries of origin and in various nongovernmental child welfare organizations has turned against international adoption. I will leave it to others to more fully debate political, legal, economic, and human rights critiques of adoption across country lines.[40] Meanwhile, I hope that a consideration of the psychological benefits to the child, and the strengths and resilience of adoptive children and families, as detailed in evidence presented here, will weigh heavily in favor of adoption.

2

Physical and Cognitive Development

When I first held Aldanysh, he was small and weak but had a memorable sparkle in his eyes. At the age of 9 months, he could not sit up and had trouble holding up his head. Our pediatricians in the United States, receiving our initial reports and pictures via email, warned that developmentally he appeared more like a 4-month-old than a 9-month-old baby. They asked us to double-check his birthdate to be sure. Although the reports of his medical history prior to that point were often vague and inconsistent, we were told at various times that he was born 2 months premature, that he had low birth-weight, that it was a very difficult birth, that his birth mother was anemic, and that he had congenital pneumonia and had been hospitalized with pneumonia three times since his birth. Official documents state that Aldanysh was relinquished at birth[1] and held in the maternity hospital for 3 months prior to being transferred to the baby house. In all these ways, he was a fairly typical orphanage baby in Kazakhstan.

The baby house was also fairly typical of such institutions in the former Soviet Union (FSU).[2] The staff paid great attention to keeping the children warm, fed, and free of disease. In our bonding visits, Aldanysh was often handed to us bundled in several layers of warm clothing, even when he was only being transferred through the internal, heated hallways from his routine care room to the heavily heated visitation room. In winter months, children never saw anything outside the baby house unless they were being taken to the hospital. "Fresh air" was not viewed positively by the staff. Food was ample but typically institutional. Mutton stew figured prominently—I once saw the sheep, still alive, being delivered to the kitchen area—and there was little in the way of fresh fruits or green vegetables. Feeding procedures were routinized. Staff had great concern about infectious disease, and children often received antibiotic injections even for conditions that were apparently viral. In our initial visits in December 2009, we were asked to purchase medicine at the local pharmacy for children in the baby house. The baby-house doctor told us that government-issued medicine for the baby house typically ran out before the end of the year.

The orphanage was very clean and neat, with significant emphasis placed on visual appearance. Fresh paint was constantly being applied, and walls and floors constantly scrubbed. The space was bright. The caregivers took pride in cleaning Aldanysh and putting him in fresh clothes just before our bonding visits. Each childcare room for children in his age bracket contained large playpens that were brightly painted and shelves full of brightly colored toys. The children never appeared to play with these toys. On one occasion, caregivers in Aldanysh's unit asked if we might be willing to buy some toys to donate to the unit, with specific instructions about the details of the desired toys. Eager to do something "to help," we excitedly rushed to the bazaar that afternoon, purchased the toys, and brought them in the next day. The toys were placed proudly on the shelves and as best we can tell, they were never used. They were for show.

Organizational aspects of the baby house were also typical of such institutions in the FSU. Caregiving staff rotated from day to day, such that the children received care from many different caregivers throughout typical weeks. Children were housed in same-age groups, and were transferred to new groups at various points that seemed unpredictable to us but that presumably were based on age or developmental milestones. Such transfers meant that the children were then introduced to a new set of rotating caregivers, disrupting any relationships the children might have formed. On the day that our son was transferred to a new group, someone wrote his name on his arm so that the staff in the new unit would know who he was. Behavioral consistency and conformity were valued. Staff told us with ambivalence that children who began bonding sessions with adoptive parents soon began to act differently, more willfully and restlessly. Despite the routinization of care and the structural impediments to establishing emotional bonds, many of the staff genuinely cared about the children. Although Kazakh culture tends toward the emotionally inexpressive, several caregivers visibly shed tears on the day we finally took custody of Aldanysh.

While my direct experience was particular to one baby house in Kazakhstan, research has repeatedly confirmed that internationally adopted children arrive in their adoptive homes with significant delays in physical growth, motor development, and cognitive development. Physical-growth delays are among the best-documented characteristics of internationally adopted children, because height and weight are easily measured and are often done so routinely in standard pediatric care. Extensive data already exist on typical patterns of physical growth in the general population, so it is easy to make comparisons. In addition to height and weight, many studies also measure head circumference, done simply by placing a measuring tape around the crown of the head. Head circumference is considered by pediatricians to be an especially important index predicting a child's future cognitive development, because it is a cheap and easy way to estimate the size of the growing brain. In a recent review of the literature, researchers concluded that delayed physical growth in institutionalized children is "a universal finding with every cohort reported to date showing moderate to severe suppression of height, weight, and head circumference."[3]

Research has consistently shown dramatic patterns of catch-up growth in children placed in adoptive homes. To address this issue, one Dutch research team conducted a *meta-analysis*, which is a combined analysis of data from various studies addressing a particular hypothesis.[4] This kind of analysis has the advantage of integrating data across many studies, each of which may have small samples and idiosyncratic drawbacks in methodology, in order to see what consistent findings emerge across the studies. The meta-analysis of physical growth in international adoptees incorporated 33 studies with a total of more than 3,000 participating children, most adopted from institutional settings. While the children's height and weight were significantly below normal upon arrival in the adoptive home, both height and weight were within the normal range upon follow-up, which occurred at an average of about 8 years post-adoption. Head circumference also displayed a pattern of significant improvement after adoption, although catch-up to normal levels was not fully complete for this measure.

The length of time a child spends in an institution is directly related to delays in physical growth. Estimates based on available data indicate that for every 3 months spent in an institution, an infant loses a month of development.[5] In the

Dutch meta-analysis, catch-up growth in both height and weight was more likely to occur for children who arrived in their adoptive families at a younger age.[6] These findings, as well as parallel findings for cognitive delays, have direct policy implications; we will return to these in the concluding chapter.

It may not be surprising that children begin to grow more rapidly in a home environment, where presumably nutrition is more adequate. Indeed, while orphanage-reared children in many places may eat adequate quantities of food, the orphanage diet may lack essential nutrients. For example, a study conducted between 2009 and 2012 by the nongovernmental organization SPOON Foundation, in conjunction with the Kazakhstan Academy of Nutrition, found that 73% of children in Kazakhstani baby houses exhibited deficiency in at least one macro- or micronutrient.[7] More than half of the children in Kazakhstani baby houses are anemic, according to another study.[8] Institutionalized children are also at risk for contracting infectious diseases and intestinal parasites that can slow growth.[9]

While nutrition is crucial, nutrition itself cannot fully explain either the delayed growth in institutionalized children or the rapid rate of catch-up once they are placed in adoptive homes. Instead, psychological factors related to nurturing are also crucial for physical growth. Psychologists have described a phenomenon known variously as psychosocial dwarfism, psychosocial short stature, or psychosocial growth failure.[10] In a nutshell, children display slower growth when raised under conditions of psychological stress or socioemotional deprivation.

Researchers have proposed a biological mechanism that explains the effect of stress on growth in terms of the body's hormone systems. Briefly, the hypothesis is that hormones released as part of the body's natural response to stress, such as cortisol and associated stress hormones, interact with the hormonal systems that control growth. Through this means, activation of stress hormones can inhibit the release or effectiveness of growth hormones. This mechanism may be adaptive in situations of acute stress, such as the "fight-or-flight" situations that our evolutionary ancestors faced. In the face of immediate danger, the body needs to mobilize essential resources to fend off the danger, rather than putting energy toward growth. However, chronic stress activates this inhibitory pathway chronically, leading to chronic inhibition of growth. Not only can psychosocial stress inhibit current growth, but it can also lead to hormonal changes that affect the timing of puberty, causing early puberty and therefore curtailing the normal period of childhood growth.[11]

Evidence that psychological factors can affect physical growth in unparented children, even when nutrition is held constant, comes from a pioneering study of psychosocial intervention in orphanages in St. Petersburg, Russia.[12] A collaborative team of Russian and American researchers, working with the cooperation of key orphanage directors, designed an intervention in which caregivers were trained to interact more responsively to the children under their care. Responsive interaction required a change in mindset, encouraging caregivers to be more emotionally expressive and to converse actively in their interactions with children during routine care, such as when cleaning, feeding, and changing the babies. An additional intervention included structural changes intended to promote more family-like bonding between caregivers and children, such as adjusting staff shifts so that children would see the same staff more consistently, decreasing the size of residential groups, and promoting a "family hour" with staff caregivers every day. One baby house implemented the responsiveness training alone, a second baby house implemented both the responsiveness training and the structural changes intended to improve bonding, and a third baby house went on with care as usual.

Results of the study showed that the interventions improved not only cognitive and behavioral measures but also the physical growth of the children. Specifically, children exposed to the combined responsiveness/structural change intervention showed more impressive physical growth than those in the responsiveness intervention alone, who in turn showed greater gains than those in the care-as-usual baby house. The results were consistent for both height and weight, and they held true for both disabled and non-disabled children. However, the interventions did not appear to affect head circumference. Because the diet was not altered by the intervention, nutrition cannot account for the different outcomes between the three baby houses. Instead, the psychosocial intervention intended to promote greater bonding relationships directly affected the children's height and weight.

As we consider developmental outcomes for children, naturally we are interested in more than just their height, weight, and head size. What has been learned about psychological and behavioral functioning in adopted children? Physical growth does bear some relationship to psychological development; some researchers have found that catch-up growth in physical size is correlated with catch-up growth in cognitive ability.[13] This should not be surprising, because the brain, like the rest of the body, depends on both adequate nutrition and nurturing in order to develop optimally. Here we consider evidence about cognitive development in adopted children, focusing on intelligence, language, attention, and higher-level thinking. We will discuss emotional and social development later, in Chapter 3, to give issues related to this area adequate space for discussion.

Generally, the pattern of "gain following loss" holds true for cognitive development as well as for physical growth. In a meta-analysis, Dutch researchers integrated findings from 62 studies, involving more than 17,000 international adoptees, that examined general cognitive outcomes, defined as IQ measures or academic achievement, after a period of years in the adoptive home.[14] In some of these studies, outcomes of adopted children were compared with those of their birth siblings or peers left in institutions in the country of origin, as well as with those of their new (non-adopted) peers in the country of rearing. International adoptees had IQ scores that were higher than those of their peers left behind and indistinguishable from those of their new peers. However, while their academic achievement outpaced that of their peers left behind, it still remained slightly behind that of their new peers. Although it is unclear why academic achievement did not show quite as much catch-up as IQ, the reason may be related to emotional and social factors (discussed in Chapter 3) that may affect school performance but not affect IQ itself.

One methodological problem with comparing outcomes of adopted children with those of children left behind is that the better-functioning children may be more likely to be adopted. This is known as the "selective adoption" effect, and it means that it is difficult for researchers to determine whether adoption actually raises IQ (compared to institutional rearing) or whether the pattern of enhanced outcomes for adopted children is simply due to the fact that they were higher functioning to begin with compared to their peers who were not chosen for adoption.

Results from a groundbreaking study strongly imply that the cognitive benefit of family care is real and cannot simply be attributed to the selective adoption effect. The research project, called the Bucharest Early Intervention Project (BEIP), involved randomly assigning unparented institutionalized Romanian children below the ages of 31 months to either continued orphanage care or care by high-quality foster parents who were carefully selected and trained by the research team.[15] Random assignment is considered to be the "gold standard" for research design, because it eliminates the possibility that pre-existing factors might explain any difference between comparison groups.

The researchers measured IQ at two subsequent time points, 42 and 54 months of age, which was approximately 1 and 2 years after placement. At both of these time points, the children randomly assigned to foster care showed significant gains in IQ compared to the group still in the orphanage. Further follow-up studies when the children reached the age of about 8 years confirmed the continued IQ benefit of the foster care intervention.[16] Additional research found that at about 8 years of age, the still-institutionalized children had abnormalities in white-matter tracts of the brain, which typically allow efficient communication between brain regions, whereas the children randomly assigned to foster care looked more similar to the control group of never-institutionalized children on these anatomical measures.[17] This research is the best evidence to date of the significant benefits in IQ and brain anatomy that result from being raised in a family setting as compared to a deprived institutional setting.

As with the study of physical growth measures, researchers studying cognitive development have been concerned with whether age at the time of adoption, which is closely tied to the length of period of deprivation, can predict a child's ultimate outcome. Do children who spend more time in institutional care generally have a harder time catching up cognitively? Although the data are somewhat mixed, generally, evidence suggests that children who are adopted earlier are better able to catch up.[18] For example, the meta-analysis study found that children adopted before 12 months of age showed better catch-up in terms of school achievement than children adopted at older ages.[19] Likewise, the BEIP team found that the foster care intervention with Romanian children was most successful in improving IQs for those who were placed into foster care before the age of 24 months.[20] This evidence strongly supports policies that promote placement of children in family settings as early in life as possible.

Research on the developing brain makes clear that stimulating environments promote better brain development than do impoverished environments. This finding fits with common sense and is clearly backed up by decades of robust evidence dating back to the 1970s.[21] Neuroscience studies of environmental enrichment have mostly focused on rodents such as rats and mice, in which the time course of development is relatively short compared to humans, and in which invasive procedures to examine the brain are deemed more ethically palatable. It is not possible to examine many aspects of brain development in the living human brain because such measurements require direct examination of the brain tissue under a microscope.

Dozens of studies on environmental enrichment in rodents and nonhuman primates have demonstrated that animals reared in enriched circumstances, such as cages with lots of playthings and playmates, have better brain development than animals reared in "standard" animal cages, that is, in social isolation and with few playthings. These benefits of enrichment have been obtained for numerous biological measures of brain development, including the thickness of the cerebral cortex, generation of new brain cells, and development of complex branching connections between brain cells.[22] These biological consequences of environmental enrichment are accompanied by benefits in learning and memory.[23] Although generalizations from other species may present challenges, it is not difficult to see the analogy between impoverished laboratory environments for animals and institutional settings for children, or between enriched environments for animals and family homes for children.

While the evidence strongly suggests a pronounced pattern of catch-up in overall cognitive skill among internationally adopted children, some researchers have looked beyond overall IQ or academic achievement to examine more specific aspects of mental function. Areas of research interest have included language development, attention, and so-called executive functions, which include skills supporting higher-level problem-solving, planning, and flexible control of behavior. As we will see, the conclusions about functioning across these domains are somewhat variable.

Language has been of central concern because in most (though certainly not all) cases of international adoption, the adoptive parents speak a different language than the one the child was exposed to in early life. For example, our son heard mainly the Kazakh language spoken by his orphanage caregivers, along with a smattering of Russian from televisions in the orphanage, prior to adoption into our English-speaking family. Language researchers refer to this kind of situation in internationally adopted children as "second first-language acquisition" to describe the task of starting over in acquiring a primary language.

Another obstacle to normal language development, beyond the issue of starting over with new sounds, words, and grammar, is that institutionalized children usually receive impoverished language input prior to adoption.[24] In institutions, children have limited interaction with adults or older children who could model various aspects of language. They particularly lack the reciprocal back-and-forth bouts of verbal and nonverbal communication that are thought to lay the essential groundwork for normal language acquisition. When we adopted our son at the age of 20 months, he had not yet said any words in Kazakh (or Russian or English), whereas typically developing children often say their first words around 12 months of age. Like many adoptive parents, we benefited from our local county's early-intervention program, which provided speech therapy services to bring our son up to age-appropriate levels in English during his first year in the United States.[25]

Consistent with our own experience, studies have generally found that within a year or two following adoption, the new language is effectively learned by adopted children, despite the fact that they often arrive in adoptive homes with mild to moderate delays even in their first language.[26] In a pattern that mirrors that of non-adopted immigrant children acquiring a second language, progress is rapid, and even enviable to any adult who has attempted to learn a second language. Children's brains are extremely adept at acquiring language spontaneously when in a language-rich environment. Within the first 2 years in the adoptive home, language performance generally achieves levels within the normal range of peers who acquired the language natively,[27] and it appears to follow the same sequential steps as in native language acquisition (for example, emphasizing concrete nouns at first, then moving on to more verbs and function words).[28] However, some adopted children do continue to exhibit more pronounced difficulties with speech and language even after some time in the adoptive home.[29]

Research has generally found that children adopted at an earlier age can more easily achieve native fluency than those adopted later.[30] It is unclear whether these age-related effects emerge because older children endured longer periods of intellectual deprivation prior to adoption, or must acquire a new language after an optimal "window of opportunity" for language learning has passed, or have reached a level of proficiency in their first language that somehow interferes with the new language acquisition. Some researchers have argued that even among early-adopted children, subtle language deficits may become apparent only as the child gets older and faces more complex linguistic challenges.[31] Nevertheless, despite these qualifications, the general pattern is one of a rapid rate of adaptation to the language of the adoptive home and country.

Fascinating recent research suggests that even among adopted children who have no conscious recollection of their birth language, the brain may still retain some traces of that language.[32] The study examined brain activity of children who had been adopted at about 12 months of age from China and placed into exclusively French-speaking homes in Quebec. At the time of the study, the children were in late childhood or adolescence (ages 9–17 years), had no recollection of Chinese, and had not been exposed to any Chinese since their adoption. Yet, when they listened to the sounds of Chinese, their brains (and in particular, the auditory cortex in the brain's left hemisphere) responded more like the brains of Chinese-French bilinguals (who had continuous exposure to both languages) and differently from brains of French monolinguals who had never had Chinese exposure. These results suggest that exposure to the birth language has biological effects that are still evident even years after the language is functionally "lost."

Other research has examined executive functions in children who were subjected to institutional care. The term *executive functions* is an umbrella term to describe a suite of goal-directed abilities that includes abstract and flexible thought, planning and sequencing, ability to control the focus of attention, and ability to override impulses. Executive functions are central to governing many aspects of everyday behavior; they contribute crucially to academic performance as well as influencing social and emotional behavior. Executive functions generally depend on the prefrontal cortex of the brain, a region that is especially well developed in people and other primates and is the last brain region to mature. Research on the developing brain suggests that maturation of the prefrontal cortex is not complete until late adolescence or later.[33] This prolonged period of development allows the prefrontal cortex to be influenced by the particular environmental context of learning, including both enriching influences (e.g., sensory and social stimulation) and disrupting influences (e.g., stress). Research in animal models has shown that development of the prefrontal cortex is affected by early-life social deprivation.[34]

Some evidence suggests that internationally adopted children continue to show subtle differences in executive functions compared to non-adopted peers, even after years in the adoptive home. For example, one study collected parent ratings of executive function difficulties among preschool and school-age children adopted from Russian orphanages. Parents completed a questionnaire indicating how often the child displayed specific problem behaviors, including problems controlling impulses; transitioning between tasks or situations; generating plans, ideas, or goals; and completing tasks in a systematic manner. Parent ratings indicated more difficulty for the school-aged adopted children than for typically developing children.[35] The deficit in parent-rated executive functions was especially pronounced for those who were adopted after the age of 18 months.

Of course, parent ratings may be biased if adoptive parents are simply more sensitive to or anxious about possible problems than non-adoptive parents. However, studies that measured actual performance on behavioral tests of executive function have also reported deficits in adopted children. For example, previously institutionalized children showed more difficulty on a task that required them to sort cards into categories according to changing sets of rules.[36] Previously institutionalized children are also more likely than comparison groups to act on impulse and to display behaviors related to those of attention-deficit disorder, reflecting difficulties in higher-level control of behavior.[37] In addition, brain imaging studies indicate disruption in prefrontal brain regions in previously institutionalized adopted children, though these studies are based on small samples.[38]

The difference in executive functions between adopted and non-adopted children is an example of something known as a "sleeper effect" in development. The sleeper effect refers to an influence that is present early in development but whose consequences don't become evident until later. Because executive functions are not really measurable in infants, differences between adopted and non-adopted children in these functions would typically not be detectable until later, for example, in middle childhood or adolescence. The existence of such sleeper effects supports a model of development in which early experiences matter even for later-developing functions. Even when a child is removed from the depriving environment, the subsequent cumulative years of experience in a more enriched environment cannot always completely overcome the effects of early adversity. As with other outcome measures, the difference between adopted and non-adopted children in executive function is influenced by age of adoption, with earlier-adopted children faring better.[39] Together, these findings support the notion of a sensitive period in early development during which family-like rearing conditions are crucial for optimal cognitive development years down the line.

Although the evidence suggests persisting challenges involving executive functions for adopted children compared to non-adopted peers, it is important to consider the alternative scenario for institutionalized children who are *not* adopted—that is, those who remain in institutions. The BEIP research group provides the best existing evidence bearing on whether such children fare worse, when it comes to executive functions, than those in family care.[40] As previously discussed, this research team randomly assigned unparented Romanian children to foster care versus orphanage care as usual. Children who received foster care subsequently performed just as well as never-institutionalized children on a behavioral task of impulse control, while the still-institutionalized children performed more poorly. Brainwave signals of attention and self-control during task performance also showed that the foster care children were more similar in this respect to never-institutionalized children than were the still-institutionalized children. The gains of the foster care group over development of still-institutionalized peers suggest the potential for family care to enhance some aspects of executive function.

When interpreting the results across all of these areas—physical development, IQ, academic achievement, language, attention, and executive functions—it is essential to keep some caveats in mind. Most importantly, development is enormously variable; each child is different. This is certainly true when considering children with typical upbringings, and even more characteristic of children with the unusual trajectories of international adoption. Numerous researchers have commented on the very diverse outcomes within their samples of internationally adopted children.[41]

The diversity of outcomes is important for at least two reasons. First, it reminds us that we must resist stereotyping and stigmatization.[42] Even in areas in which adopted children as a group may show subtle but persistent deficits or challenges—such as school achievement or executive functions—many adopted children show performance in the normal range and others even outperform their non-adopted peers. Conversely, even in areas where adopted children as a group do well, such as physical growth and overall IQ, there will still be some who struggle or lag behind.

From a scientific perspective, the broad range of outcomes exhibited by adopted children raises intriguing questions. Why do some children thrive and other children show more negative consequences when faced with adverse experiences? What are the reasons for the varied outcomes? As we have seen, one important factor is the child's age at the time of adoption, with children adopted at younger ages generally showing better outcomes than those adopted at older ages. Other relevant factors may include the type of pre-adoptive care, which varies tremendously within and between countries of origin. For example, Korean adoptees typically experienced foster rearing prior to adoption, whereas Romanian adoptees typically experienced severe, globally depriving institutional care, and this may contribute to different outcomes for these groups. Even within a particular institutional setting, children may not experience the same level of care, as some children may be staff "favorites" and receive preferential treatment.[43] Finally, researchers are beginning to consider factors intrinsic to the child, such as genetic differences that can affect the child's resilience.[44] We will return to these issues in more depth in the next chapter.

In closing this chapter, it is useful to revisit the question of the child's "best interests," often emphasized in adoption law and policies. Based on the evidence presented in this chapter, is adoption in the child's best interests? In terms of physical growth and cognitive development, surely the answer is "yes." Environments matter. Children show pronounced developmental delays at the time of adoption, delays that theoretically could be attributed either to factors intrinsic to the child (e.g., prenatal or genetic factors) or to environmental deprivation prior to adoption. The massive catch-up in both physical and cognitive growth following adoption is a striking testament to the essential importance of environment in supporting growth. Although the catch-up with non-adopted peers may not always be fully complete, due to some persistent influence of early adversity, the pronounced post-adoptive gains following pre-adoptive losses indicate that, as a whole, adoption is a highly successful path for unparented children. Furthermore, this intervention is most successful when children enter adoptive homes at a younger age. This "earlier is better" theme, robustly supported by research, has yet to be fully embraced by individuals and agencies responsible for developing adoption policies.

3 ■
Social and Emotional Development

The most wrenching aspect of our year in Kazakhstan was the separations. All of my emotions and parenting instincts told me that Aldanysh needed a primary caregiver, and intellectually I knew from the research literature the importance of attachment for normal social and emotional development during the early years. We were told that after his birth, Aldanysh remained in the maternity hospital for 3 months, spending at least part of that time in an intensive care unit. I hope he was nurtured by kind nurses and doctors, but I have no way of knowing whether this was the case. At the age of 3 months, he was transferred to the baby house, where he waited out the 6-month period during which he was eligible for adoption only by Kazakhstanis, as required by Kazakhstani law at the time. At the age of 9 months he was eligible for international adoption, and we met him and agreed to adopt him. However, the mounting legal and bureaucratic obstacles we experienced meant that he did not come into our custody until the age of 20 months.

During this period, he had no primary caregiver, but instead was cared for by a rotating staff at the baby house, coupled with our restricted daily visits.

Our daily separations happened hundreds of times over the year. We were permitted only one 2-hour visit each day, during which time my husband and I brought Aldanysh to a separate room in the baby house and played with him, under close supervision. To avoid disrupting baby house routines, we were not supposed to feed Aldanysh, nor let him fall asleep in our arms, although we did both anyway. At the end of the 2 hours, we had to return him to the baby house staff, often provoking painful transitions in which he would cry and reach out for us.

In addition to the daily separations, there were recurring lengthy separations required in order to maintain our legal permission to stay in Kazakhstan. Our visas had to be renewed periodically, and this required leaving the country, obtaining a new visa at a Kazakhstani embassy in another country (during the year we visited embassies in the United States, London, and Dubai), and then returning to Kazakhstan. After one such separation that lasted about 2 weeks, I was heartbroken to find upon my return that Aldanysh pulled away from me and would no longer look me in the eye. He was 17 months old and he had lost trust in me during my absence.

Kazakhstani adoption procedures at that time had the potential to work well for purposes of emotional bonding, but that potential was often completely undermined by how the process actually played out in many regions. Regulations required that adoptive parents first spend 2 weeks in "bonding sessions" with the to-be-adopted child at the orphanage.[1] On paper this makes sense, as the child can gradually come to know the new parents in a familiar setting, and the parents can glean clues about the baby house routines in order to understand the typical daily experiences and expectations of the child before taking custody. Upon completion of this 2-week bonding period, a local guardianship council would make a determination about the suitability of the adoption, and finally a municipal court judge needed to approve it. All of this would then be followed by paperwork required for the child's immigration—namely obtaining a passport and exit visa from the central Kazakhstani government and an entry visa from the American (or other country-of-destination) government.

In theory, if all the steps followed one another promptly, the child could be in the adoptive parents' custody shortly after completion of the bonding period. In reality, it rarely worked that way. In our case, the guardianship council made a quick determination in our favor, but then the court hearing was not scheduled until 3 months later. The judge did not issue his decision until 2 months after that. Unfortunately, the decision was negative, as the judge felt that the orphanage should have sought local adoptive families more aggressively. The negative decision led to 6 months of further delays. Our situation was extreme, but even when things went smoothly there were significant waiting periods. Most parents adopting internationally from Kazakhstan could not realistically manage the significant time in-country, away from their jobs and families, that was required to wait out the whole process. Therefore, most adopting parents made up to three trips, each separated by months—one for bonding, one for court, and one finally to take custody of the child. From the child's perspective, any bonding that happened during the first trip was completely undermined by the subsequent inexplicable disappearance of the parents. We must wonder what the child learned from this.

Psychologists have understood for decades that attachment to a primary caregiver during infancy is critical for normal development. Attachment theory was first developed in the 1950s by John Bowlby, a British psychologist who was heavily influenced by evolutionary theory.[2] Bowlby understood that for a human child, unlike the off-spring of some species who "hatch" relatively fully formed, caregiving by an adult for a fairly prolonged period of childhood is essential to the child's survival. Therefore, he proposed that evolved mechanisms served to "attach" or bond the infant to a caregiver, typically the mother, early in life. Attachment serves to keep the infant in close proximity to the mother, and is most important during a period when the infant begins to become mobile through crawling and walking but is still developmentally immature and therefore vulnerable to the dangers of the world. According to Bowlby and other attachment theorists, attachment to a primary caregiver who displays consistent patterns of responsive behavior allows the infant to begin to build a mental template of social relationships, a kind of internal model of social interactions that future relationships will be built upon.[3]

Essential to this characterization is the idea that our species is "built to bond."[4] That is, humans (and other primates) evolved to "expect" the presence of a primary attachment figure in a particular window of develop-ment.[5] We can illustrate this concept with an analogy from the brain's systems for sight.[6] Vision develops nor-mally when the brain's visual system is exposed to patterned light in early life. Because patterned light is universal everywhere on the planet, evolution could "assume" that all infants would be exposed to such light, and could then rely on that ubiquitous light trigger to stimulate normal development of the visual parts of the brain. In abnormal circumstances, such as an infant who has cataracts that prevent patterned light from reaching the eye, the development of the brain's visual system does not occur normally, underscoring the importance of a light cue in triggering optimal development.[7] Similarly, because mothers are universal, humans and other primates likely evolved developmental mechanisms that "assume" the presence of a mother during infancy and rely on that presence to stimulate normal development of the brain's systems for attachment and emotional development. According to this concept, we would predict that, analogous to the cataracts that prevent normal visual development, the absence of the expected cue—that is, the primary caregiver—would lead to difficulties in social and emotional development.

As a rule, adopted children have experienced significant disruptions in postnatal caregiving, unless they were adopted as newborns.[8] Children who are institutionalized prior to adoption may experience dozens of caregivers. Those who are fostered prior to adoption have a consistent caregiver for some period of time, perhaps followed by another if they are placed in more than one fostering arrangement consecutively, and then followed by another in the adoptive family. Therefore, the challenges in establishing an "internal working model" of relationships based on a primary caregiver are different for institutionalized children compared to fostered children. Attachment challenges may also be different for children who spent some time in the birth home before being moved to an alternative care arrangement such as foster care or institutionalization. Particularly for those unfortunate enough to experience abuse or neglect in the birth home, the issue of changing caregivers is compounded by a damaging early relationship.

Attachment is so important in the first years of life that, on this basis, prominent developmental psychologists have argued strenuously against institutional care during this period. For example, a policy paper written by key researchers in the field argued that "for important developmental reasons, these [young] children have urgent needs for regular contact with a small number of caregivers who are devoted to their well-being."[9] The same researchers wrote, "institutional care is structurally and psychologically at odds with what young children need."[10]

Not surprisingly, researchers have found that the process of attachment is disrupted in internationally adopted children, particularly those who experienced a period of institutionalization prior to adoption.[11] Attachment is measured in different ways, such as through parent questionnaires or direct observation of parent–child interactions.[12] Generally, researchers categorize attachment as either "secure" or "insecure," though some also subdivide insecurely attached children into various subcategories, such as ambivalent, avoidant, or disorganized subtypes.[13] A securely attached infant is one who shows some distress upon separation from the parent and seeks and receives comfort from the parent when reunited. The securely attached child shows a preference for parents over strangers when seeking comfort. Insecurely attached children may seem anxious or ambivalent about receiving comfort from a parent; they may be either extremely wary of strangers or indiscriminate in their responses to parents and strangers.

One representative study compared attachment security in Romanian children who had been institutionalized for at least 8 months and in those who were adopted before the age of 4 months.[14] Both of these groups, adopted by Canadians, were also compared to a non-adopted Canadian control group, and they were studied approximately 1 year after adoption. The children who were adopted before the age of 4 months did not differ from the control group, whereas those who were adopted after at least 8 months of institutional care had a higher rate of insecure attachment. These essential findings were confirmed in a follow-up study 3 years later.[15]

Previously institutionalized children also have a higher likelihood of displaying "indiscriminate friendliness."[16] This phrase describes a behavior pattern, sometimes called disinhibited attachment, in which the child seeks out attention from adults in a nonselective manner. For example, the child may approach random strangers in a store seeking hugs, and may even wander off with strangers. The ability to form quick, albeit superficial, relationships may be adaptive in an institutional setting with constantly changing caregiving staff, but is thought to reflect a poorly developed mental template for trusting relationships. For children who are not adopted but instead "age out" of an orphanage in adolescence, the characteristic of disinhibited attachment can make the child an easy target for exploitation.

Research supports an "earlier is better" model for attachment outcomes in adopted children, similar to the age-at-adoption effects for physical and cognitive development discussed in the previous chapter. A comprehensive review of the existing research examined dozens of studies of attachment and related social outcomes (e.g., attachment security, attachment disorders, social competence, and peer relationships) in international adoptees.[17] Approximately two-thirds of the studies found age-at-adoption effects: Outcomes were worse for children who were adopted at older ages. Of the one-third of studies that found no effects of age at adoption, many had smaller samples that were less likely to detect an effect. Not surprisingly, no study has ever reported that children adopted later had better outcomes than those of children adopted earlier.

The most obvious conclusion from these studies is that longer periods of institutional care have more detrimental effects on attachment and social behavior. However, a possible alternative explanation of the age-at-adoption effect is that perhaps healthier children are selected for adoption at a younger age. Under this alternative scenario, age-at-adoption effects on behavioral outcomes would actually just reflect the overall health of the child rather than the duration of institutional deprivation. However, additional evidence argues against this possibility.[18] In the BEIP study (discussed in Chapter 2), institutionalized Romanian children who were randomly assigned to high-quality foster care rather than institutional care fared better in terms of attachment outcomes, particularly if they were placed before 24 months of age.[19] This evidence implies that the environmental deprivation in early life, not some inherent quality of the child, accounts for the relationship between age-at-adoption and attachment outcomes.

While the evidence is clear that earlier is better with respect to adoptive placement, psychologists continue to research the exact nature of the relationships between the timing of early deprivation and its consequences. For example, we can ask whether there is a particular window, a specific period of time during development, during which caregiver deprivation has particularly pronounced consequences. In developmental psychology, such a window is often referred to as a "sensitive period," to reflect the idea that the developing child is especially sensitive to particular experiences, in this case interactions with a responsive caregiver, at certain stages of development. If there is such a sensitive period for the development of healthy attachment, then we would expect that deprivation within that window of time would have greater negative consequences compared to similar deprivation outside that window.

Although the evidence is a bit mixed, current data generally do support the concept of a sensitive period for attachment and related social behaviors.[20] First, for many attachment-related outcomes, the relationship between age at adoption and outcome follows a "step function," such that deprivation at early ages has negative consequences, but continued deprivation outside a critical age doesn't produce increasingly worse effects. However, the studies differ in identifying what that critical age is, namely, the age by which the child needs to experience more normal caregiving in order to have the best chance of developing normally. Existing evidence from institutionalized children suggests that the critical age for intervention may range between 6 and 24 months of age, depending on how severely depriving the institutional setting is. The timing in relation to the child's developmental stage is crucial; according to the sensitive-period concept, 24 months of caregiver deprivation in the first 2 years of life are likely to have more negative consequences for attachment than 24 months of deprivation between the ages of 2 and 4, for example.[21]

Given the centrality of research on attachment in adoption, it is easy to become fixated on attachment in infancy for its own sake and to lose sight of why attachment is considered so important in the long run. Research has shown correlations between patterns of attachment in infancy and the ability to form stable relationships later in childhood, adolescence, and adulthood.[22] Furthermore, findings on the intergenerational transmission of attachment suggest that poor attachment in childhood may make it more difficult to engage in effective parenting as an adult.[23] These findings fit with anecdotal reports that a disproportionate number of orphanage-housed children in Kazakhstan were born to mothers who themselves were orphanage-reared. Although there are likely numerous reasons for the intergenerational persistence of relinquishment (including persistent socioeconomic factors), it stands to reason that an adult who had been raised in an orphanage setting, without the opportunity to form attachment bonds, may have difficulty engaging in sensitive parenting relationships with his or her own child.

Studies of social relationships among adopted children have had mixed results in addressing whether early life adversity, followed by adoption, produces social deficits. One study in the Netherlands found that adults who were adopted internationally as children were less likely (as adults) than non-adoptees to be married, in an intimate relationship, or living with a partner. [24] However, the same study found that the adoptees generally did not differ from non-adopted adults in their self-reported level of social functioning across various other domains (e.g., friendships and professional relationships). Other research has found that social skills among early-adopted children are comparable to those of non-adopted children and better than those of children reared in institutional settings.[25] These latter findings remind us again of the resilience of children when placed in family homes.

Early-life interactions with a responsive caregiver are important not only for forming a mental template of trusting intimate relationships but also for learning how to regulate one's internal states and emotions. As all parents know, a good part of parenting in the early years is spent soothing a child. An infant's distress cries are usually perceived by the parent as quite urgent and are effective in eliciting soothing behavior.[26] In the moment, soothing may seem to have the sole purpose of immediately quieting the child by satisfying a basic need (for food, for example), but soothing has a broader purpose as well: to teach the developing child how to control internal body systems. The soothing behaviors of the caregiver prompt the child's body to shift into a less aroused or distressed state, thus teaching the child's body how to effectively make those transitions.[27]

Touch, or contact comfort, is especially helpful in calming a young child, although cues from other senses are also important. To most people, the automatic comforting response to a young child's distress is to pick up the child. Caregivers of infants are estimated to spend between 30% and 75% of their time in direct physical contact with the infant, although this varies significantly across cultures.[28] Touch, or "tactile stimulation" as researchers call it, is thought to enhance biological and behavioral outcomes for infants. For example, regular massage of premature or full-term human infants results in better outcomes such as weight gain, ease of soothing, and responsiveness to stimulation.[29] Likewise, "skin-to-skin" care of infants also enhances their developmental outcomes.[30] In other animal species in which exposure to touch can be experimentally manipulated, tactile stimulation in a critical window of development appears to be essential in triggering normal patterns of development and can affect the expression of genes that are key to developmental processes.[31]

Needless to say, institutionalized children typically do not receive prompt soothing when in distress, nor contact comfort more generally. One or two caregivers overseeing a unit of a dozen babies can hardly be expected to respond instantly to each cry in the same way a parent would. Institutionalized infants are generally not nursed, an interaction that normally provides a natural context for tactile stimulation. While parents may spend hours of the day carrying or holding an infant even when not nursing, orphanage children typically are not held except as needed for routine tasks, such as feeding, bathing, and changing. Some orphanages may feed infants with bottles propped up in cribs, such that the infants are not held by a caregiver even while bottle-feeding. Not only do such children learn that their cries are ineffective at controlling the actions of adults around them, but the absence of contact comfort means they also miss opportunities to learn adaptive means of regulating their own distress states. Presumably as a result, some orphanage children are anecdotally described as exhibiting "self-soothing" behaviors, such as picking, rocking, swaying, and other repetitive behaviors.[32]

Biological studies confirm that children raised in institutional settings have more difficulty regulating their bodies' stress states. In particular, the stress hormone cortisol, part of the body's natural fight-or-flight system, may be improperly regulated. Normally, cortisol shows a predictable pattern of daily fluctuation, with higher levels in the morning and a decline during the day. In previously institutionalized children, this typical daily rhythm is blunted, as it is in children exposed to other severe early-life stressors, such as trauma or abuse.[33] Cortisol levels may also be abnormally elevated following social interactions in adoptees. One study examined cortisol levels in preschool children (ages 4–5 years) who had been adopted out of Romanian or Russian institutions and had been in the adoptive home for about 2 to 3 years.[34] Compared to non-adopted children of the same age, the adopted children showed higher levels of cortisol, particularly after a social interaction (playing a game) with the adoptive mother. The severity of institutional neglect, as rated by the parents, was a strong predictor of this effect, such that children who experienced more severe neglect in the institution showed greater stress hormone elevation.

Studies in other species can provide information on how early-life separation from parents can affect the development of the body's stress regulation systems. Depriving an infant rat of its mother for a 24-hour period can change the infant's later hormonal response to stress, making it either hypersensitive or abnormally insensitive, depending on the timing of the deprivation.[35] These consequences of early maternal deprivation can persist even into adulthood.[36] Likewise, in monkeys, repeated separation from parents alters the monkey's physiological stress response in childhood and even later in adulthood.[37] Imposing a stressor on a pregnant mother rat affects the fight-or-flight response in her offspring, which suggests that even prenatal stress can impact subsequent development of stress regulation systems in offspring.[38] These prenatal findings have obvious relevance to adopted children if we assume that the kinds of life circumstances that lead to relinquishment are likely to be the kinds of circumstances that generate high levels of stress among birth mothers. Needless to say, there are considerable difficulties in generalizing from other species to human experiences.[39] but the basic biological mechanisms of the stress response are quite similar across mammalian species.

While many studies have focused on regulation of cortisol and other hormones,[40] other animal studies have examined the effect of maternal deprivation on *neurotransmitters*, which are chemicals used by brain cells to communicate with one another. For example, one study of monkeys found that repeated parental separations in early life resulted in higher levels of the neurotransmitter dopamine in offspring.[41] Dopamine is critically important in brain systems controlling behavioral responses to rewards and positive incentives, and it is also important in functioning of the prefrontal cortex, which governs goal-directed action. Tellingly, the elevated dopamine in early-deprived monkeys was associated with increases in impulsive behavior. This parallels the known difficulties in attention and impulse control sometimes seen in adoptees, as reviewed in Chapter 2.

In human studies, institutional rearing also appears to be associated with abnormalities in larger-scale brain structures that are important in governing aspects of emotion and social behavior.[42] For example, the amygdala, a brain structure important in learning fear associations, may be abnormally large in previously institutionalized children.[43] Another brain imaging study found that an anatomical region that is usually activated by anticipation of rewards failed to activate normally in adolescents who had experienced early institutionalization.[44] Other studies found that the brain's response to pictures of faces is blunted in such children.[45]

Although these brain imaging studies offer preliminary evidence of disruption in brain regions that are crucial for learning appropriate emotional and social behavior, their results should be interpreted with caution. Because brain imaging studies are often much more expensive than other kinds of psychological research, they are usually conducted on small samples of people. The adopted samples studied with these methods to date were drawn primarily from severely deprived Romanian adoptees. In addition, researchers still do not fully understand the relationship between the size or reactivity of particular brain structures and their role in governing real-life behavior, so the specific implications of these findings for psychological functioning are not clear. Nevertheless, the findings support the broader conclusion that early maternal deprivation appears to affect many different aspects of physiology in other species and in humans.

Recent findings from a study of institutionalized children indicate that even the chromosomes within cells are affected by early deprivation.[46] The study examined the length of *telomeres*, which are the end parts of chromosomes. Telomeres are necessary for stable functioning of the chromosome, and they typically diminish in size with normal aging and in response to psychological stressors. Findings indicated shorter telomere lengths in children who had experienced institutional care, with the greatest degree of telomere shortening evident in those children subject to the longest periods of institutionalization. This finding fits with the broader theme that early-life deprivation has serious consequences for many levels of physiology, from the micro-level, such as chromosomal structure, to the macro-level, such as the functioning of larger-scale anatomical systems like the prefrontal cortex.

Overall, these results may seem to paint a pessimistic picture of the developmental risks for children adopted from institutional settings. When considering these findings, we must appreciate the harm done to children's bodies and minds by early-life adversity yet avoid needless stereotyping of adopted children as "damaged goods," a view that is all too prevalent in some media accounts.[47] Indeed, while the evidence clearly indicates that early-life deprivation of a caregiver has negative consequences for the developing child's physiology and behavior, additional considerations prompt a more optimistic view of the possibility for resilience and recovery.

Even among studies that report negative consequences for previously institutionalized children as a group, the overall pattern is an elevated risk of a negative outcome, not a guarantee of a negative outcome. For example, in a study of severely deprived Romanian orphans adopted into British families, the researchers remarked that "[e]ven within the subgroup of children whose institutional deprivation lasted until after 2 years of age, the majority did *not* show substantial cognitive impairment (a few even showed superior cognitive functioning), and most did *not* show disinhibited attachment."[48]

Likewise, a review of studies that examined behavioral and mental health outcomes for international adoptees concluded that although adoptees faced a greater risk of externalizing behaviors ("acting out"), internalizing behaviors (anxiety and depression), and mental health referrals compared to non-adoptees, the majority of adoptees were well adjusted and did not exhibit these problems.[49] Some researchers have found that adoptees are more likely to be referred for mental health treatment than non-adoptees with the same degree of behavioral problem, suggesting a bias of parents, teachers, or counselors to refer a child for assistance simply because he or she is adopted.[50] Although certainly the mental health challenges of adoptees are important to take seriously,[51] it is equally important to keep in mind that most adoptees do not have these negative outcomes.

Despite all the challenges they face, adopted children generally seem to have normal levels of self-esteem. A meta-analysis of 88 studies including a total of more than 40,000 people (approximately 10,000 of them adopted) found no difference in self-esteem between those who were adopted and those who were not.[52] This conclusion held true regardless of whether the children were adopted domestically or internationally, whether they were the same or different race as the adoptive parents, and whether self-esteem was measured when the adoptees were children, adolescents, or adults; in all cases, there were no self-esteem differences between the adoptees and non-adoptees. Among a smaller subset of studies that compared adopted children to their peers left in institutions, the adopted children had higher self-esteem than the institutionalized children. These self-esteem findings may be particularly meaningful for parents, who often simply wish for their children to be happy and feel good about themselves, above all else.

Research on risk factors and research on resilience often go hand in hand.[53] That is, we can ask both what factors (such as early-life deprivation) may increase risk for certain negative consequences and what factors buffer children against those negative consequences. Many different factors probably contribute in complex ways to the sum total of risk and resilience operating within a particular child's life. As a starting point in understanding factors that promote resilience, we can group them into two broad categories, namely genetic and environmental factors. A child may be buffered against adverse experience due to intrinsic genetic factors that influence how that child responds to stress. Environmental factors may also buffer the child against stress if those experiences in some way compensate for the adverse experience or provide a means of coping. It is likely that genetic and environmental factors work together in complex ways; for example, genes can affect reactivity to certain experiences and experiences can in turn modify gene expression.[54]

Although it is not fully understood why some children are more emotionally resilient than others in the face of adversity, some researchers have begun to focus on known genetic differences that appear to affect stress reactivity. For example, different people possess different versions of a gene known as the *5HTT* gene, which regulates a particular neurotransmitter system in the brain, the serotonin system. People who have the "short" version of the *5HTT* gene appear to learn fear responses more quickly, pay greater attention to threatening information, and have increased risk for depression in response to very stressful life circumstances compared to people with the "long" version of the *5HTT* gene.[55] (Both variants of the gene are common in the general population.) One study found that domestic American adoptees with the long version of the *5HTT* gene had less risk of attachment difficulties than those with the short version of the gene.[56] Likewise, monkeys who experienced maternal deprivation were less likely to show negative outcomes if they possessed the long version of the gene.[57] Thus, some children may be somewhat protected against the effects of early-life adversity simply due to the luck of the draw in the genes they inherit.

The idea that different *5HTT* genotypes confer different levels of sensitivity to caregiving environments is supported by evidence from the BEIP, which followed Romanian infants randomly assigned to high-quality foster care or to continued orphanage care.[58] Children with two copies of the short version of the *5HTT* gene were most sensitive to the caregiving environment, as measured by levels of externalizing (acting out) behavior at the age of 54 months. When raised in an orphanage setting, these children showed greater externalizing (acting out) behavior than those with at least one long version of the gene; yet, when raised in foster care, those with two short versions showed *less* externalizing behavior than the other genotypes. In other words, the short *5HTT* genotype appeared to confer both greater benefits when the children were raised in homes and greater costs when they were raised in orphanages. These findings support the idea that some children may possess specific genes that make them either more or less reactive to the quality of the caregiving environment.

Environmental enrichment can also help protect against the effects of adversity, providing an important avenue for intervention that could potentially assist a wider range of children, not just those lucky enough to inherit certain genes. Biological evidence from animal studies indicates that at least some effects of early-life stress can be counteracted by later enrichment within the environment. As reviewed earlier in this chapter, maternal deprivation leads to abnormal stress physiology and altered behavior in rodents and monkeys. However, subsequently rearing the animals in an enriched environment can reverse many of these effects.

For example, one study examined the combined effects of maternal deprivation and later environmental enrichment on stress physiology in rats.[59] Rats who were in the maternal separation condition experienced 3-hour-long separations from the mother every day for the first 14 days of life, an experience known to lead to abnormalities in the stress response system in rodents. Rats in the control group were briefly handled, rather than experiencing stressful deprivation. Animals from both groups were then reared after weaning in either an enriched environment, consisting of eight peers in a large cage with burrows and toys, or an impoverished environment, consisting of two peers in a simple smaller cage with no burrows or toys.

Results revealed different consequences later in life, depending on whether the rats experienced enriched or impoverished environments after the early-life maternal deprivation.[60] For those raised in the impoverished environment, there was an expected effect of maternal deprivation, namely altered responsiveness of the stress hormone system in maternally deprived animals compared to non-deprived animals. However, this consequence of maternal deprivation was eliminated in the animals who later experienced environmental enrichment; their hormonal outcomes were normal—that is, comparable to outcomes for animals who did not experience any maternal deprivation. Similar effects held for the animals' behavior: Rats that experienced maternal deprivation followed by impoverished rearing showed deficits in exploratory behavior and increased anxiety behaviors, whereas those who experienced maternal deprivation followed by environmental enrichment showed normal behavior. Interestingly, compared to non-deprived groups, both maternally deprived groups continued to exhibit altered gene expression regardless of environment of subsequent rearing. This latter finding suggests a persisting biological marker of early maternal deprivation. Yet somehow the consequences of this altered gene expression were lessened in the enriched group, so that hormonal and behavioral indices of emotionality returned to normal levels despite the altered gene expression.

Although these findings are from studies of nonhuman animals,[61] they have direct implications for maternally deprived children. As noted earlier, humans share the basic physiology of the stress system with other mammalian species. If psychosocially stressed animals can suffer ill effects and then experience rehabilitation through enriching environments, then it stands to reason that humans can too. The challenge for future research is to determine what specific environmental features are optimal for helping children overcome the effects of early-life stress, a topic we return to in Chapter 7.

The evidence that children may have resilience against early adversity—whether through their own fortunate genetics, later environmental enhancements, or some combination thereof—should not be seen as a reason to take less seriously the toll of early deprivation. From a moral standpoint, we should not accept the premise that the damage done by institutionalization is tolerable because it can be compensated for later in life. The promise of a future possibility of rehabilitation does not give license to inflict injury. Instead, the research on resilience and recovery following early adversity indicates that development should not be written off as permanently disfigured even after experiences as drastically abnormal as institutional care. We need to balance our understanding of the ways children are affected by psychosocial deprivation with an understanding of the best ways to provide nurturing environments in which those children can thrive to their greatest potential.

4 ■
Culture, Race, and Identity

Adoptive families, particularly those with a mixed-race family composition, often face seemingly innocent remarks about race, culture, and ancestry in everyday life. "Is your husband Filipino?" asks a complete stranger at the playground, attempting to make sense of the child with Asian features who calls me, a white woman, "mommy." "No," I say, letting him ponder this for a few beats before explaining that my son was adopted. While at the hair salon, a patron stares for an inappropriately long time at my son, then says, "He is so beautiful," followed by the cringe-inducing, "Where did you get him?" "He was born in Kazakhstan," I explain politely. "Where? That's the strangest place I've ever heard of!" she exclaims, as astonished as if I had said "Mars." My son, 5 years old at the time, stared intently into the mirror as he listened to this exchange.

Even well-meaning adoptive parents have moments of painfully realizing their own implicit assumptions about the adopted child's ancestry. These assumptions can emerge at seemingly trivial moments. For example, proud that traditionally Kazakhs were admired for their expert horsemanship on the great steppes of Central Asia, I found myself disappointed that my toddler of Kazakh heritage showed absolutely no interest in pony rides at our local American fair. Did I believe that a special interest in horses would emerge in my son because his ancestors spent a lot of time on horseback? Did my eagerness to take pride in all things Kazakh lead me to expect him, even as a toddler, to "perform" Kazakh ethnicity in a certain way? In what sense, if any, is his "essence" Kazakh?[1]

The presumed importance of nationality and culture in a child's identity is reflected in the text of international human rights conventions. For example, according to the United Nations Convention on the Rights of the Child (CRC), signatory countries must "respect the right of the child to preserve his or her identity, including nationality, name and family relations as recognized by law without unlawful interference."[2] This emphasis on the importance of national identity is reflected in the CRC's preference for in-country over international placement of an unparented child.[3] Likewise, the Hague Convention on international adoption, an international treaty governing adoptions between signatory countries, allows that such adoption can only be considered "after possibilities for placement of the child within the State of origin have been given due consideration"[4] and charges authorities with giving "due consideration to the child's upbringing and to his or her ethnic, religious and cultural background."[5]

The language in human rights conventions protecting a child's nationality and cultural identity should be understood as a response to historical incidents during the 20th century in which children were forcibly transferred from one national or cultural group to another during genocidal conflicts. For example, as part of the Nazi program to strengthen the demographic power of the Aryan race, thousands of children were abducted from Poland, Ukraine, Russia, and other countries and placed in German homes for "Germanization."[6] During the Argentinian "Dirty War," children of dissidents were stolen and raised by ruling military families.[7] In both North America and Australia, large numbers of indigenous children were forcibly removed from their families and placed in white homes or institutions during the 20th century.[8] The need to protect against such atrocities is clear and uncontested.

More controversially, though, some adoption critics argue that even legal adoptions (as opposed to forced removals) across national lines should be discouraged given the purported loss of culture that can ensue. For example, one critic argues that "[c]hildren who are adopted internationally may be deprived of the right to identification with their own ethnic, cultural, or national group."[9] This line of criticism assumes that the child's "own" group is the one of their genetic ancestors. It defines belongingness on the basis of birth origins and minimizes the possibility that the adopted ethnicity, culture, or nation could also be the child's "own." The reasoning also assumes that being removed from the culture of birth amounts to deprivation that could be detrimental to the child's development and therefore counter to his or her best interests.

The goal of this chapter is to more closely examine evidence regarding how international adoptees are affected when reared in a family and culture that differs from that of their biological ancestors. Are they plagued by cultural confusion that harms development or well-being? Are they able to establish healthy identities and a strong sense of belongingness to social groups in their country of rearing? Can particular parenting strategies, community characteristics, or adoption practices support the development of a strong sense of identity in internationally adopted children and adults?

Controversial issues of race and culture in adoption are not restricted to international adoption. U.S. domestic adoption has witnessed debates about whether white parents are capable of effectively raising African-American or Native American children.[10] Anchoring one position on this issue, in the 1970s the National Association of Black Social Workers referred to transracial adoption as "cultural genocide" and argued:

> Black children should be placed only with Black families whether in foster care or for adoption. Black children belong physically, psychologically and culturally in Black families in order that they receive the total sense of themselves and develop a sound projection of their future. . . . Black children in White homes are cut off from the healthy development of themselves as people.[11]

Others in the adoption community argued in response that race-conscious placement worked to the disadvantage of African-American children, who often waited longer for permanency due to a shortage of same-race adoptive parents.[12] Research literature in the 1970s and 1980s also failed to show any evidence that transracial placement was detrimental to African-American children.[13] Emerging from this debate, the Multiethnic Placement Act, passed by Congress in 1994 and amended in 1996, now prohibits states and agencies that receive federal funds from delaying placement of a child based on his or her race or ethnicity.[14] Exceptions exist for children with Native American heritage, for whom placement within tribal families is prioritized under the Indian Child Welfare Act with the intent of preserving tribal culture.[15]

Adoptive families are caught between two broadly competing philosophical worldviews about race and culture. Both of these worldviews are prevalent in Western culture, and their apparent conflict with one another is unresolved in society at large. On the one hand, many aspire to a color-blind ideal that "people are all the same" regardless of racial or ethnic origins. Morally, each human being has the same value regardless of their place of birth, color of their skin, or shape of their eyes and noses. Legally, people of all ethnicities are entitled to nondiscriminatory treatment. Biologically, race is an artificial construct, because the genetic similarities across all humankind vastly outweigh the tiny biological differences between people born in different corners of the world. Developmentally, the needs of a child are universal, transcending race or ethnicity.

An alternative view asserts the importance of racial and ethnic group identification. In this view, even as we accept that race is not a biological construct but a social one, social constructs matter in a person's identity development. People experience the world differently according to the racial category in which others place them. A girl adopted from China and raised by white parents will be treated by others as "Chinese" on the basis of her physical features, forcing her to reconcile "Chinese" and "white" aspects of her identity. Such considerations mean that transracial adoptive families cannot simply ignore issues of race, no matter how much they believe in or strive toward a color-blind society, because society itself is not color-blind.[16]

Challenges in navigating issues of culture exist even when the adoptive parents and child are perceived to belong to the same racial category. For example, imagine a Slavic Russian child adopted by a white French family. Even though both parents and child are perceived as "white," Russian and French cultures differ. Families may struggle with the best ways to balance a sense of pride and respect for the child's birth culture with the unapologetic acknowledgement that the child now belongs to a new culture. Shift too far in one direction, and the family risks ignoring the heritage of the child's birth culture; shift too far in the other direction, and the family risks superficially "faking" the birth culture through symbolic gestures devoid of any connection to lived cultural experience.[17] A French family may aim to instill respect for and interest in Russian culture, but their home is still primarily a French home, albeit now a multiethnic French home.

Adoptive families must be prepared to handle the racial and cultural assumptions made by others in both apparently meaningless yet also deeply fraught ways. Strangers, motivated by simple curiosity, attempt to guess my son's ancestry so that they can determine "what he is." (They never guess "Kazakh.") Other adoptive parents tell anecdotes of misguided teachers who expect an adopted child to be able to sing the national anthem of his country of birth, despite the fact that the child was adopted as an infant and raised in an American family, or educational systems that forever track an internationally adopted child into English as a Second Language classes despite the fact that the child acquired native fluency in English after being adopted as a 1-year-old. Such experiences, however unintentionally, mark the "otherness" of the adopted child.[18]

If adoptive parents feel these pressures and conflicts acutely, we must recognize the even greater challenges faced by the adopted child. He or she comes to develop a sense of identity that must incorporate multiple levels of "difference"—an awareness of being adopted, an awareness of being born in another country, and in many (though not all) cases an awareness of being a racial minority in the adoptive country and a different race than the adoptive parents. In addition, the adoptee must cope with the sense of feeling inauthentic at moments when others in society expect him or her to somehow represent or embody the birth ethnicity.[19]

Many of these modes of difference are shared with other groups of people. All immigrant groups grapple with the challenges of being "different" due to birthplace and balancing their native culture with that of the country to which they have immigrated. The U.S. Census Bureau estimates that in 2010, nearly 13% of the U.S. population was foreign-born. In states such as California, New York, and New Jersey, more than 1 in 5 people are foreign-born.[20] Members of all ethnic minority groups, which currently account for approximately 37% of the U.S. population,[21] share the challenge of navigating ethnic stereotypes and discrimination. Biracial people of any origin also must integrate more than one ethnic identity into a sense of self. Domestic adoptees of any race must develop an understanding of the birth family and its role in shaping identity. While none of these challenges alone is unique to international adoptees, they all converge to make the development of identity potentially more fraught for such adoptees.

Adoptees will likely encounter these issues in different ways at different stages of development.[22] Infants, toddlers, and preschoolers are simply too young and cognitively immature to fully understand what "adoption" means or to develop a sense of identity. Nevertheless, most adoptive parents (at least those in Western countries) begin discussing the child's life story, including adoption and pre-adoptive history, as early as the time of placement in the adoptive family, so that there will be no single fraught moment when the child discovers that he or she is adopted.[23]

In the elementary school years, children begin to understand the distinction between adoptive and biological relatedness and to be aware of physical differences between people (including between themselves and their adoptive parents). They also begin to contemplate the perspective of the birth family and the loss of the birth family. In adolescence and early adulthood, people typically engage in greater self-exploration and work to establish a sense of identity. Ethnic identification typically becomes more important at this stage as part of the process of identity formation.[24] During these later stages, children and young adults also become more cognizant of societal attitudes about adoption. At younger ages, children's exposure to adoption narratives may be largely (though not exclusively) influenced by their adoptive parents, but older children, adolescents, and adults can shape their own questions and seek out information either together with or independently from adoptive parents.[25]

Recent autobiographical writing by adult adoptees has provided first-person insights into identity challenges. For example, in the introduction to a book of essays about transracial adoption, adoptees Julia Chinyere Oparah, Sun Yung Shin, and Jane Jeong Trenka write of "struggles to come to terms with the physical markers of our difference within our own families, and of the physical evidence of our maligned or exoticized African, Asian, Native, or Latin American ancestries."[26] The authors also point to the "murky waters" they must navigate:

> On the one hand, we resist being defined as victims condemned to half-lives between cultures, without meaningful connections to our families and communities. . . . [O]ur successful attempts to create new identities authentically based on our experiences are testimony that we can indeed survive and thrive. On the other hand, our experiences of racism, isolation, and abuse and our struggles with depression, addiction, and alienation indicate that adoption across boundaries of race, nation, and culture does indeed exact a very real emotional and spiritual cost.[27]

A central question, from a broader research and policy perspective, is how representative such voices are. To what extent do narratives of the "very real emotional and spiritual cost" of adoption, notwithstanding their unquestionable and powerful authenticity as individual experiences, speak for the international adoptee experience in general?

Addressing these questions requires looking beyond individual narratives to the research literature. In doing so, we must also recognize the difficulties and limitations of existing empirical research on race and culture in international adoption.[28] There are three major challenges in interpreting the research. One challenge is taking into account the rapidly changing societal contexts in which adoptees in America will experience race. A second challenge involves weighing the value judgments implicit in outcome variables related to ethnic identification. Finally, a third challenge is avoiding oversimplification of adoptees' racial categories.

The first problem in applying the existing research literature to current-day adopted populations in the United States is that the demographics of the country are rapidly changing. Current projections by the U.S. Census Bureau predict that non-Hispanic whites will be the minority ethnicity in the nation by 2050;[29] indeed, in the United States in 2011, more than half of the children under the age of 1 year were ethnic minorities.[30] While some regions of the country remain relatively homogeneously white, more than 10% of the counties in the United States, along with several entire states (California, Hawaii, Texas, and New Mexico, plus the District of Columbia) were already "majority minority" in 2011.[31]

Diversity comes through racial mixing within persons as well as within the nation at large. More than 9 million people identified themselves as "more than one race" on the 2010 U.S. Census, an increase of 32% since 2000.[32] (Presumably the biracial respondents in 2010 included the U.S. president.) Given this context of rapidly increasing racial diversification and boundary-crossing, the race-related experiences of minority-race people adopted in the 1970s, 1980s, and even 1990s, who form the basis for the published research literature, may not be easily generalized to form predictions for adoptees who are entering America now.

Empirical research on identity development in adoptees, particularly as it pertains to race and culture, is in some ways harder to interpret than the research on physical, cognitive, and emotional development covered in prior chapters, because value judgments so easily affect the interpretation of outcomes. Needless to say, values affect the interpretation of any scientific finding. But there is probably more widespread consensus about the value of outcomes related to physical and cognitive growth. Stunted growth, low IQ, and abnormal stress physiology are undesirable outcomes for a child, and we can therefore come to the straightforward conclusion that institutionalization is not in the best interests of a child. However, when it comes to racial or ethnic identification, how do we define what is "best"?

Imagine a hypothetical study that asked Korean-born adolescents adopted to America as infants how they would categorize their identity: as Korean, as American, as Korean-American, or as none of the above. Now imagine that 25% of respondents chose each of the four options. Is that a good outcome or a bad one? Should these adoptees identify as Korean? Should they identify as American? Is it a problem that a quarter of the individuals refused to accept any of the labels offered to them? Why or why not? What is "healthy" ethnic identification?

The "shoulds" regarding ethnic identification become even more complicated for children whose birth backgrounds don't fit clearly defined racial, ethnic, or cultural categories. Much research on ethnic identification in adoption has focused on seemingly clear-cut ethnic categories, such as transracially adopted African-American or Korean-American children. But for many adopted children, racial categorization and its relation to "culture" is not that simple even prior to adoption. For example, the child's biological origins may be biracial. Biracial children may be disproportionately represented among international adoptees because citizens in the country of origin prefer to adopt children who match their own ethnicity.[33] Internationally adopted children may also be disproportionately drawn from minority communities within the country of origin, both because minorities often experience more severe economic hardship that can lead to relinquishment and because minority children may be less likely to be adopted domestically. Consider a girl adopted from Russia whose birth parents are Kyrgyz migrants, an ethnic group from Central Asia that experiences severe discrimination within Russia. For "healthy ethnic identification," is the girl supposed to identify as Kyrgyz (ethnic origin of her ancestors who left Kyrgyzstan a generation ago), Russian (nationality of her birth), or American (country of her rearing)? Assertions that adoption cuts off children from their "own culture" overlook such real-life complexities in favor of simplistic assumptions about where children belong.[34]

While it is difficult to evaluate the "goodness" or "badness" of many outcomes related to ethnic identification, outcome variables such as self-esteem may be less ambiguous. Let us presume that it is generally desirable to have high self-esteem, indicated by endorsement of statements such as "I am a worthwhile person" and "I am satisfied with myself." With this in mind, we can revisit a finding about self-esteem reported in the previous chapter. Researchers combined results from 88 studies of self-esteem that included more than 10,000 adoptees and more than 30,000 non-adopted people.[35] Those who were adopted across racial lines had self-esteem equal to that of non-adoptees or those who were adopted within-race. Those who were adopted across national lines also had equally high self-esteem compared to non-adoptees or domestic adoptees. Despite all of the challenges that international and transracial adoptees face in confronting issues of identity, in the end the majority appear to develop a sense of self-worth that is comparable to that of those who were not adopted.

Research also shows that the labels that adoptees use to describe their ethnicity are unrelated to their self-esteem. Illustrating this point, one study surveyed 234 adolescent girls adopted from China to America.[36] Part of the survey included an open-ended question that asked the girls to describe their ethnicity. While the most common response was "Chinese" (endorsed by 27% of the girls), other common responses were "Asian" (13%), "Asian-American" (18%), "Chinese-American" (19%), and "White" or "Other" (8% combined). Thirteen percent of the respondents left the question blank. Crucially, the researchers found no differences in self-esteem among these groups, nor did the groups differ in their positive or negative attitudes about adoption or their academic functioning. That is, the extent to which the adoptee included "American" in her self-description (or even provided an ethnic label at all) had no bearing on her overall level of self-reported well-being.

The relationship between ethnic identification and positive outcomes in adopted people is complex at best. For example, one study compared college students who were either transracial Korean-American adoptees, Korean-Americans raised by Korean birth parents who immigrated to the United States, or international students from South Korea.[37] The students completed a questionnaire indicating their level of agreement with statements like "I feel a strong attachment toward my own ethnic group." Korean-American adoptees were less likely to endorse such statements than students who were raised in the United States by Korean immigrant parents. This could mean that the adoptees had lower ethnic identification or that, having been raised in biracial households, they experienced more ambiguity about what the questions even meant by their "own ethnic group." Interestingly, the international students who were raised in South Korea did not differ from the Korean adoptees on the ethnic identity measure; both scored lower than the non-adopted Korean-Americans. This finding raises questions about what the ethnic identification index is really measuring.[38]

Furthermore, in the same study, the adoptees did not differ from the non-adopted Korean-Americans in self-reported satisfaction with life or overall positive or negative emotion. That is, even though the adopted group indicated lower ethnic identification, that didn't necessarily make them as a group any "worse off" in terms of their emotional states and life satisfaction.[39] Recent literature reviews also detail a lack of consistent evidence that strong identification with birth ethnicity is associated with better well-being among adoptees.[40]

What may matter most for adoptees' well-being is not the degree of their identification with birth ethnicity alone, but the extent to which the adoptee perceives harmony instead of conflict between the different aspects of his or her cultural identities. The concept of bicultural identity integration was developed to understand developing identity among non-adopted people who belong in some way to more than one culture, such as biracial people or ethnic minorities within the United States. Generally speaking, research has found better well-being among people who develop a sense that the different aspects of their cultural identities coexist harmoniously.[41]

In a recent study exploring bicultural identity integration in adoptees, researchers studied 170 adolescents who were ethnic Latin Americans adopted to Italy.[42] Participants completed questionnaires regarding the extent of ethnic (Latin American) identification ("I have a strong sense of belonging to my ethnic group"), the degree of national

(Italian) identification ("I have a strong sense of belonging with the Italian people"), the extent of bicultural identity integration ("I feel part of a combined culture" as opposed to "I feel like someone moving between two cultures"), and the extent of adoptive filiation, which is the adoptee's perceived belongingness to the adoptive family ("I consider my adoptive mother and father as my parents in every respect"). Results indicated that the degree of Latin American ethnic identification by itself did not predict adoptees' well-being. Instead, better well-being was predicted by stronger national (Italian) identification, a higher degree of bicultural integration (that is, viewing Latin American ethnicity as compatible with Italian nationality), and the adolescent's perception of belongingness within the adoptive family.

One of the more extensive studies of ethnic identification in adoptees found that transracial adoptees generally do develop a strong sense of pride in their ethnicity, however they choose to define it. The study surveyed 335 adult adoptees; approximately half were Korean adoptees and half were white domestic adoptees.[43] All of the adoptees were raised by white American parents. The two groups of adoptees were statistically indistinguishable in the percent who agreed with statements indicating "I am happy with being a member of my ethnic group" (86% of Korean-American vs. 87% of white American adoptees); "I have a lot of pride in my ethnic group" (74% vs. 67%); "I feel good about my cultural or ethnic background" (84% vs. 81%); "I have a clear sense of my ethnic group background and what it means for me" (65% vs. 60%); and "I understand pretty well what my ethnic group means to me" (68% vs. 69%). These figures bode well for the ability of transracial adoptees to develop pride and self-esteem about their ethnicities. They are particularly promising given that many of these adoptees were raised in an era in which America was less ethnically diverse and less sensitive to the identity struggles of adoptees.

At the same time, the study also found that the Korean adoptees invested more effort in learning about their ethnicity, compared to the white adoptees.[44] A greater percentage of Korean-American than white American adult adoptees agreed with the following statements: "I have spent time trying to find out more about my ethnic group, such as its history, traditions, and customs" (80% vs. 45%); "In order to learn more about my ethnic group, I have often talked to other people about my ethnic group" (64% vs. 33%); and "I think a lot about how my life will be affected by my ethnic group membership" (46% vs. 21%). In addition, somewhat fewer of the Korean-Americans (52%) than white Americans (62%) agreed that "I have strong sense of belonging to my own ethnic group." This latter finding likely reflects a more divided sense of ethnic belonging when one's birth ethnicity and adoptive family ethnicity are not the same. Over 75% of the Korean adult adoptees reported, at some point in childhood, either thinking of themselves as white or wishing to be white.[45]

Other research suggests that adoptees may feel a greater sense of identification with the birth culture than their adoptive parents realize. For example, one study examined attitudes among members of Spanish families who had adopted children internationally.[46] Some of the children were adopted transracially (Asian children in white Spanish families) and others were adopted within-race (Eastern European children in white Spanish families). Adoptees were 8–12 years old at the time of the study, and the children and parents were interviewed about a variety of adoption-related issues, including the child's degree of cultural identification with the birth country. Generally, parents' and children's beliefs and attitudes were highly similar. While all members of the family indicated that the child had a strong sense of birth culture identity, the adoptees (both Asian and Eastern-European adoptees) rated themselves as having higher birth culture identification than their parents rated them as having. Although it is difficult to rule out the possibility that the parents and children were just using the rating scale differently, the findings raise the possibility that parents may underestimate their adopted child's sense of birth culture identity.

Taken together, these results imply that while transracial adoptees are capable of developing pride in their ethnicity, they often invest considerable effort in doing so, and they may work to reconcile differences between their own racial category and that of their adoptive parents. In addition, research indicates that a sense of belongingness, support, and open communication about adoption within the family are also crucial.[47] How, then, can adoptive families support and nurture the process of ethnic identity exploration and development?

In the large sample of Korean adult adoptees, more than 70% of adoptees reported that each of the following experiences was helpful in formation of identity: traveling to the birth country, having adult role models of the same race or ethnicity, attending racially diverse schools, and living in a racially diverse neighborhood.[48] Other research supports the conclusion that exposure to diverse communities and diverse cultural experiences (even if unrelated to the culture of birth) is beneficial to the self-esteem and well-being of transracially adopted individuals.[49] Presumably such experiences reduce the sense of isolation that comes from being "the one who is different."[50] Notably, fewer of the adult adoptees (49%) rated "having traditional objects from the birth country" as helpful in the formation of ethnic identity. This serves as an important reminder to adoptive parents that purchasing cultural artifacts is not as helpful as providing space for ethnically diverse social relationships.

Relationships with adults of the same ethnicity (or other minority ethnicities) may also provide opportunities for the minority-race adoptee to learn strategies for navigating racial prejudice, stereotypes, and discrimination. Unfortunately, but perhaps not surprisingly, racial minorities still experience discrimination even in a multicultural society like the United States. In a recent study of Korean-American adult adoptees, 78% of the participants reported that they had experienced race-related teasing in childhood either sometimes, often, or all the time.[51] Racial teasing was more common among those who were raised in less diverse neighborhoods. Respondents identified classmates and strangers as the most common sources of racial discrimination, but almost 40% reported experiencing discriminatory treatment by teachers and 33% reported such treatment by coworkers.

Many transracial adoptees wish that their adoptive parents could help them better navigate issues of racial prejudice.[52] For adoptees who are minority race and raised by white parents, their parents do not have firsthand experience living as a racial minority and therefore may underestimate the influence of race or feel ill-equipped to offer guidance. As transracial adoptee Jeni Wright wrote:

What I had been told about race by my parents could be summed up in three words—Love is Colorblind. My mom hand-stitched that ideal into the quilt hanging in my childhood bedroom. It is a beautiful ideal but one I had learned the limits of by first grade.[53]

Adoptive families need to confront the racial realities of minority-race adopted children, rather than leaving the children (and later adults) to fend for themselves in the face of racist experiences outside the home. In-depth interviews with a representative sample of adult Korean-American adoptees indicated that, at least for the cohort studied, adoptive parents tended to be more comfortable celebrating the cultural diversity of their children than having difficult conversations about racism and prejudice.[54] Adult adoptees reported benefiting from parents who opted to more openly acknowledge racial difference, as this validated the adoptee's experience in the world, normalized conversations about race, and contributed to a sense of shared fate among members of the adoptive family. In other words, in families who acknowledged the issue of race instead of ignoring it, the burden of confronting race-related difficulties was born by the whole family, rather than being shouldered only by the child.[55]

Largely in response to experiences narrated by adult transracial adoptees, the ethos of assimilation that characterized earlier eras in adoption has now been replaced by greater awareness of the complexities of race and culture.[56] Reading first-person adoptee accounts that encompass a wide range of experiences may help adoptive families better address similar issues in their own lives.[57] Support groups of fellow adoptees now exist, accommodating a variety of opinions on international adoption.[58] Adoptive families have access to significant in-person and online resources that did not exist a generation ago.[59] Many adoption agencies now incorporate training in race and cultural issues as required preparation before parents can be approved for international adoption.[60]

Contrary to the stereotype of the assimilationist adoptive family, many adoptive parents do seek out activities connected to the birth culture of the child. As articulated by adoptive parent Toby Alice Volkman:

> The powerful image of the network, of "kids like me" or "families like ours" "wherever we go," enacted through the everyday practices of ribbon dance classes or FCC [Families with Children from China] picnics, reflects how significantly the culture of adoption has changed in

recent years. . . . It is not that the complexities and contradictions of adoption have become any simpler. Performing "Chinese culture" surely does not erase racism; it may reinscribe or reify difference in unintended ways. But many of these complexities and contradictions are now exposed, voiced, and debated.[61]

In a study of mostly white parents from Minnesota who adopted children internationally between 1990 and 1998, more than 80% of parents reported exposing the child to birth culture experiences, through attendance at cultural camp, contact with children or adults from the same birth culture, learning the birth culture language, or celebrating a holiday or tradition associated with the birth culture.[62] The frequency of such activities by adoptive families attests to their increasing desire to maintain connections with the child's birth culture.

For international adoptees, birth culture and birth family origins are inextricably linked. Indeed, an important issue for all adoptees, whether adopted within-race or transracially, domestically or internationally, involves the role of the birth family in identity development. To what extent do adoptees struggle to integrate their biological ancestral past with their present sense of self? How important is it to have information about one's birth parents and ancestors?

Research on domestic adoptees in the United States indicates that, not surprisingly, it is important to many adoptees to learn about their birth families. A literature review estimated that between 30% and 65% of domestic adoptees either engaged in an active search for birth family information or were strongly interested in seeking such information.[63] Whereas in the not-so-distant past adoption in the United States was shrouded in secrecy that implied shamefulness, recent decades have seen growing acceptance that the child has the right to know as much as possible about his or her origins.[64] This acceptance is seen in movements to open previously sealed records, even at the risk of betraying confidentiality that may have been expected by or promised to some birth parents.[65] It is also seen in the increased incidence of open adoptions, in which continued contact with the birth parents is maintained in some form, and in the extent to which adoptees are encouraged to search for biological relatives previously unknown to them.[66]

Although one might assume that an active search for birth parents implies some dissatisfaction with the adoptive family situation, research on domestic adoptees does not support that assumption. A study comparing "searchers" with "non-searchers" found that the majority of adoptees in both groups were satisfied with their adoptive family situation.[67] The percentage who described themselves as "unhappy or uncomfortable" with their adoptive status was higher for searchers (12%) than for non-searchers (6%), and searchers tended to report slightly lower self-esteem.[68] Nevertheless, the majority in both groups reported high self-esteem and positive attitudes toward their adoptive family experience. In other words, the desire to search for origins does not reflect some kind of pathology in the adoptee or in adoptive family relationships. Motives for searching can include desire for factual information and simple curiosity, in addition to a desire for a more complete sense of identity.[69]

It is often assumed that international adoptees have no opportunity to search for biological relatives, and some critics allege that adoptive parents prefer it that way.[70] Indeed, searching for biological relatives may be more difficult for adoptees from some countries of origin because of geographical distance, language barriers, poor record-keeping, and secrecy-laden attitudes about adoption in the country of origin. Nevertheless, international adoptees, just like domestic adoptees, often want to learn about their birth family origins. For example, in a study of more than

1,400 adult international adoptees in the Netherlands, approximately one-third of the adoptees had actively searched for birth parents (and roughly half of those had experienced reunion of some kind), another one-third of adoptees were interested but not actively searching (perhaps due to structural or informational barriers), and the remaining one-third were not interested in searching.[71]

As in studies with domestic adoptees, findings from this large-scale study of international adoptees did find some differences between searchers (including those who wanted to search but were unable to) and those who were uninterested in searching.[72] There was a slightly higher likelihood of psychological difficulties, such as an anxiety or mood disorder, among those who opted or wanted to search compared to those who were uninterested. However, the differences were small in magnitude (albeit statistically significant), and the majority of both searchers and non-searchers did not experience psychological difficulties. The researchers also examined whether the adoptee's reported sense of being different from the adoptive parents was related to the desire to search for birth parents. Adoptees who perceived greater psychological or intellectual difference from the adoptive parents were more likely to search for birth parents; perceived physical difference from the adoptive parents was not related to the desire to search.

Reflecting the desire of adoptees and their adoptive parents to learn about and even make contact with biological relatives overseas, organizations have sprung up that promise to find these relatives. Investigative teams will, for a fee, attempt to locate and contact biological relatives based on clues in paperwork held by adoptive families. At least a dozen such investigative organizations currently exist for this purpose.[73] The ever-increasing use of birth search investigations by internationally adoptive parents counters the unsubstantiated charge that adoptive parents generally wish to erase their child's pre-adoptive history.[74]

Indeed, one survey found that while one-third of internationally adopting parents endorsed the item "there would be no contact with birth families" as a reason for originally choosing international adoption, some of those parents reported later wishing that they could have more birth family contact for their child's sake.[75]

While general trends in the adoption community are toward greater openness, greater support for searching for birth relatives, and greater engagement with the birth culture, it is also important to acknowledge that individual adoptees differ in their desires. Substantial minorities (30%–40%) of both domestic and international adoptees report no interest in searching for birth relatives. Based on existing evidence, those non-interested adoptees are not any worse off by any psychological measure than the interested searchers. Likewise, a study of Romanian adolescents adopted to the U.K. found that while the majority were interested in learning about Romanian culture, a sizable fraction (27%) were not.[76] Those uninterested adoptees had self-esteem that was no worse (in fact, slightly better) than the interested adoptees. Although it is not clear why some adoptees are more interested than others in exploring their "roots," reasons could include normal variation in personality among adoptees, who of course should not be expected to all think alike.

With regard to openness in adoption, it seems advisable for the adoption community to avoid replacing one rigid ideology with another. In the past, the accepted dogma of "wiping the slate clean" and ignoring or withholding information about adoptees' histories was harmful to the many adoptees who find such information essential in formulating a sense of identity. In attempting to correct this misguided practice from the past, we should avoid forcing a new, inflexible ideology that assumes that all adoptees should wish to search for birth parents and should strongly identify with the birth ethnicity and wish to explore it through culture camps, travel to the birth country, and so forth. The expectation that an adoptee must or should want to "find her roots" reflects an understanding of kinship and identity that privileges genetic essentialism, a culturally constructed belief that one's essence is genetically grounded.[77] Adoptive parents and the wider adoption community would best serve adoptees by providing ample opportunities and encouragement for self-exploration while at the same time respecting the individual desires and choices of different adoptees or even the same adoptee at different points in time.

Maintaining an open-minded attitude toward discussing the child's feelings about adoption seems to be crucial for adoptive families, regardless of their level of contact with birth families. A seminal research study examined both "structural openness" (degree of birth family contact) and "communication openness" among a sample of 73 American children, ages 8 to 13, who were adopted either domestically or internationally.[78] In the measure of family communication openness, children reported their level of agreement with statements like "My parents are good listeners when it comes to my thoughts and feelings about being adopted." The study found that higher levels of communication openness were correlated with higher self-esteem reported by the child, as well as fewer behavioral problems reported by the parents. These results, as well as other similar findings,[79] emphasize that it is important for adoptive families to empathetically listen to, acknowledge, and openly discuss the adoptee's feelings about adoption issues throughout all stages of development.

Although international adoption is sometimes criticized for severing the adoptee's relationship with the birth family, domestic adoption in some countries of origin may do the same (or worse). For example, adoption within Kazakhstan is plagued by deeply stigmatizing attitudes that mirror attitudes prevalent in the United States 50 years ago. According to locals we befriended, many Kazakhstanis view adoption as shameful. Adoption is generally hidden from both the child and the community, as the adoptive parents pretend that they are the biological parents.[80] Domestic adopters in Kazakhstan have been known to forge paperwork to support this fiction. A local Kazakh friend told us, "We don't know anyone who is adopted; but we do know women who go away for awhile and come back saying that they gave birth to a baby." In such a cultural context, somewhat ironically, policies favoring domestic over international adoption effectively favor a closed, secretive, stigmatized process in the interest of ethnic matching and preservation of "culture" over a more open process in which the fact of adoption and the biological difference between the adoptee and adoptive parents are openly acknowledged. Given these alternatives, it is not clear how domestic adoption, at least in places in which adoption is highly stigmatized, is necessarily a better avenue for upholding the right of the child to preserve identity.

In summary, then, given the evidence to date, does international adoption serve the child's best interest when we broaden our consideration of outcomes to include identity development? While the evidence related to identity development is not as straightforward as evidence related to physical or cognitive outcomes, ultimately the evidence does not amount to a persuasive argument against international adoption. Children adopted across cultural, racial, and national lines appear to generally fare well, notwithstanding the considerable work in constructing a complex sense of identity that incorporates both birth and adoptive families and ethnicities. Minority-race adoptees do report troubling racial discrimination, perhaps to a greater degree than generally realized or acknowledged by adoptive parents. But that by itself seems an odd reason to oppose international adoption. By analogy, we should not oppose immigration simply because immigrants will experience discrimination, nor should we oppose interracial marriage simply because biracial children will experience discrimination. Instead, the proper redress should be for families and communities to become more aware of racialized experiences and to work toward more just and nondiscriminatory treatment.

Some critics of adoption on the grounds of ethnic preservation have based arguments not on empirical evidence but on a more abstract articulation of human rights. Article 8 of the UN Convention on the Rights of the Child articulates the "right of the child to preserve his or her identity, including nationality, name and family relations," providing critics of adoption an opening to argue that international adoption deprives a child of these basic human rights. For example, adoption critic David Smolin argues that "[s]tripping a child of her identity and familial, community, and cultural heritage is a severe deprivation of rights."[81] Setting aside the issue of whether international adoption actually *strips* or *deprives* a child of identity (as opposed to providing the child with a more multilayered bicultural identity), any "right to culture" needs to be placed in a broader context rather than viewed in isolation. This broad context is provided in the Convention's preamble, which states the core principle that "the child, for the full and harmonious development of his or her personality, should grow up in a family environment, in an atmosphere of happiness, love and understanding."

In addition, the Convention enumerates other human rights that are fully promoted by international adoptive placement of an unparented child. Signatory countries are obliged to "ensure to the maximum extent possible the survival and development of the child" (Article 6); "take all appropriate legislative, administrative, social and educational measures to protect the child from all forms of physical or mental violence, injury or abuse, neglect or negligent treatment, maltreatment or exploitation" (Article 19); "recognize that a mentally or physically disabled child should enjoy a full and decent life, in conditions which ensure dignity" (Article 23); "recognize the right of the child to the enjoyment of the highest attainable standard of health and to facilities for the treatment of illness and rehabilitation of health" (Article 24); and "recognize the right of every child to a standard of living adequate for the child's physical, mental, spiritual, moral and social development" (Article 27).

All else being equal, an argument could be made for privileging domestic over international adoption because of the challenges of identity that the adoptee may face when placed across ethnic, racial, or national boundaries. However, all else is rarely equal. International adoption provides an avenue for realizing crucial human rights to survival, a standard of health, an adequate standard of living, and protection from violence, abuse, neglect, and exploitation—rights that, in many cases, may not be protected adequately through alternative modes of care in the child's country of origin.[82]

PART 2

Adoptive Families: Biological, Social, and Clinical Approaches

5 ■
Adoption and the Biology of Parenting

The terrible email message came on June 17, 2010, from our in-country Kazakhstani coordinator. I read it while seated in front of a computer at our favorite Internet café in Taraz, Kazakhstan:

> I [received a call] from Ministry of Education from Astana. The official staff recommend us to change region for you, and will start adoption process again with new child.

My eyes scanned the message repeatedly, my disbelief and rage instantaneous and escalating rapidly. *Start adoption process again with new child.* A mild-mannered pacifist, I had never wanted more to start punching someone or something. My husband and I had been in Kazakhstan for nearly 6 months, visiting Aldanysh in the orphanage nearly every day. We were now being told that because of the bureaucratic problems with our adoption we should start over. *With a new child.*

The Ministry of Education, which governs international adoptions in Kazakhstan, seemed to believe that to adoptive parents, children are interchangeable: There's a problem with the paperwork for that one, the one you've been holding in your arms daily for 6 months. Let's see if we can get you another one from somewhere else. It is hard to fathom that birth parents facing a crisis with a child would be told by bureaucrats, *let's give up on that child and replace him with another one.*

As difficult as it is to accept, some people believe that adoptive parents don't care as much for their children as do birth parents. Such attitudes are not restricted to Kazakhstani bureaucrats. A 2002 report on adoption attitudes by the Dave Thomas Foundation for Adoption and the Evan B. Donaldson Adoption Institute found that only 57% of Americans believed that "parents get the same satisfaction from raising adopted children as they would from raising a child born to them." Only 75% of respondents believed that adoptive parents are "very likely to love their adoptive children as much as children born to them." While this may sound like a high percentage, consider it another way: one in four Americans believe that adoptive parents are *not* very likely to love their children as much as children born to them.

In many ways I wasn't yet a parent at the moment of receiving that awful email. Legally I was not Aldanysh's mother. No one was legally his mother—he was in the care of the state. Because he was still in the orphanage, I had not yet assumed the full-time responsibilities of parenting. Other people, orphanage caregivers, were feeding him, changing him, and putting him to sleep at night. Despite that, my emotional bond with and commitment to him was indescribably strong. And I'm not unusual in that regard— I've met enough adoptive parents to know that many are fiercely committed to their children even before they legally become parents. Words that try to describe this bond sound trite: "he was mine as soon as I met him"; "it was meant to be"; "I carried him in my heart." In our case, this fierce commitment was the basis for our "going down swinging" approach to the Kazakhstani court system, where, in the months following this email, we would experience two more negative court decisions before finally winning custody.

Darwinian views of parental investment assume that parents invest in their children because they are genetically related. The "selfish gene" concept can account for the self-sacrificing behavior of parenting through the logic that parents are only doing what will allow their genes to survive into the next generation. What feels like parental love is really an adaptation that serves to propagate genes. According to some versions of this theory, males of the species have even evolved special adaptations to help them avoid cuckoldry, the "wasting" of their efforts on children whom they did not father. How, then, does one account for the peculiarly self-sacrificing behavior among internationally adopting parents, who know with certainty that they are not biologically related to the children in whom they invest so much? Does adoptive parenting fall outside the explanatory scope of evolutionary theory? If adoptive parents feel a powerful bond with their children but that bond is not genetically based, where does it come from?

Adoption appears to be too common across species and across human cultures to be written off as an evolutionary aberration or Darwinian mistake. Among human cultures, adoption (or its more temporary form, fostering) has been described in a variety of places and historical time periods.[1] In some cultures, adoption or fostering is even the norm. For example, anthropologist Erdmute Alber describes fostering as a common cultural practice among the Baatombu people in Benin, West Africa.[2] In this cultural setting, foster parents are considered preferable to biological parents. After weaning, children move to the home of the "social parent" (foster parent), who then takes responsibility for rearing and educating the child. Alber reports: "Among more than 150 older people I have spoken to on my field trips, I have only spoken with two persons who told me that they stayed during their whole childhood with their biological parents."[3] In Baatombu society, children are not considered to "belong" to their biological parents but rather to a complex social network in which gifts and exchanges, including exchanges of children, take place.

Adoption is also reported to be relatively common among Pacific Island (Oceanic) societies, and can serve as a means of social exchange or liaison between families.[4] In at least one Oceanic society, the Ifaluk, the children of high-ranking men were more likely than those of low-ranking men to be sent to another family for adoption.[5] This pattern stands in contrast to Western societies, in which children available for adoption are presumed to come from the fringes of society.[6] Explaining the frequency of adoption between families of chiefs in Hawaiian culture, Queen Liliuokalani of Hawaii, who was herself adopted, said, "[T]his alliance by adoption cemented the ties of friendship between chiefs. It spread to the common people, and it has doubtless fostered a community of interest and harmony."[7] In societies of the Northern Artic, such as the Inuit, adoption is also not uncommon; anthropologists estimate that between 20% and 70% of children are adopted.[8]

Adoptive relationships in many cultures take place within kinship networks, such as adoption by genetically related grandparents, aunts, and sisters. Indeed, adoption by kin appears to be a universal phenomenon among cultures that have been studied.[9] Kinship adoption can be easily accommodated by evolutionary theory, which would expect kin to have a stake in the survival of an orphaned or abandoned child because of the genes they share.

Indeed, evolutionary theorists have long recognized "kin selection," the more general phenomenon of making sacrifices on behalf of genetic relatives even if they are not direct offspring.[10]

While adoption is common to human societies, it is not uniquely human. At first it may seem problematic to define what adoption means in other species, because in human societies adoption often (though not always) refers to a legal status. Obviously, chimpanzee societies, as sophisticated as they are, do not have a formal system to adjudicate custody of orphaned infants or juveniles. Nor can researchers simply ask chimpanzees whether they are adopted. Instead, researchers must rely on an observational method of identifying adoptive behavior. In the study of animal behavior, the term adoption is generally applied to situations in which an animal other than the genetic parents engages, for an extended period of time, in caregiving behaviors toward a young animal who has been orphaned.[11] Such behaviors could include feeding the child, carrying the child, protecting the child from danger, and nesting with the child. Adoptive behavior in the animal world, by definition, extends over some long period of time relative to the animal's development. This long-lasting aspect of adoptive behavior distinguishes it from more temporary "babysitting" forms of caregiving (often referred to as "alloparenting") that assist rather than replace a genetic parent.[12]

While adoptive behavior has been described in birds and various mammalian species,[13] examples from primate societies are most instructive. Monkeys and apes are closely related to humans genetically, their social systems are complex like ours, and their offspring, like ours, require extended periods of care before they reach maturity. Researchers have described instances of adoption in a variety of primate species, including howler monkeys, titi monkeys, lemurs, capuchins, macaques, baboons, gorillas, and chimpanzees.[14] Indeed, the ease with which adult monkeys adopt infants has led to a common practice of cross-fostering in captive populations.[15] But adoption happens not only among animals living in captive situations, which could impose artificial influences on behavior, but in the wild as well.

As in human adoptions, many primate adoptions in the wild involve genetically related animals, which, as noted earlier, can be explained easily by evolutionary theory. Yet, just as in human societies, primate adoptions can occur between animals who are not genetically related. In one report, adoption even occurred between two different primate species in the wild—capuchin monkeys in Brazil adopted an orphaned marmoset monkey.[16]

A more extensive study reported on a total of 18 cases of adoption among a group of free-ranging chimpanzees in the African country of Cote d'Ivoire.[17] Eight orphaned youngsters were adopted by adult females, and 10 were adopted by adult male chimpanzees. The fact that adult males as well as females engage in adoptive behavior is interesting in itself, because normally parental care is the responsibility of female chimpanzees (mothers). The researchers obtained DNA samples from most of the adult male adopters and determined that in all but one of the cases, the males were not genetically related to the young-sters whom they adopted. Yet these adopting males (as well as adopting females, both related and unrelated to the child) invested in the youngsters, sharing food, carrying the youngsters on their backs for long periods of travel, protecting them in social conflicts, and in some cases shar-ing night nests with them. One adult female chimpanzee repeatedly nursed an orphaned infant who was unrelated to her. Nursing is quite costly to the adult female, so this behavior represents substantial investment in an unrelated infant. The researchers report the tremendous impact of adoption on infant chimpanzees: Orphaned infants who are not adopted almost never survive to the age of 5 years, whereas adopted infants seem capable of growing up normally.

The fact that adoption between non-kin exists in the wider animal kingdom as well as in the human species begs for an evolutionary explanation. Researchers can only speculate about why adoptive parenting evolved based on considerations of why those behaviors may be advantageous.[18] Of course, it is easy to see the advantage to the child who is adopted, but it is more difficult to see the advantage (in evolutionary terms) to the adoptive parents. Numerous possibilities have been considered, and they are not mutually exclusive. First, it is possible that adopted offspring may later help the adoptive parents, perhaps by becoming allies in future social conflicts. Alternatively, adoption investment may provide the adoptive parents with some measure of social status, which is important in many primate societies. Adoption may provide "parenting practice" that could benefit future offspring. Yet another possibility is that adoption is just one reflection of a broader pattern of altruistic behavior, in which animals in social groups make sacrifices for one another as a way to cement social bonds.[19]

Another possibility, again not mutually exclusive from other explanations, is based on the assumption that primate adoptive behavior evolved in a setting in which animals lived in kin-based groups. In such a setting, adoptive behavior might be triggered by simple physical proximity or exposure to a needy youngster, rather than depending on recognition of genetic relatedness. Under this scenario, the animals would not need to distinguish related from unrelated infants, because the nature of the social group would mean that, more often than not, an adoptive investment would benefit kin. Such mechanisms—caregiving responses to needy infants, without dependence on kin recognition—may still be operating in modern contexts that now involve much broader exposure to unrelated infants. However, these ideas remain speculative, and solid proof of why adoptive parenting evolved is difficult, perhaps impossible, to obtain.

While generally research shows that adoptive behavior occurs in nature and therefore is not "unnatural," a more nuanced question is whether adoptive parents invest the same amount in their (genetically unrelated) children as do birth parents. While anecdotal evidence of adoption in nature can serve as "existence proof" that such behavior occurs, such reports do not really address whether adoptive parenting produces the same kinds of benefits as birth parenting. A strict evolutionary perspective predicts that adoptive parents would not invest as much. Even in kinship adoptions, the degree of genetic relatedness between a child and a relative such as a grandparent or aunt is not as great as the degree of genetic relatedness between a child and parent. Therefore, kin selection theory would predict a lower level of investment by adoptive parents even when those parents are kin. Unfortunately, little empirical evidence exists one way or another on this question as it pertains to adoptive parenting in humans.

A greater body of research exists on investments made by human stepparents. For example, some evidence suggests that stepparents invest less in their stepchildren, on average, than birth parents do in their genetic children.[20] In these studies, "investment" can include financial investment (e.g., paying for college), as well as psychological investments, such as time spent with the child or emotional warmth toward the child. Abuse of children is also reportedly greater among stepfathers than biological fathers, although, of course, the vast majority of stepfathers are not abusive.[21] Such studies generally seem to support an evolutionary perspective that assumes caregivers will care less for children who are not genetically related.

However, human stepfamilies and adoptive families differ in important ways. Adoptive parents make a joint decision to initiate adoption and they exert substantial effort to become parents together. When stepparents make a decision to marry one another, children already exist and may be seen as "part of the package" that comes with being remarried. The stepparent and the spouse who is the genetic parent may have different levels of commitment to the child, resulting in conflicts in parenting. Stepparents may associate the stepchild with a rival, namely the prior partner of the spouse. Finally, at least currently in Western societies, adoptive parents are highly screened (for example, they must meet income and health requirements and pass child abuse and criminal background checks), whereas stepparents are not. For these reasons, evidence about the costs of having stepparents versus genetic parents may not directly apply to adoptive families.[22]

Very few studies to date have directly examined parental investment in adoptive versus birth families. One relevant study took advantage of a large national database of information about more than 12,000 American families whose children had reached first grade.[23] Different kinds of family structures were present in the sample, including "nuclear families" with two birth parents, two-parent adoptive families, and various other family structures. Investment in children was quantified in a variety of ways, including economic investments (e.g., number of books in the home, sending the child to private school), cultural investments (e.g., time spent reading or playing with the child), interactional investments (time spent talking with the child, eating meals with the child), and social capital (school and community involvement). Counter to the predictions of evolutionary theory, the researchers found that across most of these measures, adoptive families invested *more* in their children than did the other family types.

A large part of this adoptive-parent advantage could be attributed to demographic factors that favor investment, including parents' age and financial resources. Adoptive parents tended to be older, wealthier, and more highly educated than birth parents in the sample, which works to the advantage of adopted children, at least for the investment measures that were studied. Once these demographic factors were statistically controlled, some of the adoptive-family investment advantage disappeared—but not all.

The researchers interpreted the investment advantage for adoptive families (even after controlling for demographic factors) as supporting a "compensatory" account rather than an evolutionary account. According to this interpretation, adoptive parents are aware of the risks their children face due to poor prenatal and postnatal pre-adoptive rearing conditions, and they are aware of the social stigma that still surrounds adoption. As a result, the researchers argue, adoptive parents try harder. Regardless of whether one accepts this interpretation, the data from the study clearly indicate that evolutionary considerations involving kin selection cannot fully account for the actual investment made by adoptive parents.[24] Perhaps because of the rigorous screening process involved in modern Western adoption (a screening process that is unmatched in other primate societies, to be sure), those who actually become adoptive parents invest at high levels in the children they raise—levels that are at least as high as, if not higher than, the investment levels of birth parents.

Additional evidence also argues against the viewpoint that genetic relatedness is a precondition for high investment by parents. A recent study compared the quality of parenting between mothers who conceived naturally and mothers whose children were conceived through surrogacy, egg donation, or sperm donation.[25] Parenting quality was assessed through a standardized interview process that had previously been cross-checked against actual observations of mother–child interactions. The study found higher levels of warmth displayed by mothers of children conceived through one of the assisted reproductive technology methods (including egg donation and surrogacy) compared to the mothers of children conceived naturally. These findings suggest, again, that neither being genetically related nor gestating the child is necessary to ensure quality parenting. Instead, the authors propose a "compensatory" explanation for the higher warmth displayed by the mothers who did not conceive naturally, suggesting that perhaps they try harder to make up for the loss of biological connection.

In conversation surrounding different kinds of kinship, adoptive parents are often contrasted with "biological" parents, and adopted children contrasted with "biological" children. One problem with this terminology is obvious. All humans are biological; adoptive parents are not robots, nor are their children. This may seem like simply a semantic dispute, or an issue of colloquial versus scientific vocabulary. After all, in everyday language we use the term *organic* only for some kinds of fruits and vegetables, even though they are all organic in the scientific sense. But a deeper problem with the biological versus adoptive contrast is that it obscures the fact that all parenting relationships are biological.

That is, to call only birth parents "biological" parents is to assume that the biological part of parenting is the part that involves conception, pregnancy, and delivery. Of course, those aspects of parenting are clearly biological. But the processes of bonding and attachment are also biological. Biological mechanisms involved in bonding are separable from mechanisms of conceiving, gestating, and birthing a child. Understanding this point more fully requires delving deeper into the role of hormones in caregiving behavior.

Two key hormones that support pregnancy in all mammalian species are the sex steroids estrogen and progesterone, which increase dramatically in the mother during pregnancy and fall off sharply after delivery. In some rodent species such as rats, estrogen and progesterone are essential in triggering normal maternal behavior. "Maternal behavior" in the rat includes species-typical patterns of licking pups, nursing them, retrieving them if they become displaced from the nest, and acting aggressively toward intruders so as to protect the pups. Such behaviors appear to be restricted to female rats who have been primed with the sex steroid hormones at levels comparable to pregnancy levels. Adult males show none of these behaviors toward rat pups, nor do juvenile or adult females prior to their first pregnancy. Rats who have never given birth seem to have no idea what to do with an infant, and their initial behavior tends to be to avoid the pups or even kill them.[26]

Logically, the same situation cannot hold true in humans. If it did, we could never trust a child to a babysitter without a prior pregnancy, nor could we trust a child to its own father or any other man. Yet we do so all the time. Clearly, humans who have not given birth, unlike rats, are capable of substantial caregiving behavior. Indeed, rats may not even be the best model for other rodent species. For example, in another species of rodent known as the prairie vole, mothers and fathers share parental care, a situation that would not be possible if parenting depended on the hormones of pregnancy. In other primate species, more closely related to us than rodents, caregiving behavior toward infants is observed in juvenile females who have never given birth, as well as in males to a variable degree depending on the species.[27] Such findings have led to debate among researchers about whether primate parenting behavior is more "emancipated" from hormonal control than rodent (or at least rat) parenting behavior.[28]

Rather than assuming that parenting behavior in people (and other primates) is independent of hormones altogether, let's consider the possibility that parenting behavior may depend on hormones that are more broadly shared across members of the species rather than being specific to pregnant females.[29] Recent research has identified a hormone called oxytocin, sometimes called the "cuddle hormone" or the "love hormone," that turns out to be a much better candidate for explaining social bonding than the pregnancy hormones of estrogen and progesterone.[30] Most crucially for the topic of adoption, oxytocin is active in all people, whether male or female, pregnant or not.

Oxytocin is a hormone released by the brain's pituitary gland that can affect distant tissues (such as the uterus and breast tissues) as well as regions of the brain itself. Oxytocin appears to be critical for a variety of forms of social bonding, including both parent–child bonding and pair-bonding between adult males and females in monogamous species. In other species, interfering with the actions of oxytocin through chemical blockers can disrupt normal parental caregiving behavior,[31] and it can also disrupt pair-bonding between males and females.[32]

Oxytocin is centrally involved in childbearing, but its role is not restricted to childbearing. Oxytocin stimulates the uterine contractions involved in labor and delivery (what scientists call parturition), and it is also released in the mother during breastfeeding, contributing to the milk letdown reflex that allows for nursing. Therefore, oxytocin is active at moments thought to be critical for bonding between and mother and child.

But oxytocin is not only active in pregnant or nursing females; it can be elicited in others by exposure to infants. One study examined responses to infants in adult male prairie voles who were "reproductively naïve" (that is, had never sired an offspring).[33] Other studies had already shown that males of this species exhibit caregiving behavior to unrelated infants. This study went further by showing increased oxytocin levels in the adult males within 10 minutes of being placed in the same test cage with an unrelated infant. (Oxytocin did not increase in response to other stimuli in the same setting, such as a wooden dowel rod that was the same size as a pup.) This kind of study is particularly important because it shows that mere exposure to infants can increase the activity of a hormone that is important for social bonding. The release of the hormone is triggered not only by reproductive events but also by social contact with youngsters.

Of course, people are not prairie voles any more than people are rats. Arguably our parenting behavior is more vole-like than rat-like in some ways; humans, like voles but unlike rats, share parental care between mothers and fathers and exhibit parent-like caregiving behavior even outside of pregnancy and nursing. Nevertheless, the human brain and the social context of human behavior are much more complex than that of the tiny prairie vole. Furthermore, the fact that systems of hormonally triggered parenting behavior differ to some degree even among rats, mice, and voles, which are all rodents, should caution us against leaping to conclusions about people based on rodent studies.[34]

To understand the role of oxytocin in human parenting behavior, ideally we would examine studies of this hormone in humans. Studies of oxytocin's role in parental caregiving in people tend to be correlational studies, rather than studies in which oxytocin is directly manipulated.[35] Most parents would not want to participate in a study in which their hormone levels were intentionally raised or lowered to see if this affected their ability to bond with or tend to their children. Therefore, the existing human studies typically measure naturally occurring oxytocin levels in people's blood or saliva and attempt to associate those levels with some aspect of caregiving behavior. Strictly speaking, such studies cannot prove a cause-and-effect relationship between oxytocin and bonding, although they do provide intriguing clues.[36]

Several studies have associated oxytocin levels with aspects of caregiving behavior in human mothers and fathers. For example, one study measured oxytocin in human parents as they interacted with their 4- to 6-month-old infants.[37] Baseline oxytocin levels were similar between the mothers and fathers, again confirming that mothers have no monopoly on this particular hormone. In both parents, higher levels of oxytocin predicted higher levels of touching contact with the infant (e.g., caresses, kisses, pats, or stimulatory touch of the baby). Because the study is correlational, it cannot determine whether touching contact led to higher oxytocin or whether higher oxytocin levels led to greater touching. But nevertheless, the study and others like it establish an association between oxytocin and parenting behavior in fathers as well as mothers, emphasizing the role of this hormone outside the context of childbirth and nursing.

The obvious burning question, then, is whether this hormone is released in adoptive mothers and fathers when interacting with their children. Only one study to date appears to have addressed this question. The study examined oxytocin levels in foster mothers when interacting with their fostered infants.[38] Measurements were taken within the first 60 days of placement of the foster child and again 3 months later. Results mirrored results seen in prior studies of birth parents. Foster mothers with higher levels of oxytocin were observed to interact more positively with their infants, specifically showing more expressions of delight while playing with the infants, compared to foster mothers with lower oxytocin levels.

A related study examined how birth mothers' and foster mothers' brains responded to pictures of infants.[39] The study used electroencephalographic (EEG) methodology, which measures electrical activity from the scalp as people are exposed to different sights or sounds. Predictably, birth mothers showed a stronger EEG response to pictures of their own infant than to an unfamiliar infant. Foster mothers exhibited the same pattern; they, too, showed a preferential brain response to pictures of their own (fostered) infant, to a degree that was virtually identical to that of birth mothers. Like the study of oxytocin in foster mothers, this study shows that foster parents exhibit biological responses to their children that mirror the responses seen in birth parents.

The main point is not to argue that all of human social bonding can be explained by a single chemical or brain response. It cannot be; even scientists who take a biological approach to studying parenting behavior argue persuasively that multiple physiological systems are involved and that virtually all of those systems are responsive to experience.[40] Nor is the point that biological gestation and nursing are irrelevant. They are not; evolution built in biological mechanisms that serve to bond an infant and its birth mother under normal circumstances of gestation, delivery, and postnatal caregiving. But evolution also built in mechanisms that allow for bonding between unrelated parents and children. In circumstances in which the birth mother is unable to care for the child, others (both male and female) are prepared to do so.

In the broader context of debates about adoption, why is it crucial to consider whether all parenting, even adoptive parenting, is biological? Because like it or not, many people associate "biological" with "natural," and "natural" with "good." Numerous studies have demonstrated that people prefer "natural" over "unnatural" options in a variety of decision-making situations, and that the very word "natural" evokes positive connotations.[41] Philosophers and evolutionary theorists have long pointed out people's susceptibility to the "naturalistic fallacy," the assumption that what is natural must be morally good. In the context of adoption, labeling the birth mother as the "biological" mother primes the belief that the birth mother is the "natural" mother and therefore the "good" mother, with the implication that the adoptive mother is none of these.

Anthropologists who study adoption have described how Western cultural discourse attempts to "naturalize" adoption by framing it in biological terms.[42] Adoption agencies sometimes use language that divides the bureaucratic and emotional stages of adoption preparation into "pre-pregnancy," "pregnancy," and "birth," with the latter describing the moment of first meeting the child. Our own adoption agency used the memorable (though unfortunate) term "elephant pregnancy" to describe the long timeline of preparation for an adoption. After an adoption, family and friends often remark on the "family resemblances" between children and their adoptive parents ("he's slender just like his mom!" or "he's an explorer just like his dad!"), using resemblance as a means to legitimize adoptive relationships in a cultural context that prizes genetic relatedness.[43] In Kazakhstan, orphanage staff eagerly hastened to assure us that our (Asian) son looked just like (white) us. Such discourse underscores the presumption of genetic or "natural" relatedness as the standard against which adoptive families are often compared.[44]

Of course, not all that is natural is good, as victims of hurricanes, tornadoes, and infectious disease can attest. This is why the naturalistic fallacy is a fallacy. The argument here is not that adoptive parenting becomes good through its resemblance to "natural" parenting. The moral goodness or badness of parenting, whether by birth parents or adoptive parents, must be assessed by metrics other than whether it is biologically based. Indeed, even birth parenting, which is clearly biologically based, is not uniformly good in every instance, as sadly demonstrated by cases of abuse, neglect, and even infanticide.[45]

Instead, the argument here is that adoptive parenting is "natural" in the sense that it comes to us through evolution and involves the body's physiological systems of bonding. Adoption exists throughout the animal kingdom as well as throughout human societies, and therefore presumably is part of our species' evolutionary heritage. The biological mechanisms of bonding involved in adoptive parenting likely share much in common with the biological mechanisms of birth parenting and other strong social bonds. These considerations challenge the common belief that adoptive parenting is somehow unnatural.

6 ■

Adoptive Families in Society

Following sensational media reports of an adopted Russian child dying in an American home in 2013, tens of thousands of Russians took to the streets to demonstrate against adoption by Americans. The leader of one of the organizing groups, Russian Mothers (a Kremlin-backed group), is quoted as saying:

> We want to draw the world's attention to the forced
> confiscation of Russian children. . . . The mass media is
> full of stories that show there is an epidemic of violence
> against children in the U.S., some 6 million cases per
> year. We have child abuse in Russia too, but there is no
> such epidemic. . . . We have a different attitude toward
> children here in Russia, perhaps due to cultural
> differences, we don't treat them like cats and dogs.[1]

Russian politicians, seizing the opportunity for nationalistic grandstanding, also jumped on the America-bashing bandwagon: "Why should we send our children to certain death?" asked Svetlana Orlova, Deputy Chair of Russia's Upper House of Parliament.[2]

Data overwhelmingly contradict the accusation that American adoptive parents are likely to abuse their children. According to the *Christian Science Monitor*, out of approximately 60,000 adoptions from Russia to the United States over a period of about 20 years, there have been 19 confirmed cases of death due to abuse or neglect.[3] While clearly any child's death is horrible, especially when due to abuse, these statistics indicate a death-by-abuse rate of 0.03% among Russian children adopted by Americans. Meanwhile, the same source reports 1,220 deaths due to abuse among the 170,000 adoptions of Russian children by Russian parents, a rate of 0.72%. According to these statistics, although abuse rates are low for both groups, an adopted Russian child is almost 25 times more likely to die at the hands of an adoptive Russian family than an adoptive American family.

These data hardly support an argument against international adoption. Nevertheless, public opinion is often driven by the vividness of lurid stories, rather than by dry data. For example, in 2010, international media coverage focused extensively on the tragic return of the Russian boy Artyom by his American adoptive mother, who put him alone on a plane back to Moscow.[4] Meanwhile, Yelena Mizulina, head of the Russian parliamentary Committee on the Family, reported that approximately 30,000 children had been returned to Russian orphanages by Russian adoptive or foster parents in the prior 2 years.[5] Likewise, disturbing media reports about the abhorrent practice of "rehoming" internationally adopted children—that is, using underground networks to move an adopted child to a new and possibly abusive setting—could imply that adoptive parents are likely to abandon their children.[6] But data from a large, representative national survey, conducted by the U.S. Department of

Health and Human Services, indicate that zero percent of U.S. internationally adopting parents reported they had ever considered dissolving their adoption.[7]

A recent study in the Netherlands found that adoptive parents are actually less likely to mistreat children than other kinds of parents.[8] The study made use of records from Dutch child protective services documenting all cases of certified child maltreatment each year. The researchers compared the rates of abuse for different family types to the prevalence of those family types in the general Dutch population. Results showed that while stepparent families were overrepresented among the child maltreatment cases, adoptive families were significantly underrepresented. The risk for maltreatment among adoptive families was eight times lower than would be expected based on the frequency of adoptive families in the general population. According to these statistics, adoption is actually a protective factor, in the sense that risk of abuse decreases in adoptive families compared to other family types. Although there are probably several reasons for these low rates of abuse, one reason may be that adoptive parents (unlike birthparents or stepparents) typically must pass numerous background checks, including child abuse clearances, before being approved to adopt.

While accusations that internationally adopted children are likely to meet a "certain death" in America may seem absurd to American ears, negative attitudes toward adoption pervade American media representations as well. News stories often reinforce stereotypes about members of adoptive families, such as describing birth mothers as "callous," adopted children as "troubled," and adoptive parents as "desperate for a baby."[9] Commodification of children is a common theme in media depictions. For example, one study of newspaper reports over a 10-year period found common references to the "marketplace" of adoption, depicting the adoption process as involving "supply and demand," "baby-selling," or "trafficking."[10] News stories also tend to mark adoption as deviant even when the story's central narrative is not about adoption, for example, noting that a criminal suspect was adopted even though that information is factually irrelevant to the crime.[11] American media coverage of international adoption also varies depending on the country of origin of the child, with more negative newspaper stories about adoptions from Russia than those from China.[12]

Empirical studies suggest that American media representations of adoption are not wholly negative, instead presenting ambivalent views. A recent study examined approximately 300 news stories about adoption presented on broadcast news programs between 2001 and 2004.[13] While most of the stories intermixed both positive and negative features of adoption, they generally presented adoptive parents in a more positive light than adopted children. The study found that adoptive parents were presented as solely positive in 41% of the stories and solely negative in only 14% of the stories, but adopted children were more likely to be presented in a solely negative (22% of stories) than solely positive fashion (8% of stories). Such narratives may seem to reflect positively on adoptive parents, but they are unfair to the adopted child and may contribute to a cultural narrative about "saving troubled children" that does little good to any member of the adoptive family.

While we may expect shallow or biased coverage from mass media, scholarly representations of family issues should present a more balanced view. However, a recent study of college textbooks found that adoption is presented as a deviant form of family formation.[14] Researchers examined the contents of 37 college textbooks or anthologies intended for use in undergraduate courses about the family. The first finding was that very little attention was given to adoption at all: Less than 1% of the available page space in the textbooks was devoted to adoption, and some texts didn't even mention the topic. Furthermore, when adoption was covered in the text, the coverage tended to be negative, making on average twice as many negative as positive points about adoption. Thus, undergraduates interested in studying the family—who are nearing points in their lives when they will make their own family decisions—receive predominantly negative messages about adoption, if they learn about it at all.

Because public opinion both shapes and is shaped by media representations, it is not surprising that opinion surveys also indicate ambivalent attitudes about adoption among the general American public. In a nationwide survey in 2002, the Donaldson Institute found that nearly 95% of Americans indicated that their overall view of adoption was either "favorable" or "very favorable," and about two-thirds reported personal contact with adoption through relatives or friends.[15] At the same time, among those who reported a "very favorable" view of adoption, only about half said that they had ever seriously considered doing it themselves. As only about 1% to 2% of Americans have adopted a child, it follows that most people who support adoption are not actually doing it.

The survey respondents also indicated widespread concern about outcomes for adopted children. Nearly half (45%) of respondents endorsed the view that adopted children are more likely to have behavior problems than non-adopted children. When asked what concerns they have about adoption, 82% of respondents indicated that the possibility of a birth parent taking a child back was a "major concern" (as opposed to a minor concern or no concern at all), and 44% indicated that dealing with unexpected medical or genetic issues was a major concern. In an earlier nationwide survey, half of American respondents agreed that adoption is "not quite as good as having one's own child."[16] Altogether, the survey data indicate that while

Americans have generally positive views about adoption, they also harbor concerns that may contribute to a sense that adoption is a second-best choice for family formation.[17]

Against this background of mixed messages about adoptive families as represented in the media and public opinion, it is instructive to examine realities as reflected in actual data about those families. In what ways (aside from the means of family formation) are internationally adoptive families distinct from non-adoptive families, and in what ways are they just like any other family? The next sections consider data from studies about the demographics of adoptive families, their motivations to adopt, and family relationships.

Demographic data confirm that internationally adopting parents are, relative to the general U.S. population, disproportionately white and of higher socioeconomic status. For example, a recent study focused on a cohort of Minnesota parents who adopted a child from another country between 1990 and 1998.[18] The sample of parents was 97% white, a greater proportion than in the Minnesota population in general at the time of the survey. The parents were more highly educated than the average Minnesota parent of a newborn, with 70% holding at least a bachelor's degree (compared to 36% of all Minnesota mothers of newborns) and 30% holding a post-baccalaureate degree. The adoptive families were also wealthier than typical Minnesota parents of newborns, with 35% having household incomes greater than $100,000, and they were older on average (38 years at time of placement) than non-adoptive Minnesota mothers.[19]

Similar findings about the race and socioeconomic status of adoptive parents were documented in a nationwide survey conducted by the U.S. Department of Health and Human Services.[20] This 2007 survey, referred to as the National Survey of Adoptive Parents (NSAP), included a representative sample of all adoptive parents (both domestic and internationally adopting). Ninety-two percent of internationally adopting parents were non-Hispanic whites, compared to 71% of those engaging in private domestic adoption and 63% adopting from U.S. foster care. More than 93% of internationally adopting parents reported household income levels greater than 200% of the poverty level, compared to 60% of all families with children in the United States. Conversely, while nearly 20% of all U.S. families with children report incomes below the poverty line, less than 1% of internationally adopting families fall into that category. Even compared with parents adopting children through private domestic adoptions or foster care, those adopting internationally had higher incomes. Likewise, more than 95% of internationally adopting parents reported being educated beyond the high school level, compared to 68% of all U.S. families with children.

These data support the common assumption that internationally adopting families tend to be privileged, at least in terms of income and educational status. Given the costs of international adoption and the considerable paperwork burden, it is not surprising that those who successfully navigate the process tend to be those with more financial and educational resources. Supporters of adoption may interpret these data as reinforcing the degree to which such adoptive families are able to provide their children with many material advantages. The economic advantages of such families may be particularly important for children with special medical needs, discussed in more detail in the next chapter. At the same time, critics of international adoption may interpret the data about socioeconomic status in a different frame, contending that internationally adoptive parents, because of their privilege, may have difficulty appreciating the life circumstances of the child's birth parents in the country of origin.[21] Indeed, the role of money and privilege as potentially corrupting influences in adoption has been an issue of much discussion, as addressed in Chapter 8.

The same nationwide survey reported a number of neighborhood characteristics in which there were either no differences between adoptive families and the general U.S. population or slight advantages for the adoptive families. For example, virtually the same percentage (roughly 80%) of all U.S. families and internationally adoptive families were categorized as living in a metropolitan area. Nearly all families, adoptive or not, reported living in neighborhoods with amenities, such as parks, community centers, or libraries. Slightly greater percentages of internationally adopting families, compared to the general population, reported living in a "safe neighborhood" or a neighborhood with "no characteristics of poor physical condition," a result presumably tied to socioeconomic variables that favor internationally adoptive families.

Are internationally adopting parents more likely to be religious than non-adoptive parents? Demographic data suggest not, countering recent reports of a growing contingent of adoptive parents motivated by Christian evangelical teachings.[22] The NSAP survey found that 66% of internationally adoptive parents reported attending religious services at least monthly, compared to 70% of parents in the general U.S. population. In fact, parents adopting from U.S. foster care were the most likely to report monthly religious attendance (87%). Doubtlessly, some evangelical and other faith-based organizations vocally promote adoption, but it doesn't seem that internationally adopting parents as a group are likely to be more religiously observant than other comparison groups.

Further research, based on the NSAP and other studies, has tried to better ascertain why parents choose to adopt internationally. When the NSAP survey asked this question directly, 90% of internationally adopting parents (compared with 70% of domestic adopters) endorsed the option "to provide a permanent home for a child"; 92% (compared with 60% of domestic adopters) endorsed "to expand family"; and 72% (compared with 52% of domestic adopters) endorsed "inability to have a biological child." Thus, while infertility was certainly a commonly endorsed motivation, nearly 30% of the internationally adopting parents did not attribute their choice to infertility, and the endorsement of infertility as a motivation was lower than the endorsement of items related to family expansion and providing a home for a child.

Prior experience with adoption also appears to influence the likelihood of choosing adoption to form a family. In the NSAP sample, 90% of internationally adopting parents reported having previous experience with adoption, such as having an adopted relative or friend. (The survey item did not specify whether the adopted relative or friend was internationally or domestically adopted.) In a separate study that examined a random sample of non-adoptive married adults in two Midwestern cities, prior exposure to adoptive relationships (e.g., self, spouse, sibling, or other relative was adopted) was a significant predictor of self-reported willingness to adopt a child, even when demographic factors such as education, gender, and age were statistically controlled.[23]

Parents adopting internationally have some choice in countries of origin, and their choices have been scrutinized by critics who suspect ulterior, racially based motives for particular choices.[24] Because internationally adopting parents have chosen not to adopt from U.S. foster care, some critics may believe that the (mostly white) parents are biased against black children, who are disproportionately represented in U.S. foster care. The recent upsurge in adoptions from Ethiopia to the United States directly undermines this assumption[25] and suggests instead that other aspects of foster care besides the children's race may drive adopting parents away from choosing that option.[26]

However, even some who acknowledge that internationally adopting parents are now choosing African children in high numbers seem to persist in race-based criticism of the motives of adoptive parents. For example, while recognizing adoptions from Africa as a "fifth wave" of trends in international adoption, demographer Mary Ann Davis writes:

> "White" or "honorary White" children adopted through intercountry adoption can be passed off to strangers as biological children.... Asian children ... are assumed to have superior intelligence.... Black children from a developing nation may give the adopter prestige as saviors or rescuers, the moral imperative of a developed nation.[27]

It seems that internationally adopting parents cannot win; no matter the choice, some critics assume that it reflects racial stereotypes or race-based hierarchies of value.

It is difficult to determine how much adoptive families' choices are actually driven by racial preferences. Some narrative accounts based on interviews with adoptive parents do reflect the parents' concern about how a minority-race child would fit into the adoptive family or community.[28] However, it is not clear whether those narratives are representative, nor whether parents should be faulted for thinking through the impact of a transracial placement on the child and family. Data from the nationally representative NSAP sample found that less than 7% of internationally adopting parents said their primary reason for adopting from abroad was "wanting a child of the same race/ ethnicity as family," compared to 34% of domestically adopting parents who endorsed that statement.[29] Further, data from the 2000 U.S. Census indicate that minority-race parents are more likely to adopt a same-race child than are white parents.[30] These data, together with the fact that 84%

of international adoptions to America are transracial placements (compared with 21% of private domestic adoptions),[31]
contradict the oversimplified and illogical narrative that
white adoptive parents choose to adopt internationally so
that they can raise a child who looks like them.

Adoptive parents' choices regarding a specific country
of origin are likely based on a complex interplay of factors,
including a country's availability of children of various
ages, the reputed health status of the children, the time
frame of the adoption process in that country, the cost and
travel requirements, the parents' ancestral or personal connection to particular cultures, and political and historical
factors causing countries to open and close to international
adoption. In our case, our decision was based largely on
the available programs through the agency we selected.
Having decided that we wanted to adopt internationally,
we first selected an agency with an excellent reputation for
ethical placements and humanitarian work in countries of
origin. All of that agency's open programs at that time happened to be in Asia. Our final outcome, which was to adopt
a child of Asian ethnicity, therefore reflects these factors,
rather than some false (and offensive) belief that Asian
children are smarter or could somehow "pass" as white.

Regardless of what motivates adoptive parents, studies
suggest that their families function quite well after placement. One study of both adoptive and (non-relinquishing)
birth families found that on a variety of measures of family
functioning, adoptive families fared as well as or better
than birth families after the arrival of a child in the family.[32] The study culled data from a large nationwide sample
of U.S. families, called the National Survey of Families and
Households. Families were interviewed at two time points
approximately 5 years apart. Among families who gained a
child through birth or adoption between the first and second time point, both birth and adoptive families reported
less depression and increased support from extended

families following the child's arrival, compared to before the child's arrival. Self-reported quality of the marriage went down in families formed through birth but up in adoptive families following arrival of the child. Adoptive parents also reported greater satisfaction with their families and greater family cohesion. Although this large-scale study did not differentiate between international and domestic adoptive families, other studies have found slightly higher well-being, better marital relationship quality, and higher levels of social support in internationally adoptive families than among families formed through birth.[33]

Of course, it is important to acknowledge the distinct challenges that adoptive families may face. For example, one study found that hospitalization of a child was experienced as more stressful by adoptive families than by families formed by birth, presumably because most adoptive families lack medical information about the child's genetic ancestors.[34] Another study found that adopted adolescents had slightly more conflict with their parents than non-adopted adolescents, although the adoptive and non-adoptive parents themselves displayed similar levels of warmth.[35] Nevertheless, despite findings such as these, adoptive parents report high levels of satisfaction with their families. For example, in the NSAP sample, 96% of internationally adopting parents reported that knowing what they now know, they would still make the same adoption decision.[36] Together these findings suggest a high level of resilience and commitment among adoptive families.

Although it is challenging to assess the quality of parenting behavior, existing data suggest that parental competence is at least as high, if not higher, among adoptive compared to non-adoptive parents. For example, a study of Spanish families found that parents who had adopted children from Russia showed higher levels of positive emotion and reflectiveness about their parenting and relationship with the child, compared to families formed by birth with similar education levels.[37] The American NSAP sample found that, compared to U.S. parents in general, internationally adopting parents reported higher rates of reading to the child every day, singing or telling stories to the child every day, and eating family meals together most days of the week.[38] While it is problematic to argue, based on such data, that one set of parents is "better" than another in any general sense, there is certainly nothing in the data to suggest that adoptive parents are worse.[39]

The majority of internationally adopting families involve a married couple, but diversification in family structure has led to increasing numbers of single parents and same-sex couples who adopt children or wish to do so. According to the nationwide NSAP survey, the percent of American children living with married parents in 2007 was 82% for children adopted internationally, 70% for those adopted from foster care, and 59% for those adopted through private domestic means; for comparison, in the general U.S. population, about 71% of children live with married parents.[40] The issue of nontraditional family adoptions has special policy relevance in the context of international adoption, because most countries of origin for international adoptions prohibit adoption by same-sex couples and only a few allow single-parent adoption. With this policy context in mind, it is useful to review evidence about how children fare in families with different kinds of parents.

Existing evidence supports the conclusion that internationally adopted children do just as well in single-parent as in in dual-parent adoptive homes. One study compared Chinese girls adopted to Canadian or American families headed by either a single parent or two parents.[41] The study included 415 dual-parent families and 126 single-parent families (consisting of a never-married mother). At the time of the study, the children ranged from 1.5 to 11 years of age. Parents completed a questionnaire that asked about a variety of problem behaviors in the child, ranging from anxiety and depression to rule-breaking and aggression. Scores were virtually identical for the children from single-parent and dual-parent households. In fact, children in both the single-parent and dual-parent adoptive families were reported to have fewer problem behaviors than in the general population.

These findings are somewhat limited because the single parents in the sample were limited to women raising Chinese girls; neither adopted boys nor single fathers were included. The focus on adopted girls in this study is a consequence of the fact that the vast majority of adopted Chinese children are girls, due to Chinese cultural preferences for boys, combined with China's one-child policy. Furthermore, nearly all of the research on single-parent adoption has focused on single mothers, because instances of single-father adoption are rare (in part because they are infrequently allowed). Future research involving single-parent families with different gender compositions could provide a fuller picture of whether family structure matters for internationally adopted children.[42]

Nevertheless, sociological data from decades of research on non-adoptive families indicate that single-parenthood is only a risk factor for children insofar as it is tied to socioeconomic disadvantages that tend to co-occur with single-parenthood. In other words, once economic factors are accounted for, there is little to no negative consequence of being raised by a single parent. For example, one large-scale study in Great Britain examined a variety of health, educational, and behavioral outcomes for a nationwide representative sample of more than 15,000 children.[43] Children living with single parents at the time of the survey had worse outcomes than those living with two parents on measures such as having a longstanding illness, having an identified educational special need, and having been suspended or expelled from school. Single-parent families in the sample also faced more economic hardship according to various measures. The most important finding of the study was that the economic factors explained virtually all of the differences in health and behavioral outcomes between children from single- versus dual-parent households; once economic hardship was statistically controlled, the effect of household type on children's outcomes (for both boys and girls) vanished.

These findings, although they are taken from studies of non-adoptive families, have implications for understanding outcomes for children adopted into single-parent homes. As reviewed previously, internationally adopting families tend to be economically privileged, a characteristic that holds for both single-parent and dual-parent adoptive families. Adoptive families are screened for income in two ways. First, typically the family must reach a certain income threshold in order to be eligible for adoption (depending on the agency and country of origin to which they are applying). Second, the high cost of international adoption tends to be a deterrent for low-income families. Though it may be unfair, the net result is that internationally adoptive families, including single parents, are economically advantaged. This means that single-parent adopters look quite different, economically speaking, from single-parent families in the general population. Given that economic hardship appears to largely account for the negative impact of being raised in a single-parent (non-adoptive) family, we may extrapolate the conclusion that any adverse outcomes of single-parenthood are much less likely among single parents who are in the privileged position of adopting internationally.

Additional research has focused on adoption by same-sex partners. In the United States in 2007, an estimated 65,000 legally adopted children lived in families headed by same-sex partners, including children living with one birth parent and that person's partner, as well as children living with two same-sex partners who are not biologically related to the child.[44] These numbers have likely risen even higher since that report, as social policy related to same-sex partners has continued to liberalize in the United States. While statutes vary from state to state, at the time of this writing the vast majority of U.S. states legally recognize same-sex domestic adoptions, and same-sex marriage has been made legal in all 50 states by the Supreme Court.[45]

Children raised by same-sex parents generally fare just as well as children raised by opposite-sex parents. Studies of children's outcomes have examined a variety of measures, including mental health, educational achievement, social relationships, and personality development, in numerous samples in a variety of countries.[46] The evidence finding essentially no effect of parental sexual orientation on children's outcomes is so conclusive that the American Psychological Association (APA), the premiere professional organization for psychologists, endorsed a public policy statement "that the adjustment, development, and psychological well-being of children is unrelated to parental sexual orientation . . . [C]hildren of lesbian and gay parents are as likely as those of heterosexual parents to flourish."[47] The APA further resolved that it "opposes any discrimination based on sexual orientation in matters of adoption, child custody and visitation, foster care, and reproductive health services."[48] Similar position statements have been articulated by other major professional organizations, including the American Medical Association, American Bar Association, American Academy of Pediatrics, and Child Welfare League of America.[49]

Reasons for choosing adoption may be somewhat different for same-sex parents than for opposite-sex parents, since the traditional biological option for family formation is simply not available to same-sex couples. Several studies have reported that same-sex adoptive parents are less likely to have pursued fertility treatments, more likely to report that they "did not have a strong desire for biological children," and more open to transracial adoption compared to opposite-sex adoptive parents.[50] Researchers have speculated that same-sex parents may be more willing to consider adoption as a first choice for family formation because they already tend to live in communities that are open to diversity more generally.[51]

Consistent with common sense, what best predicts children's adjustment is the quality of relationships within the family, not the parents' sexual orientation. For example, one study of opposite-sex and same-sex adoptive parents found that children's externalizing ("acting out") behaviors were associated with aspects of the parenting relationship, not the family structure.[52] The lowest levels of acting-out behaviors occurred in children whose parents engaged in more supportive co-parenting, as rated by researchers who coded the parents' pleasure, interactivity, and cooperation during a videotaped family play session. The association between parenting relationship and child's behavior held regardless of whether the parents were opposite-sex or same-sex partners. Other studies have also found that variables such as parenting stress are better predictors of a child's behavioral problems than the family structure itself.[53]

The fundamental question of what it means to be a family lurks behind all research on adoption from a social perspective. Indeed, ambivalence in public opinion about adoption may reflect conflicted conceptions about the ideal family. Some definitions of *family* focus on structural aspects of family groups, and others focus on emotional aspects.[54] A structural definition of *family* is one that defines a family according to the specific people who are in it and their blood or legal relationships to one another. For example, according to the U.S. Census Bureau definition, "family households contain at least one person related to the householder by birth, marriage or adoption."[55] Family households are contrasted with "nonfamily households," which can involve either a person living alone or a person living with an unmarried partner, friend, or roommate. While this kind of structural definition is specific and easy to apply objectively, it leaves out certain groupings that may functionally act as a family. For example, unmarried partners, whether opposite-sex or same-sex, are not categorized as "family" under this kind of definition. Likewise, the focus by the Census Bureau on the household unit excludes families that may be distributed across more than one residence, such as the grandparents who live next door, the separated parents who share custody of a child, or the birth mother who maintains a relationship with an adoptive family through an open adoption.

Research suggests that when people think about what it means to be a family, they emphasize emotional rather than structural features. One study asked a large sample of American undergraduates to list all the features that define *family*.[56] The researchers then presented the resulting list of 70 features to a second sample of people who were asked to rate each one according to "how central the feature is in your concept of family." The features that were rated as most central were emotional features: love, trust, respect, and support. "Always there" and "lifelong/forever" were also rated as highly central to the concept of family. Among all 70 features, the feature that people rated as *least* central to the concept of family was "blood-related."[57]

At the same time, laypeople do tend to think of certain social groups as more prototypical of the concept of family.[58] When presented with phrases describing groups of people and asked to indicate how much each resembled "a family," participants predictably rated "two biological parents and children" most highly (average rating of 5.75 on a 6-point scale). The rating for "two adoptive parents and children" was close behind (average rating of 5.31).

Two-parent groups and opposite-sex-partner groups tended to be rated as resembling the concept "family" more than single-parent or same-sex-partner groups, indicating that, when forced to consider family structure alone, the respondents tended to favor traditional forms.[59] (Not surprisingly, "orphanage" received a very low rating for resemblance to the concept of family.)

These results, taken together, suggest two competing strains of thought in the average American's concept of what it means to be a family. When not prompted to think about specific structures, people emphasize emotional connections in the definition of family. However, when attention is drawn to specific family forms in the absence of any other information, people deem some forms to be more family-like. A lesson for advocates of nontraditional families hoping to adopt, such as single parents or same-sex partners, may be to frame public representations of their families in emotional terms: Such families can have all of the emotional characteristics that people strongly associate with family (love, trust, respect, "always there"), even if the specific family form is nontraditional.

In sum, adoptive families may be troubled at times by ambivalent social attitudes about adoption, biased media coverage of adoptive families, and perceived cultural ideologies that privilege genetic relationships and traditional family forms. Nevertheless, collectively we can contribute to changing societal discourse about adoption and developing a more expansive concept of family that encompasses diverse family forms.[60] Awareness of prevailing preconceptions about the family in the broader culture can be a first step toward resisting those constraining ideas and articulating more inclusive conceptions. As one research study participant stated succinctly, "The most important thing that we can communicate about adoption is that we are a family—we are defined by our relationships, and our relationships are always loving."[61]

7 ■
Special Needs and Interventions

During our preparations to adopt, I encountered a statement online that troubled me: "All adopted children are special needs children," someone wrote authoritatively. The author was underscoring that parents need to be attentive to the special considerations in adopted children's development, whether or not the child has identifiable medical needs. It was difficult to locate the precise reason for my discomfort with the statement at the time. I didn't like how it pathologized adoption, implying that all adopted children are somehow inherently problematic. I knew adopted children and adults who seemed perfectly healthy and "normal." But the statement also triggered anxiety about whether I had the ability to successfully parent a child with "special needs," whatever that might mean.

Adoptive parents, like all parents, are centrally concerned with ensuring the well-being of their children. Yet knowing that a child has experienced early-life deprivation can add a unique dimension to adoptive parenting. For example, in a focus-group study of adoptive parents, one mother said:

> When I observe her having difficulties or strong emotions, I'm always wondering "Is this normal for her, or is this the result of the neglect she experienced in the orphanage?" Every day I have this persistent overhanging sense of anxiety that I can't do enough, be enough, give enough to make up for what she didn't have when she was in the orphanage.[1]

Other parents in the focus group were concerned about assumptions that others would make about the child's psychological needs:

> One mother shared how she felt when an acquaintance assumed that her daughter had an attachment disorder simply because she was adopted from Russia. She said, "I was enraged. I calmly said to him, 'My daughter is really very normal and healthy.' But I wanted to punch him."[2]

Adoptive families must achieve a difficult balance between recognizing and addressing real needs when they arise, and resisting a vision of their children that focuses on potential pathology.

The purpose of this chapter is to examine more closely the needs of internationally adopted children and how those needs can be addressed within adoptive families and communities. Overlapping issues arise whether the child's needs are medical or psychological and whether they qualify as "special" needs or just regular needs of children who have experienced the early-life disruptions and deprivations involved in out-of-family care. The chapter introduces dilemmas and ambiguities surrounding special needs in international adoption, reviews evidence regarding the prevalence of special needs in adoptive populations, and considers issues of disability in countries of origin and receiving countries. Finally, the chapter reviews evidence related to interventions that can assist adoptive families in coping with the needs of a child who has encountered early adversity.

Some of the most morally disconcerting moments in our adoption process involved issues of special needs. As part of required preparatory paperwork, our adoption agency gave us a long list of medical conditions to consider. For each condition (birthmark, asthma, HIV, cleft palate, hepatitis, missing limb, hearing impairment, and so on), we had to check "yes," "no," or "maybe" to indicate whether we would accept a child with that condition. Completing that checklist in the abstract was painful enough, but meeting specific children with clear medical needs was even more heartbreaking.

At the time we adopted our son, Kazakhstan was a "travel-blind" country, meaning that the adoptive parents traveled to the country without a specific referral (or match). The parents were then brought to an orphanage and shown a few children available for adoption. In some cases, orphanage officials had already picked out a child for a particular family, and they used children with more severe special needs as foils in the rigged selection process. For example, in a proceeding with a Soviet-style predetermined conclusion, officials might show the prospective adoptive parents a young boy with missing limbs, a toddler with a cleft palate, and then a relatively healthy-looking infant, with the expectation that the parents would choose the last of the three. In other cases, adoptive parents who were promised a "healthy infant" arrived in-country to be shown only older children with obvious medical needs. The parents then had to decide, on the spot, whether to accept a child with medical conditions that the parents had previously ruled out.

Needless to say, many adoptive parents voluntarily choose to adopt children with identified special needs because they feel prepared and compelled to offer such children homes. Yet, identifying and addressing the needs of an adopted child is an ongoing process for all adoptive families, whether they seek to adopt a special needs child, discover after the adoption that their child has previously unknown medical or psychological needs, or have a relatively healthy child who still must navigate the developmental and emotional challenges inherent in those who experienced early adversity and family dislocation. The rewards can be great for both the child and parent, but the challenges need to be acknowledged and potential sources of intervention identified.

Several factors complicate the issue of defining and identifying "special needs" within various child welfare systems. First, while adoptions are sometimes dichotomized as either "special needs" or "non-special needs" (read: "healthy"), children's needs exist along a continuum. Some children who are classified as "special needs" may need only a single surgery to correct a physical malformation, whereas others may have chronically disabling or potentially life-threatening conditions. Furthermore, medical needs that seem "special" in a country of origin with limited medical infrastructure may seem minor and manageable in the context of a country with advanced medical care. In some systems, otherwise healthy children may be categorized as "special needs" if they are older, under the assumption that older children may have more rocky transitions into adoptive homes. Finally, as reviewed in Chapters 2 and 3, virtually all institutionalized children begin to show developmental delays as a consequence of the deprived institutional setting. Do experience-based developmental delays count as "special needs," even if they reflect a normal response to deprivation? If so, then any previously institutionalized child could indeed be characterized as "special needs."

Adding to this ambiguity is the unreliability of medical information conveyed to prospective parents by officials in many countries of origin. Our translator told us that in Kazakhstan at the time we adopted, orphanages received more money from the government to care for children with medical diagnoses than for those without diagnoses. As a result, every child in the baby house had some sort of diagnosis. Empirical studies of children adopted from former Soviet countries document the widespread use of vague neurological diagnoses, such as "perinatal encephalopathy," that are often later disconfirmed in the adoptive country.[3] At the same time, children from the post-Soviet region may be especially vulnerable to the effects of maternal alcohol consumption, given the high rate of alcohol abuse in the region,[4] and these effects, unless severe, can be difficult to detect in infancy.[5] In addition, in many countries of origin, infrastructure is simply not sufficient to support adequate medical testing, diagnosis, or record-keeping. To this already confusing mix, add the challenge of accurately translating medical terminology between languages. The end result is effectively a roll of the dice on the part of adoptive parents, notwithstanding any carefully considered pre-adoptive paperwork checklists.[6]

The Hague Convention on intercountry adoption attempts to address some of these challenges by expecting that sending countries (at least those that have ratified the Hague) will provide a specific child referral that includes adequate medical information.[7] In addition, the Hague requirements place special emphasis on the need to appropriately identify and provide pre-adoption training to parents whose goal is to adopt children with special needs.[8] These provisions are crucial in protecting both adoptive parents and children, as it is presumably better for children to be placed in families who feel prepared to address the child's medical and emotional needs. Yet, even the well-intentioned Hague provisions cannot fully anticipate or address medical and developmental issues that may arise in adopted children. (For that matter, no one gives families formed through birth any kind of guarantee of the lifelong health and well-being of their children either.)

Several studies have attempted to document the prevalence of medical special needs among international adoptees. One study took advantage of U.S. Census data to capture information from a nationally representative sample of international adoptees, domestic adoptees, and all non-adopted children in the United States in the year 2000.[9] Parents reported whether children in their household currently had one of four disability categories: sensory disability (vision or hearing impairment), physical disability (substantial limits in physical activities such as walking and climbing stairs, etc.), mental disability (difficulty learning, remembering, or concentrating), or "self-care" disability (inability to dress, bathe, etc.). In this dataset, which included more than 13,000 international adoptees and 155,000 domestic adoptees, the rate of disability was estimated at 11.7% for international adoptees, 12.2% for domestic adoptees, and 5.8% for non-adopted children.

In addition to finding a rate of disability that was twice as high among adopted than non-adopted children, the researchers also noted variations in this pattern. For example, international adoptees were more likely than domestic adoptees to have sensory or physical disabilities and less likely than domestic adoptees to have mental disabilities. Furthermore, among international adoptees, the disability rates varied widely depending on the country of origin, with relatively lower rates among adoptees from China and Korea and relatively higher rates among adoptees from Russia and Eastern Europe.[10]

This study has the methodological advantage of drawing from a representative sample of U.S. families, rather than sampling from clinics or adoption support groups, which could overrepresent children with disabilities.

However, the main limitation of the study is that it is now dated, as it relied on data from the 2000 U.S. Census and included children who were adopted as many as 15 years prior to that census (now 30 years ago). The findings from this study likely underrepresent the proportion of special needs children currently being adopted internationally, as reports suggest increasing trends toward special needs adoptions in recent years.[11]

Results from the nationally representative National Survey of Adoptive Parents (NSAP), conducted by the U.S. Department of Health and Human Services in 2007, also provide some information about the prevalence of disability among international adoptees.[12] According to this dataset, 29% of internationally adopted children were reported by their parents to have "special health care needs," which was defined rather broadly, compared to 19% of children in the general U.S. population. At the same time, 93% of internationally adopting parents reported that their child's health status was either "excellent" or "very good," a number higher than in the general population (84%). While these two sets of numbers may seem contradictory (relatively high rate of disability combined with high health status), one interpretation is that internationally adopted children have a relatively high likelihood of special medical needs, but that available treatment for those medical conditions has led to a positive health status. Additional data from the survey indicated that internationally adopting families were more likely to have health insurance than the general U.S. population, likely reflecting the socioeconomic status of families who adopt internationally.

Another study, conducted by the Donaldson Institute in 2012–2013, sampled from more than 1,000 internationally adopting families recruited from the organization's website, from online adoption groups, and from solicitations through adoption agencies.[13] The researchers acknowledge that the sampling method may overrepresent families with children having special needs. Among the respondents, nearly half (47%) reported having an adopted child who had special needs at the time of the survey. Of those children with disabilities, about half were diagnosed in the country of origin (pre-adoption) while the other half had a disability that was not diagnosed until later, after the child was in the adoptive country. In other words, about half of the children with a disability were adopted by parents who did not know explicitly about the disability at the time of the adoption.[14] Diagnoses within the country of origin tended to fall into the category of medical and physical disabilities, whereas later-diagnosed conditions were more likely to be psychological disabilities, presumably because those are less likely to be detected in infancy.

The survey also found that parents of children with special needs were skeptical of the medical information they received from the child's country of origin.[15] More than half of the parents reported that they had received inaccurate medical information. The majority of the parents attributed the inaccuracies to the fact that the medical systems in the country of origin were simply inadequate in terms of diagnostic expertise and ability to maintain records. Some parents of special needs children also suspected that orphanage personnel or adoption officials had intentionally misrepresented the child's medical condition, although there is no way to verify such doubts. Large majorities of parents of special needs adoptees reported concerns about insufficient care and treatment of their child's condition prior to adoption, specifically noting limitations in pre-adoptive medical care, adult caring and nurturing, and feeding and nutrition.

It is instructive to consider how disability is perceived, experienced, and addressed in countries of origin in order to understand the prevalence of disability among children available for adoption.[16] The former Soviet world provides an illustrative example, although medical infrastructure and attitudes differ, of course, across the wide range of countries-of-origin of adoptees. In Russia and other former Soviet countries, people with disabilities face nearly insurmountable obstacles to full participation in society. A 2013 Human Rights Watch report detailed physical barriers to accessibility in Russia, including apartment buildings that commonly have no elevators or ramps (or have dangerously steep ramps) as well as largely inaccessible public transit, sidewalks, public buildings, and medical facilities.[17] The report gives as an example a 26-year-old woman with limited mobility living in Sochi, which was then poised to host the 2014 Paralympic Games, who could not leave her apartment for months because she had no reliable way to get down the stairs. In Kazakhstan I personally witnessed all of these physical barriers, in addition to the much-maligned unshoveled sidewalks and unplowed streets, as I watched a fellow adoptive parent attempt to navigate the city in his wheelchair.

Literally adding insult to injury, discriminatory attitudes toward the disabled derive from a Soviet mentality that considered disabled people as inherently "defective" and unlikely to contribute as citizens.[18] Sadly, Russian mothers of newborns with apparent disability have reportedly been pressured by doctors to place their children in state-run institutions, or *internats*,[19] where the children are permanently warehoused with little attempt at therapeutic intervention to help them reach their human potential.[20] Even those disabled children who are formally relinquished for adoption (as opposed to those who are placed in institutions without a legal relinquishment) are unlikely to be adopted domestically within Russia. Human Rights Watch reports that the common practice of pressuring Russian women to relinquish disabled infants works against domestic adoption in general, as prospective Russian adopters assume that all relinquished children must have a "defect" that led to the relinquishment.[21]

While it is problematic to make sweeping generalizations about medical care and quality of life for disabled children across the wide range of countries of origin for international adoption, some evidence suggests that the barriers faced by disabled children and adults in Russia and the other former Soviet countries are not unique.[22] For example, Human Rights Watch issued a report on the barriers to education for special needs children in China, arguing that "[d]iscrimination against children and young people with disabilities permeates all levels of education in the mainstream system."[23] Human Rights Watch issued a similarly depressing portrait of life for children with disabilities in Nepal.[24] The non-governmental organization Disability Rights International has documented widespread systemic abuses of individuals with intellectual disabilities in countries as diverse as Vietnam, Peru, Republic of Georgia, and Romania.[25] Implementing accessible systems of treatment, education, and employment for people with disabilities can be expensive, and many countries of origin of adoptees simply do not have the resources at the present time. This lack of public support for families who themselves have limited financial resources presumably contributes to heartbreaking decisions for birth parents to relinquish children whom they perceive to be disabled or unhealthy.

Even in countries of origin with more financial resources, like South Korea, negative and shame-infused attitudes toward disability can limit the potential of children to thrive in family and community settings. For example, a series of studies based on interviews with middle-class Korean and Korean-American immigrant families that included a disabled child found striking differences in the degree of support for families. Korean-American families reported greater social support and more positive community attitudes toward disability than families in Korea.[26]

Comparisons of medical resources and attitudes toward disability in countries of origin versus Western receiving countries can run headlong into the "rescue narrative" about international adoption. Numerous adoption scholars have challenged the rescue narrative, the idea that adoptive parents are "saving" a child from a horrible fate in the country of origin.[27] The narrative deserves to be challenged: In its most strident forms, it smacks of imperialism, the belief that all things are inherently superior in the West and that rich Westerners are duty-bound to save the poor and unlucky elsewhere in the world. The rescue narrative can oversimplify both the desperation of the birth country and the idealized perfection of a Western life. For this reason, many in the adoption community find the rhetoric of "rescue" or "saving children" deeply problematic. Yet, we must still acknowledge that, in fact, medical care differs dramatically across the globe, as does quality of life for people with disabilities.

Common sense tells us that parenting a child with a disability may be more challenging than parenting a generally healthy child, even among affluent parents who have access to the best treatment resources. To what extent is this common-sense view supported by empirical evidence? As context, the nationally representative NSAP survey asked adoptive parents how having the child in the family compared with expectations. Among internationally adopting parents, 62% reported that their experience was better than expected, 24% reported it was about what they expected, and 14% indicated that it was more difficult than they expected.[28] Can specific child or family characteristics predict which parents will have a more difficult time than expected?

Existing studies present a mixed and complex picture of the relationship between a child's disability and various family outcome measures. In general, the distinction between medical needs and emotional-behavioral needs is important in understanding challenges for adoptive families. These two categories of needs do not always overlap. For example, one study investigated a sample of more than 1,000 children adopted from China, of whom 124 were categorized as special needs children.[29] The "special needs" in these children consisted primarily of physical or medical conditions, such as cleft palate, limb abnormalities, and heart defects. The researchers compared these special needs children to non-special needs Chinese adoptees on a commonly used measure of emotional well-being that assesses both internalizing behaviors (depression, anxiety) and externalizing behaviors ("acting out"). The researchers found that the special needs children scored no worse than the comparison group. Thus, at least in this sample, medical special needs did not predict poorer emotional-behavioral adjustment for the children.

Other studies have assessed parent-reported stress as an outcome measure. One general finding is that, on average, adoptive parents do not necessarily have higher stress levels compared to samples of non-adoptive parents.[30] This is an important reminder that adoption should not be seen as an inevitable "problem" within a family. Other studies have been more interested in understanding what predicts the wide variation of stress levels among adoptive families, rather than simply comparing them as a group to non-adoptive families. In several studies of adoptees from a variety of countries of origin, a common finding is that the presence of medical special needs did not predict parents' stress levels, but the presence of emotional-behavioral special needs did predict higher stress levels for parents.[31]

High parental stress may put children at risk for less than optimal parenting, and indeed children with behavioral problems may be especially vulnerable to disrupted or dissolved adoptions.[32] Therefore, supporting adoptive families whose children who are experiencing psychological or behavioral problems should be a paramount concern for child welfare professionals. Addressing these kinds of special needs can be more complex and fraught than addressing physical or medical special needs. Psychological or behavioral special needs may be more challenging to treat. They may also pose a greater threat to the quality of relationships inside and outside the adoptive family, an issue of special concern in a population deprived of reliable parental relationships prior to adoption. Much intervention research has therefore focused on the parenting relationship and family environment as playing an important role in addressing the psychological needs of adopted children.

Some researchers have examined parents' expectations for their children, under the assumption that realistic parental expectations will help to ensure more positive outcomes for the family. The presumed importance of parental expectations also underpins aspects of the pre-adoptive training that is required by most agencies and now by the Hague guidelines. Of course, forming or even defining a "realistic expectation" for an adopted child in general is challenging when adoptees' circumstances, characteristics, and outcomes vary tremendously.[33] Furthermore, there is a paucity of data from controlled studies demonstrating that direct manipulations of parental expectations can have an actual impact on families' outcomes.

A unique series of studies followed a sample of internationally adopting parents longitudinally to see whether pre-adoption characteristics, including parents' expectations, could predict children's and families' adjustment to the adoption. The first phase of the study reported on parents' expectations,[34] and found that parents generally endorsed highly positive expectations, as indicated by strong agreement with statements such as "I expect that my child will bond with me fairly quickly" and "I expect my child will be accepted by our friends and family." Parents also strongly endorsed items acknowledging the possibility of mild transitional needs, for example, agreeing with statements such as "I expect my child to have mild problems with eating or sleeping" and "I expect my child to have mild, short-term problems with attachment." In general, parents were less likely to agree with statements indicating an expectation of more serious problems, such as "I expect my child to have serious, long-term difficulties with language development" or "I expect my child to have serious, or significant long-term medical problems." The study found that the parents' self-reported degree of pre-adoption training was unrelated to their expectations for the adoption. However, parents anticipating adoption of an older child expected more challenges than did those anticipating adoption of a younger child, and those whose referral suggested more serious medical needs indeed reported greater expectations for medical problems. These latter findings indicate a reassuring degree of realism.

Interestingly, when families were followed longitudinally, the relationship between pre-adoption expectations and post-adoption parental stress levels displayed a surprising pattern.[35] Common wisdom might suggest that parents with the highest positive expectations before adoption are most naïve, and therefore would have the highest levels of stress when facing realities after adoption. Counter to this line of thought, the researchers found that higher post-adoption stress (6 months after the adoption) was predicted by more pessimistic pre-adoption expectations. Those parents who, pre-adoptively, expected to have more post-adoption problems tended to report higher levels of stress after the adoption.

Because the study was a correlational study, it is difficult to tease apart the possible causal relationships between negative expectations and subsequently high stress levels. One possibility is that both variables reflect stable personality traits among the parents, such that people who are pessimistic at the pre-adoption time point tend to be pessimistic about their stress levels at the later time point. Another possibility, perhaps more worrisome, is that more negative expectations for a child's outcome could actually make the outcome worse, perhaps through a sort of self-fulfilling prophecy. Because this is the only study to date that directly examined these issues prospectively in internationally adopting families, and because the effect was correlational and relatively small in magnitude, it is important not to overplay the results. Nevertheless, they suggest that the relationship between "realistic expectations" and family outcomes may be more complex than the simple idea that families will adjust better when they anticipate more problems.

Numerous studies have found correlations between attributes of the adoptive parents and outcomes for children, suggesting that certain parenting styles may be more or less suited to promoting positive outcomes within the family. Many of these studies have been conducted with domestic adoptions, so we can only assume that their conclusions would apply as well to international adoptions. For example, one study found fewer behavioral problems and lower depression levels among adoptees whose parents described family interactions as predictable, meaningful, and manageable.[36] Another found that the parents' greater endorsement of child-centering parenting (e.g., "I often tell him how proud I am of him," "I make spending time with him a high priority") predicted more adaptive social behavior and academic achievement in the adopted child.[37] Other research found that high quality of a child's relationship with an adoptive parent strongly predicted lower likelihood of conduct problems such as skipping school.[38]

Because parents are affected by their children as well as the other way around, it can be difficult to disentangle the cause-and-effect impact of parenting on children's outcomes based on such correlational studies. For example, it can be hard to tell whether a child's behavior problems may be the result of poor parent–child relationships or the cause of poor parent–child relationships, or some mixture of both. One study found that a poor parent–child relationship may serve as the path that connects the experience of early-life adversity to negative behavioral and educational outcomes.[39] For example, being older at the time of adoption (which serves as a rough indicator of extent of adversity) predicted more negative outcomes, and at least part of that association could be statistically accounted for by the poorer parent–child relationship that tended to occur with an older adopted child. This study concurs with other correlational studies in identifying the quality of the parent–child relationship as a key locus for potential intervention to promote resilience in adoptive families.

Parenting strengths may even protect children's bodies from the adverse biological effects of stress associated with early deprivation. As reviewed in Chapter 3, children exposed to early adversity display shortened telomeres, which are the end parts of chromosomes within cells that serve to protect the DNA. Severe stress is thought to damage telomeres. In a fascinating study, researchers examined both telomere shortening and parenting styles among a sample of families in the U.S. child welfare system whose children were at risk for maltreatment.[40] Confirming prior findings, the study found that children in this high-risk group had shorter telomeres than those in a low-risk control group of children. Even more fascinating, the degree of telomere shortening within the high-risk group was predicted by how the parents (who were all birth parents of the children) interacted with the children during a videotaped play session. Some parents' behaviors were more "child-centered," responding in a well-timed, synchronous manner to their children's actions and expressions, whereas other parents' behaviors were more distant, unresponsive, or disconnected from the child's activities. High-risk children whose parents interacted in a more "child-centered" manner had less telomere shortening than those whose parents were more detached. While the study was a correlational study, it suggests that high-quality parenting may help to buffer children against the adverse biological effects of early-life stress.

Research has begun to move beyond correlational studies, with their inherent problems in determining the directions of causation, toward controlled experimental studies of the effects of parenting interventions on adoptive or foster family outcomes. In such studies, families are randomly assigned to either an intervention group or a control group, and after some period of time the groups are compared on outcome variables of interest. The beauty of the experimental method is that, because of the random assignment to conditions, any difference in outcome between the groups must logically be caused by the experimental intervention.

Several studies with children in the U.S. foster care system have found that interventions focused on responsive parenting have beneficial consequences for the children's biology and behavior. For example, one intervention, referred to as the "Attachment and Biobehavioral Catch-up," or ABC, intervention, focuses on helping children develop the ability to regulate their stress physiology and behavior. Foster parents in the intervention group received 10 sessions of therapist-led training in responsive and nurturing parenting techniques, while parents in the control group received 10 sessions intended to support cognitive development. Children whose parents received the parenting training were subsequently better able to regulate the release of the stress hormone cortisol, exhibited fewer behavior problems, and showed enhanced performance on tasks of cognitive flexibility compared to those in the control group.[41] The researchers are currently conducting a similar study with internationally adopting families, and preliminary data indicate more responsive parent–child interactions and better child cognitive functioning among those in the intervention group.[42] (Full disclosure: our family participated in the study.) Other research teams working with children in foster care have independently confirmed the beneficial effects of sensitive-parenting interventions on children's physiology and behavior.[43]

While most intervention studies have focused on children within the U.S. foster care system, a few have examined parenting interventions with internationally adoptive families. For example, Dutch researchers reported on an intervention conducted with families in the Netherlands who had adopted children internationally before the age of 6 months.[44] The intervention focused on building attachment relationships between the parent and child. One condition involved giving the parents a book of written materials promoting sensitive and playful interactions with a child; a second condition involved giving the parents written materials plus, in three separate sessions, videotaping the mother–child interaction and providing feedback about parenting behaviors in the video; and a third condition, the control condition, involved providing written materials about adoption that did not necessarily address sensitive-parenting issues. When assessed several months later, children whose mothers received the book plus the video feedback displayed better attachment behavior than that of the children in the other two groups.

These intervention studies consistently imply that a focus on positive parenting can help adopted children better regulate their behavior. The studies are promising in part because the intervention methods occurred over short periods of time (3 to 10 sessions). Although the interventions typically involve multiple sessions guided by trained personnel such as therapists, after training the sensitive-parenting techniques can be sustained by families for free. In other words, families do not need to be affluent to engage in positive parenting techniques. Still, numerous questions remain for future research, including identifying exactly which parenting behaviors are most essential in helping children of different ages (e.g., infancy, middle childhood, or adolescence).[45] It will also be crucial to determine how long-lasting any beneficial effects may be, and whether such interventions are consistently successful across a range of internationally adopting families whose children are typically quite diverse in characteristics such as age at adoption and nature of pre-adoptive experiences.

While promoting positive relationships within the adoptive family is crucial, it is also important that adoptive families be able to obtain assistance from trained experts in a variety of professions. Depending on the child, needs may include speech therapy, occupational therapy, special education, or psychotherapy. For example, data from the NSAP survey found that among parents of internationally adoptive families with children over the age of 5 years, 35% reported receiving mental health care for the child and 36% reported accessing a tutor for the child.[46]

Obtaining the expertise of trained professionals is especially important for families whose children have more severe behavioral problems. As reviewed in earlier chapters, the vast majority of adopted children fall within the normal range on various outcome measures, but some children pose extreme challenges for even the most sensitive and positive of parents. A small minority of children exposed to prenatal insults, severe deprivation, abuse, or lack of nurturing may develop dangerous and problematic behaviors that cannot be handled by the parents alone. In such cases, parents should have the assistance of trained professionals who are competent in addressing the needs of adoptive families.[47]

Yet, it must be acknowledged that rigorously tested psychotherapy treatments specifically focused on more severe behavioral problems in adoptees do not exist at the current time. Of course, empirically supported therapies have been developed in the non-adoptive context to address many psychological conditions, such as depression, anxiety, conduct problems, and attentional problems. While therapeutic approaches have been developed specifically for previously institutionalized children,[48] at the present time the support for such therapies comes from case reports and uncontrolled outcome studies, rather than in the form of rigorously controlled intervention studies. This does not imply that the therapies are necessarily ineffective, but rather that their effectiveness has yet to be demonstrated in scientifically rigorous studies.

For example, an intervention known as "trust-based relational intervention" has shown some promise in addressing the special emotional and behavioral needs of previously institutionalized or severely neglected children. The therapy emphasizes establishing an environment of "felt safety" for the child (calm and predictable environments), encouraging relational engagement between parent and child (e.g., through eye contact and active listening), and training parents to help their children make better behavioral choices.[49] One study followed 19 children, most adopted from orphanages in Eastern Europe, who attended a summer camp for special needs children that focused on this intervention strategy. The camp included a combination of attachment-promoting activities, provision of an environment rich in sensory activities, and exercises in appropriate social behavior. Researchers found that parent reports of aggressive behavior decreased and positive attachment behaviors increased during the camp experience.[50] Subsequent research also reported a reduction in the stress hormone cortisol in children who attended the camp.[51] Other case reports also attest to the effectiveness of this therapeutic approach,[52] though outcome studies that include a control group for comparison (the gold standard in clinical research design) have not yet been reported.

Even for clinical conditions that have been well recognized by the psychological community as relevant to adoptive populations, there is unfortunately little clarity on the best treatment options or even on the proper diagnoses. For example, the concept of "reactive attachment disorder," presumed to be a phenomenon of severely disordered behavior caused by faulty attachment in early life, is controversial among scholars.[53] Some researchers have questioned whether poor attachment (as opposed to deprivation more generally) is even the key mechanism leading to the behaviors labeled as "reactive attachment disorder"; others have expressed concern that the label is too often applied to adoptees who may be better described by other diagnoses such as conduct disorder, attention-deficit disorder, or post-traumatic stress disorder.[54] Even those researchers who support the validity of the "reactive attachment disorder" diagnosis have acknowledged that currently there are no evidence-based treatments for it.[55] This leaves families with a stressful evidence gap. To address the needs of adoptive families, particularly those whose children exhibit severe behavioral problems, research must begin to address the effectiveness of therapies in an empirical fashion.

Without evidence of treatment effectiveness, parents who are eager to ensure their child and family's well-being in the face of severe stresses are sometimes, unfortunately, drawn to dramatic and poorly supported interventions. In such instances, the best outcome may be wasted time and money, and the worst outcome may be a harmful effect on the child. The classic example of this phenomenon is the case of "holding therapy" to treat presumed attachment problems. The following story of this discredited technique should serve as a cautionary tale for parents.

"Holding therapy" is a phrase used to describe a range of therapeutic techniques that involve the therapist physically holding the child who is presumed to suffer from attachment difficulties. The most ethically problematic forms involve physically coercive holding, though any form of physical contact with a therapist may be psychologically coercive. Some versions of the therapy propose that the child be forcibly restrained until he or she feels extreme shame or rage. The rationale behind holding therapy is loosely based on attachment theory in the sense that attachment in infancy is thought to derive in part from physical contact. Yet, as others have pointed out, holding therapy actually makes no sense from the perspective of attachment theory, because it provides physical touch from a stranger (the therapist) in a coercive and threatening way rather than providing touch from the desired attachment figure (the parent) in a nurturing way that could build trust.[56]

Aside from the poor theoretical base and ethically problematic components, holding therapy is not supported by any research on effectiveness. In fact, it can actually cause physical and psychological harm to the child. The most notorious case of harm was the case of Candace Newmaker, a child who was smothered by coercive restraint in a form of holding therapy known as "rebirthing."[57] While holding therapy appears to be on the wane, it is possible that other questionable treatments will emerge into the vacuum as researchers struggle to identify empirically supported treatments. Adoptive parents would be well advised to be aware of "red flags" indicating poorly validated treatments. For example, if a treatment is only presented and discussed on the Internet, rather than in the pages of scholarly journals, and if it is heavily promoted by an individual or group with possible financial or reputational gain, without being independently verified as effective, it may do more harm than good.

A key issue for the adoption community is making sure that families know where to turn for assistance with post-adoption challenges—whether those challenges are medical, educational, or psychological, acute or chronic, mild or severe, and regardless of whether the challenges emerge in the immediate post-adoption period or many years later.[58] Existing studies suggest that families who access specialized services benefit from them. For example, data from the nationally representative NSAP survey found that among those internationally adoptive parents who reported using mental health services, roughly half found the service "very helpful" and only 10% reported that the service was "not very helpful" (the remainder, approximately 40%, reported that the service was "somewhat helpful").[59] Another study of families with children adopted from U.S. foster care found that accessing educational resources and parent support groups decreased the likelihood of an adoption dissolution.[60]

Ideally, adoption agencies should serve as coordinating centers for post-adoption services and referrals for adoptive families, but agencies vary widely in quality. Furthermore, the recent decline in international adoptions has led some agencies to shutter their doors altogether. As a result, adoptive families must be proactive in seeking services from other providers when needed. For example, in the Donaldson survey of adoptive parents of special needs children, 57% of the parents indicated that they had to seek out services themselves, rather than having those services provided or referred by the adoption agency.[61] In the NSAP survey, only 50% of internationally adoptive parents reported having met with someone at their adoption agency to discuss post-adoption services.[62] In the same dataset, 29% of internationally adopting parents reported that "at least one needed adoption-specific support was not received post-adoption."[63] These findings suggest unmet needs for a significant proportion of families. Adoption agencies and child welfare professionals should continue to improve awareness and access to services to ensure the best interest of the adopted child.

In sum, adoptive parents, like all parents but perhaps even more urgently, must proactively advocate for their children's needs. While surveys indicate that adoptive populations have a higher than average incidence of special needs, the vast majority of adoptees are healthy or have treatable needs. Through adoption, international adoptees have generally gained access to First-World medical care and residence in countries that, while surely not immune from stereotypes and stigmatization of disabled individuals, have legislative mandates intended to reduce discrimination and increase accessibility for people with a range of disabilities. Even adopted children without diagnosed medical needs may benefit from interventions that emphasize child-centered and responsive approaches to parenting. The most difficult special needs to address are emotional-behavioral challenges, which are most likely to occur in older children who have endured the most severe and prolonged deprivation prior to adoption.[64] While the adoption community awaits empirically validated treatments for such individuals, policy should focus on prevention, which amounts to placing children in family settings as early in life as possible to minimize the well-established effects of psychological deprivation.

8 ■
Conclusions and Policy Considerations

Research reviewed in this book overwhelmingly affirms the conclusion that international adoption benefits children. The stable, supportive environments of family homes have an enormous positive impact on development, allowing children who suffered adversity early in life the opportunity to dramatically make up lost ground physically, cognitively, and emotionally. While some adopted children may still lag behind non-adopted peers developmentally, most lingering delays or challenges are attributable to the early-life adversity that preceded adoption, not to adoption itself. Adopted children may face challenges as they grapple with the role of birth family and birth culture heritage in their identity formation, but there is no systematic evidence that these issues have any long-lasting negative consequence for the vast majority of adoptees. Finally, contrary to myths perpetuated in media stories and public opinion, adoptive parents are just as committed to, bonded with, and invested in their children as birth parents, and they possess significant resources that can be directed to the benefit of their children as needed.

Several recommendations for policymakers, researchers, and adoptive parents follow directly from the evidence reviewed in these chapters. First, policies that significantly delay the placement of children in homes across national borders while searching for in-country solutions can directly harm children. It is nonsensical to require an institutionalized child to be rejected month after month by potential domestic adopters when willing and able families, ready to welcome the child with open arms, are waiting across a national boundary. Research clearly demonstrates that early-placed children have the best opportunity for developmental catch-up across all psychological domains that have been studied. If policies significantly delay family placement in order to prioritize residence in a country of origin, those who support such policies must recognize and defend the reality that such policies are designed to serve political ends rather than the developmental needs of the child.

Policymakers should also ensure that bureaucratic steps involved in adopting a child do not inadvertently complicate the formation of an attachment relationship between the child and adoptive parents. For example, in some countries of origin, regulations require prospective adoptive parents to make several trips separated by months. Any bonding with the child that happens on the first trip is difficult to sustain over months from thousands of miles away, to the detriment of the child. Once a legally adoptable child has been introduced to parents with legal permission to adopt the child, regulations should facilitate the development and maintenance of an attachment relationship rather than undermining that relationship through bureaucratic delays. This recommendation follows from psychological research on the importance of bonding with primary caregivers early in life.

A third set of recommendations pertains to living conditions for children who have not yet been placed for adoption. Even when adoption is facilitated in a timely manner, there will often be some period of time, hopefully as brief as possible, between the point of separation from birth parents and placement in an adoptive family. During this window of time, the child should receive not only food, warmth, and adequate medical care but also socioemotional nurturing, which is essential for healthy child development. Fostering or improved orphanage conditions could both serve this end, provided that they are not seen as a permanent course of care for a child, but rather a temporary stopgap until a permanent family home for the child is established. Empirical work on interventions in Russian orphanages suggests that promoting greater caregiver–child bonding through structural changes in orphanages (e.g., emphasis on emotional expressivity by caregivers, staff shifts that encourage formation of relationships) can be beneficial for children.[1] Additional research indicates that fostering can have significant benefits over institutionalization, provided that foster parents are highly qualified and trained.[2] Nevertheless, permanent family-home placement should be prioritized as the ultimate goal.

Research also encourages a more liberal approach to the definition of *family*, even as many countries of origin are becoming more restrictive in allowable family structures for adoptive placement. Existing evidence to date suggests that families who depart from the traditional structure, such as single parents or same-sex-partnered parents, provide homes in which adopted children can thrive.[3] Consistent with common sense, what matters for a child is the emotional support and parenting style within a family, not the family structure per se. Screening of potential adoptive parents should focus as much as possible on assessing emotional resilience, support, and commitment in the adoptive parents, rather than using family structure as a proxy for those more important variables.

Fifth, policymakers could better serve adoptive families by creating central information portals for post-adoption services. Many families are well supported by their agencies through the stages of pre-adoption preparation and navigating the maze of paperwork required to legally complete the adoption but find themselves on their own in the adoption's aftermath. Adoptive families, even with their generally above-average education and financial resources, can sometimes find themselves uncertain about where and how to locate early-intervention or educational services, information on relevant medical treatments, or advice on best parenting practices for children who experienced institutionalization or neglect. Some of these needs may arise years after the adoption is completed—for example, as a child enters adolescence and begins to grapple more directly with issues surrounding race, culture, and identity.[4] Given the current instability in international adoption, agencies may open and close over the time period when families could benefit from services. Therefore, central information gateways that are not tied to specific agencies could better support adoptive families.

A sixth recommendation pertains to adoptive parents, who are advised to address thoughtfully, as most already do, the relationship between the adoptive family and the country, culture, and race of the child's origins. Despite normative proscriptions that seem to proclaim "the right way" for adoptive parents to address issues of culture,[5] there is no one-size-fits-all solution for how to nurture the developing identity of a child whose genetic roots lie across the world. Each adopted child, and later adult, will have unique ways of navigating a rich and complex identity. Parents can help by being partners in the process of identity formation, by supporting the child's (or adult's) desire to make contact with birth families and communities if and when that desire arises, by sharing responsibility for connecting respectfully with the culture of origin, and, in cases of transracial adoptions, by embracing the multiracial composition of the family. Although many adoptive families are already attentive to these issues, some critics or others in the general public may not be aware of the extent to which the adoption community has moved beyond assimilationist practices of the past. As adoptive families, we have the responsibility to educate others in thoughtful and respectful ways.

A final set of recommendations pertains to research. While the findings reviewed in this book represent the formidable contributions of a large number of researchers, there is still more to be learned. One key area for future research is the area of intervention. For example, not enough is known about effective treatment approaches for families whose adopted child is experiencing severe behavioral problems resulting from abuse, neglect, and deprivation. Although these children are a minority among adoptees, their adoptions are at most risk for dissolution. Families need reliable evidence about how best to manage the needs of such children.

Another currently underdeveloped area of research focuses on outcomes for unparented children within countries of origin. While a large body of evidence attests to the positive outcomes of international adoption, there is less systematic evidence pertaining to how children fare when they spend entire childhoods in institutions, in foster care, or in domestic adoption in their countries of origin.[6] This imbalance in the research literature exists for obvious reasons: research infrastructure is better in receiving countries than in countries of origin, and adopted children are easier to track (for example, through agency contacts) than children released from orphanages, who may disappear into the margins of society. Anecdotal evidence suggests very undesirable outcomes among those who have "aged out" of orphanages, such as high levels of social isolation, unemployment, criminal involvement, and suicide.[7] Kazakhstani politician Dariga Nazarbayeva, daughter of President Nursultan Nazarbayev, has been quoted as saying of Kazakhstani orphanage graduates that "70 percent of the boys raised in this system end up in jail and 60 percent of girls turn to prostitution,"[8] though the source of these numbers is unclear. Discussions about best options for child welfare would be immensely advanced if there were more systematic data detailing the long-term prospects for children exiting from a wide range of alternative care possibilities. Such data could help move discussions about placement options away from ideological positions and toward those that are both child focused and data driven.

Given the vast literature attesting to the benefits of international adoption, it is striking that a number of influential nongovernmental organizations as well as policies in some countries of origin clearly relegate international adoption to "last resort" option for unparented children.[9] Some countries with significant populations of unparented children do not permit international adoption at all. If international adoption can benefit children, why is there not more universal and enthusiastic support?

There may be myriad reasons that individuals, organizations, or nations oppose international adoption, but they seem to fall into three broad categories. The first category is nationalistic sentiment or other political motivation. For example, Russia banned adoption to America in 2012 to retaliate after the U.S. government passed a bill seeking sanctions against Russian human rights violators (unconnected to adoption).[10] The subordination of children's best interests so that adults may feel more patriotic and political leaders may garner nationalistic support is deeply troubling from a moral and humans rights perspective.[11]

Political or nationalistic motives must be understood as reflecting often complex and fraught histories and relationships between and within nations.[12] For example, although Kazakhstan does not have a colonial relationship with the United States or Europe (Kazakhstan was colonized by Russia), there is a sentiment (not unjustified) among many local people that more powerful nations, such as Russia, China, and Western nations, are helping themselves to vast resources such as oil and gas from Kazakhstan. Local opposition to foreign adoption can thus resonate with anti-foreign sentiment that originates from other issues. In another example, opposition to foreign adoption in Guatemala should be seen in the context of a nation that suffered a brutal civil war in which the abduction of children was used as a tool of war. Beliefs in Guatemala that children were being abducted and "adopted" by foreigners for the purpose of organ harvesting may seem less outrageous when one appreciates the extreme levels of violence that Guatemalans experienced during the civil war and its aftermath.[13] Advocates for adoption must recognize and respect these complex realities, which differ from nation to nation, and situate advocacy efforts appropriately within such contexts.

A second category of reasons for opposing international adoption, or at least strictly limiting its scope, is the preference for placement of the child in the country of origin through either domestic adoption, foster care, or other residential care alternatives. Arguably the benefits that adoption brings to a child, as reviewed in earlier chapters, ought to pertain to domestic as well as international adoption. Laudable efforts have been made to increase rates of domestic adoption in various countries of origin (such as Romania and Korea), even where such efforts run counter to widespread cultural resistance or stigmatization of adoption. Such efforts should be supported by those concerned with the problem of unparented children world-wide, including internationally adoptive families.

At the same time, resource limitations in some countries of origin, especially those that include economically stressed populations, may limit the number of families who can afford to take an additional child into the home. A recent study of domestic adoption in Romania, Ukraine, India, Guatemala, and Ethiopia found modest but not overwhelming increases in domestic adoption during periods in which programs to support such adoption were implemented.[14] For example, in the early 2000s Romania was forced to ban international adoption as a condition of integration into the European Union, following concerns about illegal activity in connection with international adoption; efforts to promote domestic adoption were undertaken in the years before and have been made since. Between 1998 and 1999, the number of domestic adoptions doubled in Romania (and international adoptions also occurred at a high rate). However, since that time, levels of domestic adoption have leveled off despite continuing need for more adoptive families. The study's authors report:

> It should be of concern that the rate of domestic adoptions in Romania has been at a standstill since 2006. More children are abandoned by birth parents than there are families to adopt them. For example, from 2006 to 2011, there were 6,620 adoptions, but there also were 7,958 abandoned children. This still left approximately 1,300 infants in another form of alternative care. . . . The increase of children in institutional care is inconsistent with Romania's national priorities and the best interests of children.[15]

The authors report somewhat higher rates of domestic adoption in Ukraine, which they attribute to better infrastructure than in Romania and promotion of adoption by

Ukraine's then-president Viktor Yushchenko. Nevertheless, in a note of caution, it is also reported that adoption in Ukraine is culturally surrounded by secrecy, such that more than half of the adoptive families surveyed had not told the children they were adopted and nearly a quarter said they never planned to tell them.[16] Likewise, attempts to promote domestic adoption in South Korea have faltered due to cultural taboos against raising children who don't carry forth the family bloodline.[17] Those who privilege domestic adoption over international adoption due to concerns about a child's identity development must acknowledge that domestic adoption can pose its own challenges.

Virtually no research to date compares outcomes between children adopted internationally and those adopted domestically within the same country of origin, so there is no robust evidence for making arguments about which option is actually better for a child. The one exception is a study that examined outcomes for Indian children adopted either internationally (to the United States or Norway) or domestically within India.[18] The study found better outcomes (as reported by the parents on a standard questionnaire) for those who were adopted abroad than those adopted domestically in India. Policy cannot rationally rest on a single study, as any study has inherent limitations in methodology and generalizability. Nevertheless, the results should at least give pause to those who assume that domestic adoption within the country of origin will inevitably produce better outcomes for the child than international adoption. The privileging of domestic adoption may be based primarily on political notions of sovereignty and adults' focus on cultural heritage rather than on evidence that it is actually better for children.

Furthermore, children with disabilities face dismal prospects for domestic adoption in many countries. For example, in a 2014 report, Human Rights Watch described how Russian child welfare officials actively discouraged prospective Russian families from adopting or fostering disabled children, based on cultural assumptions that such children have no potential to develop.[19] There is virtually no community support for families attempting to raise children with disabilities in Russia. With minimal prospects for domestic adoption and with international adoption largely banned by Russia, such children remain in institutions that in many cases can only be described as physically and psychologically abusive. Human Rights Watch reports cases of institutionalized children with disabilities being tied to furniture, beaten by staff, isolated from other children, or housed in "lying down rooms" in which they are never permitted to move about.[20] Given this reality, it is absurd to argue that unparented children with disabilities are better off staying in Russia because their cultural heritage could be maintained there.

While there may be good reasons to support both domestic and international adoption as alternatives for unparented children, other alternatives, such as in-country foster care or various forms of residential care, are more controversial, even as large numbers of children reside within such systems. For example, in Romania in 2011, data indicate that 19,376 children were in foster care and 23,240 children were in institutions (for comparison, in that year, 1,083 Romanian children were adopted domestically and 0 were adopted internationally).[21] While a systematic review of foster care is outside the scope of this book, we can simply note that foster care is not a permanent solution for a child, but rather a temporary one. Although foster care can produce better outcomes than institutionalization when foster families are rigorously selected and trained,[22] other research indicates that adoption produces better long-term outcomes for children than long-term fostering.[23] Significant problems resulting from the impermanency of foster care, even in well-resourced countries like the United States, have been well described elsewhere,[24] even as most people recognize foster care as potentially appropriate in situations in which later reunification with birth families may be possible. Similarly, efforts to provide small-group residential care options for unparented children are laudable and preferable to life in a large institution, on the streets, or with an abusive birth family. Yet, it is difficult to see why residential care options would be preferable to adoption for children who are legally adoptable.[25]

In addition to nationalism and a preference for domestic care options, a third category of reasons for opposing international adoption is a set of concerns centering around money, corruption, and potential trafficking. Some raise these concerns more obliquely through references to the "market" for adoptable children or by highlighting the significant expense involved in adoption and the relative affluence of adoptive families compared with that of birth families in countries of origin.[26] Others articulate a similar set of concerns through more strident statements asserting that international adoption amounts to human trafficking.[27]

This category of concerns is important to take seriously, as the potential for corruption always coexists with significant financial exchanges. Adoptive families need to have awareness (and many do) of the significant economic disparities present in most scenarios of international adoption and the resulting power dynamics that can develop. Prospective adoptive parents should also ask hard questions of their agencies about how a child's legal eligibility for adoption is verified in the countries in which the agency works. Regulatory structures need to ensure, as best as possible, that children being offered for adoption are truly legally available for adoption, with birth parents having either formally relinquished the child or having had rights terminated through a fair legal process. For these reasons, the Hague Convention on international adoption includes safeguards that are sensible responses to the need to prevent fraud.[28]

At the same time, sometimes the zeal to cast out corruption goes too far, with negative consequences for genuinely abandoned children caught up in a challenged system. For example, adoption advocates argue that the U.S. Department of State prematurely halted adoptions from Nepal in 2010 in the face of allegations of fraud that were never confirmed by any credible evidence and were often based on misunderstandings of the local context and culture.[29] While caution may intuitively seem the best strategy anytime corruption is suspected, it must be recognized that adoption suspensions and lengthy investigations attempting to uncover evidence of corruption take a measurable toll on children who remain without families during crucial developmental time periods. Unsubstantiated rumors about corruption should not be allowed to derail a child's placement in a family.

Volumes could be and have been written about the topic of corruption in various societies.[30] While the topic is largely beyond the scope of this book, I raise two points for consideration. First, Western critics of adoption often fail to distinguish between two distinct kinds of corruption: petty corruption that is the bread and butter of many economies, and genuine human trafficking. Making an "unofficial payment" to an official who expects such payment to move along required paperwork may be corruption, but in many countries it is utterly common and mundane, simply the routine way of doing any kind of business.[31] Such petty corruption is not equivalent to kidnapping or "baby buying," such as making coercive payments to birth families in exchange for a child whom they would otherwise not relinquish. Most people would agree that kidnapping and other forms of coerced relinquishment are morally indefensible, and protections must be in place to prevent their occurrence. At the same time, if we require that international

adoption only be practiced in places that have been puri-
fied of mundane, petty corruption, we do a disservice to
unparented children born into countries where such activities are commonplace.

Secondly, when castigating corruption in international
adoption, critics often fail to examine whether other child
welfare alternatives in a particular country are themselves corrupt. When the director of our son's baby house
was arrested in 2011, it was for corruption involving a
domestic Kazakhstani adoption (forging paperwork to
represent a domestic adoptive parent as if she were the
birth mother, to hide the stigma of adoption).[32] Existing
systems of institutional care for children in many places
are already infiltrated by corruption. For example, corrupt
patronage interests in vast, established orphanage systems in the former Soviet Union fuel resistance to de-
institutionalizing reforms.[33] In such a context, halting
international adoptions does not eliminate petty corruption in child welfare systems; it just concentrates corruption in other sites, such as institutional care.

Some critics also point to the expense of international
adoption, as if the mere dollar amount itself were clear evidence of wrongdoing, or at least something very troubling.[34] When we hear that an international adoption costs
(for example) $30,000, we may envision an adoptive parent
simply handing over a wad of bills totaling $30,000 to a
shady intermediary somewhere in the developing world
and receiving a baby in return. Media reports that dwell
on the commodification of adoption (the adoption "market," "supply and demand" for babies, and so on) perpetu-
ate this myth of a shady back-alley deal involving tens of
thousands of dollars.

To be sure, some of the money we paid for our adoption
went to local intermediaries in Kazakhstan. These intermediaries included two coordinators who shepherded us
through the bureaucratic process (which we could not have

done on our own, given the opacity of post-Soviet bureaucratic structures), a translator who was needed to translate both written documents and conversations among English, Kazakh, and Russian on a daily basis, and a driver to transport us to the baby house and to official meetings. None of these people should be expected to work for free. Much of the cost of our adoption took the form of travel expenses paid to airlines, local hotels, and local restaurants. Costs imposed by U.S. regulations were another major source of expenditure, though these costs are justifiable in ensuring the legality and ethics of the adoption process. We paid for a home study by a certified social worker in the United States, for fingerprinting and background checking by three different governmental agencies (state police, FBI, U.S. Citizenship and Immigration Services), and for innumerable documents, certificates, and notarizations. The expense of international adoption is indeed burdensome for many families. However, just because adoption costs money does not make it equivalent to "baby buying."

Critics sometimes use the phrase "adoption industry" to describe the network of people who devote some or all of their professional time to facilitating adoption.[35] By referring to adoption as an "industry," the critics aim to portray adoption as an impersonal, faceless enterprise in which families are artificially manufactured for commercial gain. Nothing could be further from my personal experience with the compassionate social workers who staffed our adoption agency. These were people who cared about supporting children and families, and none of them was getting rich doing so. To describe our agency as part of the "adoption industry" is as sensible as describing an obstetrician as part of the "baby manufacturing industry." Of course, there are some money-making opportunists in the world of adoption, just as in any human endeavor. But we need to recognize the phrase "adoption industry" as a rhetorical device intended to delegitimize and depersonalize the network of people whose work is needed to support adopted children and families.

Some critics also allege that the international adoption "industry" actually creates orphans.[36] By this reasoning, according to the simple laws of supply and demand, where the demand exists, supply will follow; when rich Westerners want children, available children will be "created" to meet that demand. Of course, it is common and accepted practice for children to be created to meet adults' desires to become parents (for example, in typical biological parenting, in vitro fertilization, and surrogacy). However, the critics' contention that children become "orphans" to meet Western demand is a troubling one, particularly if it implies, as it is often meant to, that children who otherwise would be living with their functional birth families are stolen from those families to serve the needs of richer people who want them. I would wager that no adoptive parent would want to adopt a child obtained under such circumstances. And tragically, there have been reports of birth families whose children were kidnapped or otherwise coercively taken and later emerge as available for foreign adoption.[37] Where critics and advocates disagree is in whether such instances are localized to particular times and places or whether they are systemic problems pervasive enough to delegitimize international adoption everywhere.[38] This is a question crying out for evidence to address it, but unfortunately there is little systematic data on the prevalence of kidnapping or coercion of birth parents. In the absence of objective data, predetermined ideologies about adoption fill the gap.

A recent empirical study purported to show that international adoption "creates" orphans, but the study's methodologies and conclusions have been sharply disputed by other scholars.[39] Based on a sample of only seven countries in Europe in 2003, the authors reported a statistically significant correlation between the number of children under the age of 3 years in institutions and the number of out-going international adoptions. Countries with more institutionalization reported more children adopted out to other countries. From these meager data, the report concluded that "rather than reduce the number of children in institutions, international adoption may contribute to the continuation of this harmful practice."[40]

Aside from the limited database on which this conclusion was based—a handful of European countries, none of which is a major source of internationally adopted children, sampled in only one year—the conclusion falls prey to a classic error in reasoning: drawing a cause-and-effect conclusion from correlational data. As generations of professors in research methods classes have drilled into their students, correlation does not equal causation. Correlations, or patterns of associations, may have come about through many causal pathways. Yet, the researchers in this study jumped to the conclusion that international adoption *causes* high levels of institutionalization just because the two are correlated. On purely logical grounds, it is equally possible that the causal arrow goes in the other direction: high levels of institutionalization *cause* high levels of international adoption. (Plausibly, international adoption seems more likely to follow from high numbers of children available in institutions rather than the other way around, but the point is that correlational data cannot distinguish these two possibilities.) Additional explanations could involve other hidden variables; for example, perhaps in some countries cultural attitudes about state responsibility lead to both higher levels of institutionalization and low levels of domestic adoption, thus leaving the door open for higher levels of international adoption. In any case, the data from this study could be explained in many ways. The authors' conclusion—that international adoption creates high levels of institutionalization—seems to have been determined by pre-existing biases rather than by critical evaluation of the data.

With respect to issues of money, corruption, and potential trafficking, adoption critic David Smolin writes: "Significant segments of the adoption community are in deep denial about the prevalence and seriousness of abusive practices in intercountry adoption."[41] I do not count myself among them. After living for year in Kazakhstan, a country ranked as one of the most corrupt in the world,[42] and after navigating the Kazakhstani judicial system for a significant part of that year, I no longer consider myself naïve. I do, however, object to the wholesale depiction of international adoption as "trafficking," a term that aims to obscure nuances and complexity through its emotional power. *Trafficking*, by standard definitions, is the buying and selling of people for purposes of exploitation (such as slavery or sexual exploitation).[43] Orphanages themselves, not adoptions, create the greatest threat of genuine trafficking. Orphanages release into the world adolescents who are unmoored from family and community supports, have little to no financial safety net, have been deprived of the opportunity for normal development of cognitive and social skills, and therefore are at very high risk for exploitation by traffickers. Castigating all international adoption as "trafficking" detracts from the genuine problems of trafficking in the developing world.[44]

A final, though crucially important, issue in the discussion of adoption is the role of the birth parents. As others have pointed out, birth parents are often the invisible part of the adoption picture, the ghosts or lacunae in adoption stories.[45] Written accounts of adoption typically take the viewpoint of adoptive parents, as in this book, or the viewpoint of the adoptee, as in recent first-person accounts of adoption. Birth parents who relinquish children are less likely to write books about their experience, presumably because the decision to relinquish a child is deeply personal, often complex, sometimes secret, and often stigmatized, or because birth parents in many situations live challenging lives in which the time to write is an unthinkable luxury.

Increasingly, though, journalists and researchers are hearing and telling their stories. For example, Chinese radio host Xinran relays stories of Chinese women compelled to relinquish (or even kill) female infants in a time when China's one-child policy and male preference led to large-scale abandonment of girls.[46] Fieldwork interviews with Chinese birth mothers also emphasize the role of oppressive Chinese government policy in restricting birth mothers' choices.[47] Journalist Erin Siegal tells the harrowing story of a Guatemalan mother whose daughter was essentially kidnapped and wound up in the foreign adoption pipeline.[48] Other stories remind us that anti-adoption politicians are not above exploiting birth mothers for political gain. For example, after a Russian boy died in an American adoptive home in 2012, Kremlin-controlled state media trotted out the boy's birth mother, whose parental rights had been terminated due to alcoholism, for orchestrated television interviews as part of a campaign against American adoption.[49]

Systematic evidence about birth parents in countries of origin for international adoption is generally lacking, but some researchers have studied characteristics of birth parents in domestic adoptions in the West. Findings generally confirm what common sense would tell us—namely that many mothers who relinquish a child (or have parental rights terminated) find the experience to be extremely painful and can struggle for years with feelings of guilt, loss, anger, and anxiety about the child's current well-being.[50] Some evidence suggests that an important factor in birth mothers' resolution of these emotions is the degree to which she perceives the relinquishment or termination as an exercise of her own choice instead of a "choice" that was coerced by circumstances. The birth mother's satisfaction with the level of contact with the adopted child may also mitigate some of these negative consequences.[51] Birth mothers tend to have high rates of emotional difficulties such as anxiety and depression, though it is very challenging to ascertain to what extent those emotional problems are caused by the relinquishment or termination itself or by other life circumstances (poverty, poor social support, oppression of women, violence or abuse, addiction) that tend to surround and precede relinquishment.[52] Evidence from studies of birth fathers is even more meager, but it must be remembered that they, too, are part of the so-called adoption triad of birth families, children, and adoptive families.[53]

The absence of the birth parents' perspective from debates about international adoption can have two kinds of negative consequences. On the one hand, the potentially adverse impact of systems of international adoption on birth parents may be neglected or ignored, as researchers focus exclusively on what is good for children and, to a lesser extent, what is good for adoptive families. On the other hand, the lack of systematic information about birth families leaves a vacuum that may be filled with overly romanticized views. For example, not knowing much about the complexity of birth parents' situations may allow us to entertain the idea, which in most cases is likely an appealing fiction, that if only someone would give the birth parents a bit of money, the problems that led to relinquishment would be solved.[54]

Sadly, a review of literature on outcomes of alternative-care placements concluded that children who were reunified with birth parents following alternative care had poorer outcomes than those who were adopted or fostered, and reunified children had only marginally better outcomes than those remaining in institutions.[55] Realistic assessments of the viability of reunification or birth family preservation must recognize the need for a whole suite of family support services (such as employment, mental health, addiction, and abuse prevention services), as well as changes in cultural attitudes about out-of-wedlock births, disability, cross-ethnic relationships, and women's access to reproductive services, to realize the worthy aim of keeping as many children with stable birth families as possible and ensuring that they thrive within those families. These are difficult problems to solve, and children wait while the world flounders at solving them.

My son's baby house was named Umit, as are many similar institutions in Kazakhstan. In the Kazakh language, *umit* means "hope." My hopes for my son include the normal parental hopes: that he remains happy, healthy, and enveloped by love throughout his life. I hope he continues to develop self-respect as an American with origins in Kazakhstan. In the darkest moments of our journey in Kazakhstan, when I thought we would lose him, I hoped desperately that whoever was awarded the privilege of raising him would be kind and decent. But now my hopes have broadened beyond our family. I hope that in some future world, there are no longer institutions poignantly named Umit. I hope that the children who would populate such future Umits will be instead held in the arms of parents, whether those parents are related by birth or adoption and regardless of where they live.

Notes ■

Front Matter

1. Excerpt from *The Handmaid's Tale* by Margaret Atwood. Copyright (c) 1986 by OW. Toad, Ltd. Reprinted by permission of Houghton Mifflin Harcourt Publishing Company. All rights reserved.

2. Brief quote from p. 417 from *Tales of Burning Love* by Louise Erdrich. Copyright (c) 1996 by Louise Erdrich. Reprinted by permission of HarperCollins Publishers.

Chapter 1

1. Batty, D. (2010, April 10). U.S. mother sparks outrage after sending adopted child back to Russia alone. *The Guardian*; Associated Press (2010, April 16). Russia suspends U.S. adoptions after 7-year-old boy returned. *Moscow Times.*

2. Rich, L. (2010, September 30). *Kyrgyzstan: American adoptions still stalled.* Retrieved from http://www.eurasianet.org/node/62055.

3. Levy, C. J. (2010, November 23). Unwrapping red tape to find the gift of family. *New York Times*, A12.

4. For similar beliefs in Russia and elsewhere, see Khabibullina, L. (2009). International adoption in Russia: "Market," "children for organs," and "precious" or "bad" genes. In D. Marre & L. Briggs (Eds.), *International adoption: Global inequalities and the circulation of children.* New York: New York University Press.

5. See, for example, Briggs, L., & Marre, D. (2009). Introduction: The circulation of children. In D. Marre & L. Briggs (Eds.), *International adoption: Global inequalities and the circulation of children.* New York: New York University Press; King, S. (2009). Challenging monohumanism: An argument for changing the way we think about intercountry adoption. *Michigan Journal of International Law, 30,* 413–470. For a more nuanced view, see Perry, T. L. (1998). Transracial and international adoption: Mothers, hierarchy, race, and feminist legal theory. *Yale Journal of Law & Feminism, 10,* 101–397.

6. According to the United Nations Convention on the Rights of the Child, which was ratified by Kazakhstan on August 12, 1994, "In all actions concerning children, whether undertaken by public or private social welfare institutions, courts of law, administrative authorities or legislative bodies, the best interests of the child shall be a primary consideration" (United Nations Convention on the Rights of the Child, Part I, Article 3). The Hague Convention on international adoption also privileges the "best interest of the child" in several sections (e.g., Hague Convention on Protection of Children and Co-operation in Respect of Intercountry Adoption, Preamble; Chapter I, Article 1; Chapter II Article 4; Chapter IV Article 16; Chapter V, Article 24). For discussion of the origins and use of the term "best interest of the child," see Cantwell, N. (2014). *The best interest of the child in intercountry adoption, Innocenti Insight.* Florence: UNICEF Office of Research.

7. See, for example, Smolin's view in Bartholet, E., & Smolin, D. (2012). The debate. In J. L. Gibbons & K. S. Rotabi (Eds.), *Intercountry adoption: Policies, practices, and outcomes.* Surrey, UK: Ashgate; Hollingsworth, L. D. (2003). International adoption among families in the United States: Considerations of social justice. *Social Work, 48,* 209–217.

8. See, for example, Bartholet's view in Bartholet, E., & Smolin, D. (2012). The debate. In J. L. Gibbons & K. S. Rotabi (Eds.), *Intercountry adoption: Policies, practices, and outcomes.* Surrey, UK: Ashgate; Bartholet, E. (2007). International adoption: Thoughts on the human rights issues. *Buffalo Human Rights Law Review, 13,* 151–255; Carlson, R. (2010). Seeking the better interests of children with a new international law of adoption. *New York Law School Law Review, 55,* 733–1191.

9. For review, see Carlson, R. (2010). Seeking the better interests of children with a new international law of adoption. *New York Law School Law Review, 55,* 733–1191.

10. Bergquist, K. J. S. (2012). Implications of the Hague Convention on the humanitarian evacuation and "rescue" of children. In J. L. Gibbons & K. S. Rotabi (Eds.), *Intercountry adoption: Policies, practices, and outcomes.* Surrey, UK: Ashgate; Gailey, C. W. (2010). *Blue-ribbon*

babies and labors of love. Austin: University of Texas Press, p. 100; Williams, P. (2010, December 20). Save the children? Adoption has become a form of trafficking in and of itself. *The Nation.*

11. Graff, E. J. (2008). The lie we love. *Foreign Policy, 169,* 58–66.

12. Briggs, L. (2012). *Somebody's children.* Durham, NC: Duke University Press, pp. 3, 16–17; for more nuanced discussion, pp. 234–236; Gailey, C. W. (2010). *Blue-ribbon babies and labors of love.* Austin: University of Texas Press, p. 107.

13. Briggs, L., & Marre, D. (2009). Introduction: The circulation of children. In D. Marre & L. Biggs (Eds.), *International adoption: Global inequalities and the circulation of children.* New York: New York University Press, pp. 17–19.

14. See, for example, Gailey, C. W. (2010). *Blue-ribbon babies and labors of love.* Austin: University of Texas Press, p. 93.

15. According to Selman (2012), among the 15 countries sending the most children for international adoption between 2003 and 2010, only 3 (Russia, Ukraine, and Poland) could be described as having a mainly white population, while the remaining 12 have a mainly nonwhite population. Of the 256,175 children adopted internationally during this period, approximately 75% were from countries with primarily nonwhite populations. Selman, P. (2012). The rise and fall of intercountry adoption in the 21st century: Global trends from 2001 to 2010. In J. L. Gibbons & K. S. Rotabi (Eds.), *Intercountry adoption: Policies, practices, and outcomes.* Surrey, UK: Ashgate. Furthermore, according to the U.S. National Survey of Adoptive Parents, in 2007, only 19% of international adoptees were non-Hispanic whites, whereas 50% of private domestic adoptees were non-Hispanic whites. Additional statistics from the same survey indicate that 84% of internationally adopted children were adopted transracially. Vandivere, S., Malm, K., & Radel, L. (2009). *Adoption USA: A chartbook based on the 2007 National Survey of Adoptive Parents.* Washington, DC: U.S. Department of Health and Human Services.

16. Mackey, R. (2009, April 3). Malawi court bars new Madonna adoption. *New York Times.*

17. Levy, C. J. (2010, April 9). Russia calls for halt on U.S. adoptions. *New York Times,* A1.

18. Herszenhorn, D., & Eckholm, E. (2012, December 28). Russia's plan to bar adoptions upends families. *New York Times,* A1.

19. See, for example, Siegal, E. (2011). *Finding Fernanda: Two mothers, one child, and a cross-border search for the truth.* Oakland: Cathexis Press, pp. 86–88.

20. See, for example, Dillon, S. (2007). Missing link: A social orphan protocol to the United Nations Convention on the Rights of the Child. *Human Rights & Globalization Law Review, 1,* 39; Graff, E. J.

(2008). The lie we love. *Foreign Policy, 169,* 58–66; Oreskovic, J., & Maskew, T. (2008). Red thread or slender reed: Deconstructing Prof. Bartholet's mythology of international adoption. *Buffalo Human Rights Law Review, 14,* 71–128; see also Kim, E. J. (2010). *Adopted territory: Transnational Korean adoptees and the politics of belonging.* Durham, NC: Duke University Press, Ch. 7, for discussion of the concept of "orphan" as a sentimental object for Westerners.

21. U.S. Citizenship and Immigration Services (n.d.). *Orphan process.* Retrieved from http://www.uscis.gov/adoption/immigration-through-adoption/orphan-process.

22. For example, research by the nonprofit group EveryChild found that among institutionalized children in former Soviet and Soviet-bloc countries, less than 5% were orphans by the narrow definition. Carter, R. (2005). *Family matters: A study of institutional childcare in Central and Eastern Europe and the former Soviet Union.* London: EveryChild.

23. For articulation of the need for global policy on social orphans from a human rights perspective, see Dillon, S. (2007). Missing link: A social orphan protocol to the United Nations Convention on the Rights of the Child. *Human Rights and Globalization Law Review, 1,* 39.

24. Carter, R. (2005). *Family matters: A study of institutional childcare in Central and Eastern Europe and the former Soviet Union.* London: EveryChild.

25. UNICEF (2010). *At home or in a home? Formal care and adoption of children in Eastern Europe and Central Asia.* UNICEF Regional Office for Central and Eastern Europe and the Commonwealth of Independent States (CEE/CIS). Carter (2005) argues that such figures are likely to be underestimates and puts the number in excess of 1.3 million children. Carter, R. (2005). *Family matters: A study of institutional childcare in Central and Eastern Europe and the former Soviet Union.* London: EveryChild.

26. Carter, R. (2005). *Family matters: A study of institutional childcare in Central and Eastern Europe and the former Soviet Union.* London: EveryChild.

27. UNICEF (2010). *At home or in a home? Formal care and adoption of children in Eastern Europe and Central Asia.* UNICEF Regional Office for Central and Eastern Europe and the Commonwealth of Independent States (CEE/CIS).

28. Briggs, L. (2012). *Somebody's children.* Durham, NC: Duke University Press; Graff, E. J. (2008). The lie we love. *Foreign Policy, 169,* 58–66.

29. Smolin's view in Bartholet, E., & Smolin, D. (2012). The debate. In J. L. Gibbons & K. S. Rotabi, (Eds.), *Intercountry adoption: Policies, practices, and outcomes.* Surrey, UK: Ashgate.

30. See, for example, Davis, M. A. (2011). *Children for families or families for children.* Dordrecht: Springer, pp. 189–201; Gailey, C. W. (2010). *Blue-ribbon babies and labors of love.* Austin: University of Texas Press.

31. Siegal, E. (2011). *Finding Fernanda: Two mothers, one child, and a cross-border search for the truth.* Oakland: Cathexis Press; Graff, E. J. (2008). The lie we love. *Foreign Policy, 169,* 58–66; Oreskovic, J., & Maskew, T. (2008). Red thread or slender reed: Deconstructing Prof. Bartholet's mythology of international adoption. *Buffalo Human Rights Law Review, 14,* 71–128.

32. Oreskovic and Maskew argue that sending countries with strong central governmental systems, such as China, Russia, and South Korea, are less prone to abusive practices than those countries with weak central control, and they estimate that 82% of adoptions are from centrally controlled countries. Oreskovic, J., & Maskew, T. (2008). Red thread or slender reed: Deconstructing Prof. Bartholet's mythology of international adoption. *Buffalo Human Rights Law Review, 14,* 71–128.

33. For perspectives from different sending countries, see chapters in Gibbons, J. L., & Rotabi, K. S. Eds. (2012). *Intercountry adoption: Policies, practices, and outcomes.* Surrey, UK: Ashgate.

34. For review of the situation in China, see Johnson, K. (2012). Challenging the discourse of intercountry adoption: Perspectives from rural China. In J. L. Gibbons & K. S. Rotabi, (Eds.), *Intercountry adoption: Policies, practices, and outcomes.* Surrey, UK: Ashgate.

35. For review of child welfare in Romania, see Nedelcu, C., & Groza, V. (2012). Child welfare in Romania: Context and processes. In J. L. Gibbons & K. S. Rotabi (Eds.), *Intercountry adoption: Policies, practices, and outcomes.* Surrey, UK: Ashgate.

36. Tobis, D. (2000). *Moving from residential institutions to community-based social services in Central and Eastern Europe and the former Soviet Union.* Washington, DC: World Bank; Carter, R. (2005). *Family matters: A study of institutional childcare in Central and Eastern Europe and the former Soviet Union.* London: EveryChild; Levy, C. J. (2010, May 4). Russian orphanage offers love, but not families. *New York Times,* A1; Herszenhorn, D. (2012, December 24). Citing broken system, critics fight Russia's adoption ban. *New York Times,* A1; Whewell, T. (2013, April 2). Russia: Are efforts to help thousands of 'abandoned' children being resisted? *BBC News.*

37.   Beegle, K., et al. (2009). Orphanhood and the living arrangements of children in sub-Saharan Africa. *Research Working Papers, 1*, 1–40; Nyambedha, E. O., et al. (2003). Changing patterns of orphan care due to the HIV epidemic in western Kenya. *Social Science & Medicine, 57*(2), 301–311; Roby, J. L., & Shaw, S. A. (2006). The African orphan crisis and international adoption. *Social Work, 51*, 199–210.

38.   Perlez, J. (1994, October 27). Bucharest journal; Little care, less love: Romania's sad orphans. *New York Times.*

39.   U.S. Department of State, Bureau of Consular Affairs (2015, March 31). *FY 2014 annual report on intercountry adoption.*

40.   See, for example, Bartholet, E. (2007). International adoption: Thoughts on the human rights issues. *Buffalo Human Rights Law Review, 13*, 152; Dillon, S. (2003). Making legal regimes for intercountry adoption reflect human rights principles: Transforming the United Nations Convention on the Rights of the Child with the Hague Convention on Intercountry Adoption. *Boston University International Law Journal, 21*, 179–257; Dillon, S. (2008). Missing link: A social orphan protocol to the United Nations Convention on the Rights of the Child. *Human Rights and Globalization Law Review, 1*, 39. Dwyer, J. G. (2014). Intercountry adoption and the special rights fallacy. *University of Pennsylvania Journal of International Law, 35*, 189–267; Graff, E. J. (2008). The lie we love. *Foreign Policy, 169*, 58–66; Smolin, D. M. (2005). Intercountry adoption as child trafficking. *Valparaiso Law Review, 39*, 281–325.

Chapter 2

1.   Details about our son's birth family are not provided here because we wish to protect the privacy of our son's birth story and the people involved in it, for his sake and theirs. This absence of discussion of the birth family does not imply an attempt to "erase" that part of the larger context, as adoptive parents are sometimes accused of doing (e.g., Briggs, L. [2012]. *Somebody's children.* Durham, NC: Duke University Press).

2.   See comparable descriptions in St. Petersburg-USA Orphanage Research Team (2008). The effects of early social-emotional and relationship experience on the development of young orphanage children. *Monographs of the Society for Research on Child Development.* Boston: Wiley-Blackwell. For similar descriptions from another part of the world, see Groark, C. J., McCall, R. B., & Fish, L. (2011). Characteristics of environments, caregivers, and children in three Central American orphanages. *Infant Mental Health Journal, 32*, 232–250.

3. Johnson, D. E., & Gunnar, M. R. (2011). Growth failure in institutionalized children. *Monographs of the Society for Research on Child Development, 76*, 92–126; see also Miller, L. C. (2012). Medical status of internationally adopted children. In J. L. Gibbons & K. S. Rotabi (Eds.), *Intercountry adoption: Policies, practices, and outcomes*. Surrey, UK: Ashgate.

4. Van IJzendoorn, M. H., et al. (2007). Plasticity of growth in height, weight, and head circumference: Meta-analytic evidence of massive catch-up after international adoption. *Journal of Developmental & Behavioral Pediatrics, 28*, 334–343.

5. Miller, L. C. (2012). Medical status of internationally adopted children. In J. L. Gibbons & K. S. Rotabi (Eds.), *Intercountry adoption: Policies, practices, and outcomes*. Surrey, UK: Ashgate.

6. Van IJzendoorn, M. H., et al. (2007). Plasticity of growth in height, weight, and head circumference: Meta-analytic evidence of massive catch-up after international adoption. *Journal of Developmental & Behavioral Pediatrics, 28*, 334–343.

7. SPOON Foundation (2012). *2012 progress report*. Retrieved from http://www.spoonfoundation.org/about-us/SPOON_Foundation_2012_Progress_Report.html.

8. Kroupina, M. G., Toemen, L., Aidjanov, M. M., Georgieff, M., Hearst, M. O., Himes, J. H., et al. (2015). Predictors of developmental status in young children living in institutional care in Kazakhstan. *Maternal and Child Health Journal, 19*, 1408–1416.

9. Miller, L. C. (2012). Medical status of internationally adopted children. In J. L. Gibbons & K. S. Rotabi (Eds.), *Intercountry adoption: Policies, practices, and outcomes*. Surrey, UK: Ashgate; Saiman, L., et al. (2001). Prevalence of infectious diseases among internationally adopted children. *Pediatrics, 108*, 608–612.

10. Johnson, D. E., & Gunnar, M. R. (2011). Growth failure in institutionalized children. *Monographs of the Society for Research on Child Development, 76*, 92–126.

11. Johnson, D. E., & Gunnar, M. R. (2011). Growth failure in institutionalized children. *Monographs of the Society for Research on Child Development, 76*, 92–126; Mul, D., et al. (2002). Early puberty in adopted children. *Hormone Research in Paediatrics, 57*, 1–9.

12. St. Petersburg-USA Orphanage Research Team (2008). The effects of early social-emotional and relationship experience on the development of young orphanage children. *Monographs of the Society for Research on Child Development*. Boston: Wiley-Blackwell. See similar results for Eritrean orphanages: Wolff, P. H., et al. (1995). The solomuna orphanage: A historical survey. *Social Science & Medicine, 40*, 1133–1139; Wolff, P. H., & Fesseha, G. (1998). The orphans of Eritrea: Are orphanages part of the

problem or part of the solution? *American Journal of Psychiatry*, *155*, 1319–1324.

13. Johnson, D. E., & Gunnar, M. R. (2011). Growth failure in institutionalized children. *Monographs of the Society for Research on Child Development, 76*, 92–126.

14. van IJzendoorn, M. H., & Juffer, F. (2005). Adoption is a successful natural intervention enhancing adopted children's IQ and school performance. *Current Directions in Psychological Science, 14*, 326–330; Van Ijzendoorn, M. H., et al. (2005). Adoption and cognitive development: A meta-analytic comparison of adopted and nonadopted children's IQ and school performance. *Psychological Bulletin, 131*, 301–316. The length of time in the adoptive home varied quite a bit across the studies reviewed in the meta-analysis, but for most of the studies children were adopted as infants or toddlers and assessed at school age, adolescence, or adulthood.

15. Nelson, C.A., et al. (2007). Cognitive recovery in socially deprived young children: The Bucharest Early Intervention Project. *Science, 318*, 1937–1940. For a full account of the project, see Nelson, C., Fox, N., & Zeanah, C. (2014). *Romania's abandoned children: Deprivation, brain development, and the struggle for recovery.* Cambridge, MA: Harvard University Press.

16. Fox, N. A., et al. (2011). The effects of severe psychosocial deprivation and foster care intervention on cognitive development at 8 years of age: Findings from the Bucharest Early Intervention Project. *Journal of Child Psychology and Psychiatry, 52*, 919–928.

17. Bick, J., Zhu, T., Stamoulis, C., Fox, N. A., Zeanah, C., & Nelson, C. A. (2015). Effect of early institutionalization and foster care on long-term white matter development: A randomized clinical trial. *JAMA Pediatrics, 169*, 211–219.

18. Dalen, M. (2012). Cognitive competence, academic achievement, and educational attainment among intercountry adoptees: Research outcomes from the Nordic countries. In J. L. Gibbons & K. S. Rotabi (Eds.), *Intercountry adoption: Policies, practices, and outcomes.* Surrey, UK: Ashgate; Julian, M. M. (2013). Age at adoption from institutional care as a window into the lasting effects of early experiences. *Clinical Child and Family Psychology Review, 16*, 101–145.

19. van IJzendoorn, M. H., & Juffer, F. (2005). Adoption is a successful natural intervention enhancing adopted children's IQ and school performance. *Current Directions in Psychological Science, 14*, 326–330; Van Ijzendoorn, M. H., et al. (2005). Adoption and cognitive development: A meta-analytic comparison of adopted and nonadopted children's IQ and school performance. *Psychological Bulletin, 131*, 301–316.

20. Nelson, C. A., et al. (2007). Cognitive recovery in socially deprived young children: The Bucharest Early Intervention Project. *Science, 318*, 1937–1940.

21. Diamond, M. C. (1988). *Enriching heredity: The impact of the environment on the anatomy of the brain.* New York: Free Press; for review, see Sale, A., et al. (2009). Enrich the environment to empower the brain. *Trends in Neurosciences, 32*, 233–239.

22. See, for example, Kempermann, G., et al. (1997). More hippocampal neurons in adult mice living in an enriched environment. *Nature, 386*, 493–495; Kozorovitskiy, Y., et al. (2005). Experience induces structural and biochemical changes in the adult primate brain. *Proceedings of the National Academy of Sciences U. S. A., 102*, 17478–17482; see review in Sale, A., et al. (2009). Enrich the environment to empower the brain. *Trends in Neurosciences, 32*, 233–239.

23. van Praag, H., et al. (2000). Neural consequences of environmental enrichment. *Nature Reviews Neuroscience, 1*, 191–198.

24. Tirella, L. G., Chan, W., Cermak, S. A., Litvinova, A., Salas, K. C., & Miller, L. C. (2008). Time use in Russian baby homes. *Child: Care, Health and Development, 34*, 77–86.

25. Evidence indicates relatively high use of early-intervention services for speech and language among internationally adoptive families, e.g., Loman, M. M., et al. (2009). Postinstitutionalized children's development: Growth, cognitive, and language outcomes. *Journal of Developmental and Behavioral Pediatrics, 30*, 426–434.

26. Glennen, S. L. (2007). Predicting language outcomes for internationally adopted children. *Journal of Speech, Language and Hearing Research, 50*, 529–548; Scott, K. A., et al. (2008). Oral and written language development of children adopted from China. *American Journal of Speech-Language Pathology, 17*, 150–160.

27. See, for example, Tan, T. X., et al. (2012). Second-first language acquisition: Analysis of expressive language skills in a sample of girls adopted from China. *Journal of Child Language, 39*, 365–382; Cohen, N. J., et al. (2008). Children adopted from China: A prospective study of their growth and development. *Journal of Child Psychology and Psychiatry, 49*, 458–468.

28. Snedeker, J., et al. (2007). Starting over: International adoption as a natural experiment in language development. *Psychological Science, 18*, 79–87; Snedeker, J., et al. (2012). Disentangling the effects of cognitive development and linguistic expertise: A longitudinal study of the acquisition of English in internationally adopted children. *Cognitive Psychology, 65*, 39–76.

29. Glennen, S., & Bright, B. J. (2005). Five years later: Language in school-age internationally adopted children. *Seminars in Speech and Language, 26,* 86–101.
30. Cohen, N. J., et al. (2008). Children adopted from China: A prospective study of their growth and development. *Journal of Child Psychology and Psychiatry, 49,* 458–468; Scott, K. A., et al. (2011). How well do children who are internationally adopted acquire language? A meta-analysis. *Journal of Speech, Language and Hearing Research, 54,* 1153–1169; Loman, M. M., et al. (2009). Postinstitutionalized children's development: Growth, cognitive, and language outcomes. *Journal of Developmental and Behavioral Pediatrics, 30,* 426–434.
31. Scott, K. A., et al. (2011). How well do children who are internationally adopted acquire language? A meta-analysis. *Journal of Speech, Language and Hearing Research, 54,* 1153–1169.
32. Pierce, L. J., Klein, D., Chen, J. K., Delcenserie, A., & Genesee, F. (2014). Mapping the unconscious maintenance of a lost first language. *Proceedings of the National Academy of Sciences U. S. A., 111,* 17314–17319; see also Hyltenstam, K., Bylund, E., Abrahamsson, N., & Park, H. S. (2009). Dominant-language replacement: The case of international adoptees. *Bilingualism: Language and Cognition, 12,* 121–140; Oh, J. S., Au, T. K. F., & Jun, S. A. (2010). Early childhood language memory in the speech perception of international adoptees. *Journal of Child Language, 37,* 1123–1132.
33. See, for example, Casey, B. J., et al. (2008). The adolescent brain. *Annals of the New York Academy of Sciences, 1124,* 111–126; Huttenlocher, P. R., & Dabholkar, A. S. (1997). Regional differences in synaptogenesis in human cerebral cortex. *Journal of Comparative Neurology, 387,* 167–178; Yurgelun-Todd, D. (2007). Emotional and cognitive changes during adolescence. *Current Opinion in Neurobiology, 17,* 251–257.
34. Kolb, B., et al. (2012). Experience and the developing prefrontal cortex. *Proceedings of the National Academy of Sciences U. S. A., 109,* 17186–17193.
35. Merz, E. C., & McCall, R. B. (2011). Parent ratings of executive functioning in children adopted from psychosocially depriving institutions. *Journal of Child Psychology and Psychiatry, 52,* 537–546.
36. Hostinar, C. E., et al. (2012). Associations between early life adversity and executive function in children adopted internationally from orphanages. *Proceedings of the National Academy of Sciences U. S. A., 109,* 17208–17212.
37. See, for example, Lindblad, F., Weitoft, G. R., & Hjern, A. (2010). ADHD in international adoptees: A national cohort study. *European Child & Adolescent Psychiatry, 19,* 37–44; McLaughlin, K. A., et al. (2010). Delayed maturation in brain electrical activity partially explains the association between early

environmental deprivation and symptoms of attention-deficit/hyperactivity disorder. *Biological Psychiatry, 68,* 329–336; McLaughlin, K. A., Sheridan, M. A., Winter, W., Fox, N. A., Zeanah, C. H., & Nelson, C. A. (2014). Widespread reductions in cortical thickness following severe early-life deprivation: A neurodevelopmental pathway to attention-deficit/hyperactivity disorder. *Biological Psychiatry, 76,* 629–638; Stevens, S. E., et al. (2008). Inattention/overactivity following early severe institutional deprivation: Presentation and associations in early adolescence. *Journal of Abnormal Child Psychology, 36,* 385–398.

38. See, for example, Behen, M. E., et al. (2009). Abnormal fronto-striatal connectivity in children with histories of early deprivation: A diffusion tensor imaging study. *Brain Imaging and Behavior, 3,* 292–297; Chugani, H. T., et al. (2001). Local brain functional activity following early deprivation: A study of postinstitutionalized Romanian orphans. *Neuroimage, 14,* 1290–1301; Mueller, S. C., et al. (2010). Early-life stress is associated with impairment in cognitive control in adolescence: An fMRI study. *Neuropsychologia, 48,* 3037–3044.

39. Julian, M. M. (2013). Age at adoption from institutional care as a window into the lasting effects of early experiences. *Clinical Child and Family Psychology Review, 16,* 101–145.

40. McDermott, J. M., et al. (2012). Early adversity and neural correlates of executive function: Implications for academic adjustment. *Developmental Cognitive Neuroscience, 2,* S59–S66.

41. Beckett, C., et al. (2006). Do the effects of early severe deprivation on cognition persist into early adolescence? Findings from the English and Romanian adoptees study. *Child Development, 77,* 696–711; Rutter, M., & O'Connor, T. G. (2004). Are there biological programming effects for psychological development? Findings from a study of Romanian adoptees. *Developmental Psychology, 40,* 81–94; Scott, K. A., et al. (2011). How well do children who are internationally adopted acquire language? A meta-analysis. *Journal of Speech, Language and Hearing Research, 54,* 1153–1169. Tottenham, N. (2012). Risk and developmental heterogeneity in previously institutionalized children. *Journal of Adolescent Health, 51,* S29–S33.

42. Van IJzendoorn, M. H., et al. (2011). I. Children in institutional care: Delayed development and resilience. *Monographs of the Society for Research in Child Development, 76,* 8–30.

43. Smyke, A. T., et al. (2007). The caregiving context in institution-reared and family-reared infants and toddlers in Romania. *Journal of Child Psychology and Psychiatry, 48,* 210–218.

44. Stevens, S. E., et al. (2009). Dopamine transporter gene polymorphism moderates the effects of severe deprivation on ADHD

symptoms: Developmental continuities in gene–environment interplay. *American Journal of Medical Genetics Part B: Neuropsychiatric Genetics, 150,* 753–761.

CHAPTER 3

1. Current procedures reportedly now require a 30-day bonding period.
2. See, for example, Bowlby, J. (1969). *Attachment and loss,* Volume 1. New York: Basic Books. For articulation of key points vis-à-vis attachment and institutionalization, see Dozier, M., Zeanah, C. H., Wallin, A. R., & Shauffer, C. (2012). Institutional care for young children: Review of literature and policy implications. *Social Issues and Policy Review, 6,* 1–25.
3. Bretherton, I., & Munholland, K. A. (2008). Internal working models in attachment relationships: Elaborating a central construct in attachment theory. In J. Cassidy & P. Shaver (Eds.), *Handbook of attachment,* 2nd ed.: *Theory, research, and clinical applications.* New York: Guilford Press.
4. Zeifman, D. (2013). Built to bond. In C. Hazan & M. I. Campa (Eds.), *Human bonding: The science of affectional ties.* New York: Guilford Press.
5. For more discussion of the concept of "experience-expectant" development, see Greenough, W. T., et al. (1987). Experience and brain development. *Child Development, 58,* 539–559; Rutter, M. (2011). Biological and experiential influences on psychological development. In D. P. Keating (Ed.), *Nature and nurture in child development.* Cambridge, UK: Cambridge University Press.
6. For a similar analogy, see Nelson, C. A. (2011). Neural development and lifelong plasticity. In D. P. Keating (Ed.), *Nature and nurture in child development.* Cambridge, UK: Cambridge University Press.
7. Lewis, T. L., & Maurer, D. (2009). Effects of early pattern deprivation on visual development. *Optometry & Vision Science, 86,* 640–646.
8. Dozier, M., & Bick, J. (2007). Changing caregivers: Coping with early adversity. *Psychiatric Annals, 37,* 411–415; Dozier, M., & Rutter, M. (2008). Challenges to the development of attachment relationships faced by young children in foster and adoptive care. In J. Cassidy & P. Shaver (Eds.), *Handbook of attachment,* 2nd ed.: *Theory, research, and clinical applications.* New York: Guilford Press.
9. Dozier, M., et al. (2012). Institutional care for young children: Review of literature and policy implications. *Social Issues and Policy Review, 6,* 1–25, p. 2.

10. Dozier, M., et al. (2012). Institutional care for young children: Review of literature and policy implications. *Social Issues and Policy Review, 6,* 1–25, p. 2.

11. See, for example, Vorria, P., et al. (2006). The development of adopted children after institutional care: A follow-up study. *Journal of Child Psychology and Psychiatry, 47,* 1246–1253; Zeanah, C. H. (2000). Disturbances of attachment in young children adopted from institutions. *Journal of Developmental and Behavioral Pediatrics, 21,* 230–236; O'Connor, T. G., et al. (2003). Child–parent attachment following early institutional deprivation. *Development and Psychopathology, 15,* 19–38; Kreppner, J. M., et al. (2001). Can inattention/overactivity be an institutional deprivation syndrome? *Journal of Abnormal Child Psychology, 29,* 513–528; Dobrova-Krol, N., et al. (2010). The importance of quality of care: Effects of perinatal HIV infection and early institutional rearing on preschoolers' attachment and indiscriminate friendliness. *Journal of Child Psychology and Psychiatry, 51,* 1368–1376. For reviews, see Bakermans-Kranenburg, M. J., et al. (2011). Attachment and emotional development in institutional care: Characteristics and catch-up. *Monographs of the Society for Research in Child Development, 76,* 62–91; van den Dries, L., et al. (2009). Fostering security? A meta-analysis of attachment in adopted children. *Children and Youth Services Review, 31,* 410–421.

12. Solomon, J., & George, C. (2008). The measurement of attachment security and related constructs in infancy and early childhood. In J. Cassidy & P. Shaver (Eds.), *Handbook of attachment,* 2nd ed.: *Theory, research, and clinical applications.* New York: Guilford Press.

13. Ainsworth, M. S. (1979). Infant–mother attachment. *American Psychologist, 34,* 932–937; Weinfield, N. S. et al. (2008). Individual differences in infant–caregiver attachment. In J. Cassidy & P. Shaver (Eds.), *Handbook of attachment,* 2nd ed.: *Theory, research, and clinical applications.* New York: Guilford Press.

14. Chisholm, K., Carter, M. C., Ames, E. W., & Morison, S. J. (1995). Attachment security and indiscriminately friendly behavior in children adopted from Romanian orphanages. *Development and Psychopathology, 7,* 283–294.

15. Chisholm, K. (1998). A three-year follow-up of attachment and indiscriminate friendliness in children adopted from Romanian orphanages. *Child Development, 69,* 1092–1106.

16. See, for example, Rutter, M., et al. (2007). Early adolescent outcomes for institutionally deprived and non-deprived adoptees. I: Disinhibited attachment. *Journal of Child Psychology and Psychiatry, 48,* 17–30; for review, see Julian, M. M. (2013). Age at adoption from institutional care as a window into the lasting effects

of early experiences. *Clinical Child and Family Psychology Review,* *16*, 101–145.

17.   Julian, M. M. (2013). Age at adoption from institutional care as a window into the lasting effects of early experiences. *Clinical Child and Family Psychology Review, 16*, 101–145.

18.   Julian, M. M. (2013). Age at adoption from institutional care as a window into the lasting effects of early experiences. *Clinical Child and Family Psychology Review, 16*, 101–145.

19.   Smyke, A. T., et al. (2010). Placement in foster care enhances quality of attachment among young institutionalized children. *Child Development, 81*, 212–223.

20.   Julian, M. M. (2013). Age at adoption from institutional care as a window into the lasting effects of early experiences. *Clinical Child and Family Psychology Review, 16*, 101–145.

21.   Julian, M. M. (2013). Age at adoption from institutional care as a window into the lasting effects of early experiences. *Clinical Child and Family Psychology Review, 16*, 101–145.

22.   See, for example, Berlin, L. J. et al. (2008). The influence of early attachments on other relationships. In J. Cassidy & P. Shaver, P. (Eds.), *Handbook of attachment,* 2nd ed.: *Theory, research, and clinical applications.* New York: Guilford Press; Thompson, R. A. (2008). Early attachment and later development. In J. Cassidy & P. Shaver (Eds.), *Handbook of attachment,* 2nd ed.: *Theory, research, and clinical applications.* New York: Guilford Press; Weinfield, N. S. et al. (2008). Individual differences in infant–caregiver attachment. In J. Cassidy & P. Shaver (Eds.), *Handbook of attachment,* 2nd ed.: *Theory, research, and clinical applications.* New York: Guilford Press.

23.   Serbin, L., & Karp, J. (2003). Intergenerational studies of parenting and the transfer of risk from parent to child. *Current Directions in Psychological Science, 12*(4), 138–142; Serbin, L. A., & Karp, J. (2004). The intergenerational transfer of psychosocial risk: Mediators of vulnerability and resilience. *Annual Review of Psychology, 55*, 333–363; Van Ijzendoorn, M. H. (1992). Intergenerational transmission of parenting: A review of studies in nonclinical populations. *Developmental Review, 12*, 76–99.

24.   Tieman, W., et al. (2006). Social functioning of young adult intercountry adoptees compared to nonadoptees. *Social Psychiatry and Psychiatric Epidemiology, 41*, 68–74.

25.   Almas, A. N., Degnan, K. A., Radulescu, A., Nelson, C. A., Zeanah, C. H., & Fox, N. A. (2012). Effects of early intervention and the moderating effects of brain activity on institutionalized children's social skills at age 8. *Proceedings of the National Academy of Sciences U. S. A., 109*, 17228–17231; Palacios, J., Moreno, C., & Román, M. (2013). Social competence in internationally adopted

and institutionalized children. *Early Childhood Research Quarterly, 28,* 357–365.

26. Zeifman, D. M. (2001). An ethological analysis of human infant crying: Answering Tinbergen's four questions. *Developmental Psychobiology, 39,* 265–285.

27. Hofer, M. A. (1994). Hidden regulators in attachment, separation, and loss. *Monographs of the Society for Research in Child Development, 59,* 192–207; Hofer, M. A. (2006). Psychobiological roots of early attachment. *Current Directions in Psychological Science, 15,* 84–88; Barr, R. G. (2011). Mother and child: Preparing for a life. In D. P. Keating (Ed.), *Nature and nurture in child development.* Cambridge, UK: Cambridge University Press.

28. Hertenstein, M. J. (2002). Touch: Its communicative functions in infancy. *Human Development, 45,* 70–94; Barr, R. G. (2011). Mother and child: Preparing for a life. In D. P. Keating (Ed.), *Nature and nurture in child development.* Cambridge, UK: Cambridge University Press.

29. For review, see Caulfield, R. (2000). Beneficial effects of tactile stimulation on early development. *Early Childhood Education Journal, 27,* 255–257; Underdown, A., et al. (2010). Tactile stimulation in physically healthy infants: Results of a systematic review. *Journal of Reproductive and Infant Psychology, 28,* 11–29; Jump, V. K., et al. (2006). Impact of massage therapy on health outcomes among orphaned infants in Ecuador: Results of a randomized clinical trial. *Family & Community Health, 29,* 314–319.

30. Feldman, R., et al. (2002). Comparison of skin-to-skin (kangaroo) and traditional care: Parenting outcomes and preterm infant development. *Pediatrics, 110,* 16–26; Martínez, J. C. (2007). International perspectives: Skin-to-skin contact: A paramount contribution to the modern neonatal paradigm. *NeoReviews, 8,* e55–e57.

31. Champagne, F. A. (2010). Early adversity and developmental outcomes: Interaction between genetics, epigenetics, and social experiences across the life span. *Perspectives on Psychological Science, 5,* 564–574; Kaffman, A., & Meaney, M. J. (2007). Neurodevelopmental sequelae of postnatal maternal care in rodents: Clinical and research implications of molecular insights. *Journal of Child Psychology and Psychiatry, 48,* 224–244. See also Weller, A., & Feldman, R. (2003). Emotion regulation and touch in infants: The role of cholecystokinin and opioids. *Peptides, 24,* 779–788.

32. For evidence regarding diminishment of such repetitive behavior following removal from institutional care, see Bos, K. J., et al. (2010). Stereotypies in children with a history of early institutional care. *Archives of Pediatrics & Adolescent Medicine, 164,* 406–411.

33.   Gunnar, M. R., & Loman, M. M. (2011). Early experience and stress regulation in human development. In D. P. Keating (Ed.), *Nature and nurture in child development*. Cambridge, UK: Cambridge University Press; see also Kroupina, M. G., Fuglestad, A. J., Iverson, S. L., Himes, J. H., Mason, P. W., Gunnar, M. R., et al. (2012). Adoption as an intervention for institutionally reared children: HPA functioning and developmental status. *Infant Behavior and Development, 35*, 829–837.

34.   Fries, A. B. W., et al. (2008). Neuroendocrine dysregulation following early social deprivation in children. *Developmental Psychobiology, 50*, 588–599.

35.   For reviews, see Gunnar, M. R. & Loman, M. M. (2011). Early experience and stress regulation in human development. In D. P. Keating (Ed.), *Nature and nurture in child development*. Cambridge, UK: Cambridge University Press; Gunnar, M., & Quevedo, K. (2007). The neurobiology of stress and development. *Annual Review of Psychology, 58*, 145–173.

36.   Kaffman, A., & Meaney, M. J. (2007). Neurodevelopmental sequelae of postnatal maternal care in rodents: Clinical and research implications of molecular insights. *Journal of Child Psychology and Psychiatry, 48*, 224–244.

37.   Dettling, A. C., Feldon, J., & Pryce, C. R. (2002). Repeated parental deprivation in the infant common marmoset (*Callithrix jacchus*, primates) and analysis of its effects on early development. *Biological Psychiatry, 52*, 1037–1046; Pryce, C. R., et al. (2005). Long-term effects of early-life environmental manipulations in rodents and primates: Potential animal models in depression research. *Neuroscience & Biobehavioral Reviews, 29*, 649–674; Sánchez, M. M., et al. (2005). Alterations in diurnal cortisol rhythm and acoustic startle response in nonhuman primates with adverse rearing. *Biological Psychiatry, 57*, 373–381.

38.   Champagne, F. A. (2010). Early adversity and developmental outcomes: Interaction between genetics, epigenetics, and social experiences across the life span. *Perspectives on Psychological Science, 5*, 564–574.

39.   For discussion of this issue in relation to attachment, see Coan, J. A. (2008). Toward a neuroscience of attachment. In J. Cassidy & P. Shaver (Eds.), *Handbook of attachment*, 2nd ed.: *Theory, research, and clinical applications*. New York: Guilford Press.

40.   See also work on peptide hormones oxytocin and vasopressin: Fries, A. B. W., et al. (2005). Early experience in humans is associated with changes in neuropeptides critical for regulating social behavior. *Proceedings of the National Academy of Sciences U. S. A., 102*, 17237–17240.

41. Pryce, C. R., et al. (2004). Evidence for altered monoamine activity and emotional and cognitive disturbance in marmoset monkeys exposed to early life stress. *Annals of the New York Academy of Sciences, 1032,* 245–249; Pryce, C. R., et al. (2004). Deprivation of parenting disrupts development of homeostatic and reward systems in marmoset monkey offspring. *Biological Psychiatry, 56,* 72–79.

42. For review, see Nelson, C. A., et al. (2011). The neurobiological toll of early human deprivation. *Monographs of the Society for Research in Child Development, 76,* 127–146.

43. Mehta, M. A., et al. (2009). Amygdala, hippocampal and corpus callosum size following severe early institutional deprivation: The English and Romanian Adoptees study pilot. *Journal of Child Psychology and Psychiatry, 50,* 943–951.

44. Mehta, M. A., et al. (2010). Hyporesponsive reward anticipation in the basal ganglia following severe institutional deprivation early in life. *Journal of Cognitive Neuroscience, 22,* 2316–2325.

45. Moulson, M. C., et al. (2009). The effects of early experience on face recognition: An event-related potential study of institutionalized children in Romania. *Child Development, 80,* 1039–1056; Parker, S. W., & Nelson, C. A. (2005). An event-related potential study of the impact of institutional rearing on face recognition. *Development and Psychopathology, 17,* 621–639; Parker, S. W., & Nelson, C. A. (2005). The impact of early institutional rearing on the ability to discriminate facial expressions of emotion: An event-related potential study. *Child Development, 76,* 54–72. See also Moulson, M. C., Shutts, K., Fox, N. A., Zeanah, C. H., Spelke, E. S., & Nelson, C. A. (2015). Effects of early institutionalization on the development of emotion processing: A case for relative sparing? *Developmental Science, 18,* 298–313.

46. Drury, S. S., et al. (2011). Telomere length and early severe social deprivation: Linking early adversity and cellular aging. *Molecular Psychiatry, 17,* 719–727.

47. See, for example, Graff, E. J. (2013, February 22). Fatal adoption: Did Max Allen Shatto's mother kill him? Retrieved from http://www.slate.com/articles/double_x/doublex/2013/02/max_allen_shatto_adopted_from_russia_killed_by_his_mother.html.

48. Rutter, M., & O'Connor, T. G. (2004). Are there biological programming effects for psychological development? Findings from a study of Romanian adoptees. *Developmental Psychology, 40,* 81–94; quote from pp. 90–91, emphasis in original.

49. Juffer, F., & van IJzendoorn, M. H. (2005). Behavior problems and mental health referrals of international adoptees. *JAMA, 293,*

2501–2515; see also Bimmel, N., et al. (2003). Problem behavior of internationally adopted adolescents: A review and meta-analysis. *Harvard Review of Psychiatry, 11,* 64–77.

50.   Warren, S. B. (1992). Lower threshold for referral for psychiatric treatment for adopted adolescents. *Journal of the American Academy of Child & Adolescent Psychiatry, 31,* 512–517.

51.   Hjern, A., et al. (2002). Suicide, psychiatric illness, and social maladjustment in intercountry adoptees in Sweden: A cohort study. *Lancet, 360,* 443–448.

52.   Juffer, F., & Van IJzendoorn, M. H. (2007). Adoptees do not lack self-esteem: A meta-analysis of studies on self-esteem of transracial, international, and domestic adoptees. *Psychological Bulletin, 133,* 1067–1083.

53.   For overview of theoretical and empirical approaches to resilience, see Rutter, M. (2013). Annual research review: Resilience: Clinical implications. *Journal of Child Psychology and Psychiatry, and Allied Disciplines, 54,* 474–487.

54.   For review of biological approaches to resilience, see Feder, A., et al. (2009). Psychobiology and molecular genetics of resilience. *Nature Reviews Neuroscience, 10*(6), 446–457. See also Cicchetti, D. (2013). Annual research review: Resilient function in maltreated children: Past, present, and future perspectives. *Journal of Child Psychology and Psychiatry, 54,* 402–422.

55.   Canli, T., & Lesch, K. P. (2007). Long story short: The serotonin transporter in emotion regulation and social cognition. *Nature Neuroscience, 10,* 1103–1109.

56.   Caspers, K. M., et al. (2009). Association between the serotonin transporter promoter polymorphism (5-HTTLPR) and adult unresolved attachment. *Developmental Psychology, 45,* 64–76; van IJzendoorn, M. H., et al. (2010). Methylation matters: Interaction between methylation density and serotonin transporter genotype predicts unresolved loss or trauma. *Biological Psychiatry, 68,* 405–407; Drury, S. S., et al. (2012). Genetic sensitivity to the caregiving context: The influence of 5httlpr and BDNF val66met on indiscriminate social behavior. *Physiology & Behavior, 106,* 728–735; Bakermans-Kranenburg, M. J., et al. (2011). DRD4 genotype moderates the impact of parental problems on unresolved loss or trauma. *Attachment & Human Development, 13,* 253–269.

57.   Suomi, S. J. (2006). Risk, resilience, and gene × environment interactions in rhesus monkeys. *Annals of the New York Academy of Sciences, 1094,* 52–62.

58.   Brett, Z. H., Humphreys, K. L., Smyke, A. T., Gleason, M. M., Nelson, C. A., Zeanah, C. H., et al. (2015). Serotonin transporter linked polymorphic region (5-HTTLPR) genotype moderates the longitudinal impact of early caregiving on externalizing

behavior. *Development and Psychopathology, 27,* 7–18; see also Brett, Z. H., Sheridan, M., Humphreys, K., Smyke, A., Gleason, M. M., Fox, N., et al. (2014). A neurogenetics approach to defining differential susceptibility to institutional care. *International Journal of Behavioral Development, 39,* 150–160.

59. Francis, D. D., et al. (2002). Environmental enrichment reverses the effects of maternal separation on stress reactivity. *Journal of Neuroscience, 22,* 7840–7843.

60. Francis, D. D., et al. (2002). Environmental enrichment reverses the effects of maternal separation on stress reactivity. *Journal of Neuroscience, 22,* 7840–7843.

61. For similar results, see also Morley-Fletcher, S., et al. (2003). Environmental enrichment during adolescence reverses the effects of prenatal stress on play behaviour and HPA axis reactivity in rats. *European Journal of Neuroscience, 18,* 3367–3374; Fox, C., et al. (2006). Therapeutic and protective effect of environmental enrichment against psychogenic and neurogenic stress. *Behavioural Brain Research, 175,* 1–8; Laviola, G., et al. (2008). Effects of enriched environment on animal models of neurodegenerative diseases and psychiatric disorders. *Neurobiology of Disease, 31,* 159–168.

Chapter 4

1. For critique of essentialist thinking about race in adoption, see Homans, M. (2002). Adoption and essentialism. *Tulsa Studies in Women's Literature,* 257–274.

2. United Nations Convention on the Rights of the Child, Article 8.

3. United Nations Convention on the Rights of the Child, Article 21b.

4. Convention on Protection of Children and Co-operation in Respect of Intercountry Adoption, Article 4b.

5. Convention on Protection of Children and Co-operation in Respect of Intercountry Adoption, Article 16b. For critique of the CRC and the Hague treaty, see Dwyer, J. G. (2013). Intercountry adoption and the special rights fallacy. *University of Pennsylvania Journal of International Law, 35,* 189–267.

6. Heberer, P. (2011). *Children During the Holocaust.* Lanham, MD: AltaMira Press; Heinemann, I. (2004). "Until the last drop of good blood": The kidnapping of "racially valuable" children and Nazi racial policy in occupied Eastern Europe. In A. D. Moses (Ed.), *Genocide and settler society: Frontier violence and stolen indigenous children in Australian history.* New York: Berghahn Books; see also Zahra, T. (2011). 'A human treasure': Europe's displaced children between nationalism and internationalism. *Past & Present,*

210, 332–350; Zahra, T. (2011). *The lost children*. Cambridge, MA: Harvard University Press.

7. Gandsman, A. (2009). "A prick of a needle can do no harm": Compulsory extraction of blood in the search for the children of Argentina's disappeared. *Journal of Latin American and Caribbean Anthropology, 14*, 162–184.

8. Jacobs, M. D. (2009). *White mother to a dark race: Settler colonialism, maternalism, and the removal of indigenous children in the American West and Australia, 1880-1940*. Lincoln: University of Nebraska Press; Jacobs, M. D. (2014). *A generation removed: The fostering and adoption of indigenous children in the postwar world*. Lincoln: University of Nebraska Press; Moses, A. D., Ed. (2004). *Genocide and settler society: Frontier violence and stolen indigenous children in Australian history*. New York: Berghahn Books.

9. Hollingsworth, L. D. (2003). International adoption among families in the United States: Considerations of social justice. *Social Work, 48*, 209–217, pp. 212–213.

10. Kennedy, R. (2004). *Interracial intimacies: Sex, marriage, identity, and adoption*. New York: Pantheon.

11. As cited in Bartholet, E. (1991). Where do black children belong? The politics of race-matching in adoption. *University of Pennsylvania Law Review, 139*, 1163–1256.

12. See, for example, Bartholet, E. (1999). *Nobody's children: Abuse and neglect, foster drift, and the adoption alternative*. Boston: Beacon Press.

13. See, for example, Silverman, A. R. (1993). Outcomes of transracial adoption. *The Future of Children, 3*, 104–118; Simon, R. J., & Altstein, H. (1996). The case for transracial adoption. *Children and Youth Services Review, 18*, 5–22.

14. See chapter 44 in Cahn, N. R., & Hollinger, J. H., Eds. (2004). *Families by law: An adoption reader*. New York: New York University Press. For continued debate, see Griffith, E. E. H., & Bergeron, R. L. (2006). Cultural stereotypes die hard: The case of transracial adoption. *Journal of the American Academy of Psychiatry and the Law, 34*, 303–314; Bartholet, E. (2006). Commentary: Cultural stereotypes can and do die: It's time to move on with transracial adoption. *Journal of the American Academy of Psychiatry and the Law, 34*, 315–320; Schetky, D. H. (2006). Commentary: Transracial adoption—changing trends and attitudes. *Journal of the American Academy of Psychiatry and the Law, 34*, 321–323.

15. See chapter 51 in Cahn, N. R., & Hollinger, J. H. (2004). *Families by law: An adoption reader*. New York: New York University Press; see also Hearst, A. (2012). *Children and the politics of cultural belonging*. Cambridge, UK: Cambridge University Press.

16.   See, for example, Hübinette, T., & Tigervall, C. (2009). To be non-white in a colour-blind society: Conversations with adoptees and adoptive parents in Sweden on everyday racism. *Journal of Intercultural Studies, 30,* 335–353; see also Katz, J., & Doyle, E. K. (2013). Black and white thinking? Understanding negative responses to transracial adoptive families. *Adoption Quarterly, 16,* 62–80.

17.   Quiroz, P. A. (2012). Cultural tourism in transnational adoption: "Staged authenticity" and its implications for adopted children. *Journal of Family Issues, 33,* 527–555.

18.   See concept of "racial micro-aggressions," in Tuan, M., & Shiao, J. L. (2011). *Choosing ethnicity, negotiating race.* New York: Russell Sage Foundation, p. 141.

19.   Baden, A. L., Treweeke, L. M., & Ahluwalia, M. K. (2012). Reclaiming culture: Reculturation of transracial and international adoptees. *Journal of Counseling & Development, 90,* 387–399; Lee, R. M. (2003). The transracial adoption paradox: History, research, and counseling implications of cultural socialization. *Counseling Psychologist, 31,* 711–744.

20.   Grieco, E. M., et al. (2012). The foreign-born population in the United States: 2010. *American Community Survey Reports.* U.S. Department of Commerce, Economics and Statistics Administration, U.S. Census Bureau.

21.   U.S. Census Bureau. (2012, May 17). *Most children younger than age 1 are minorities, Census Bureau reports.* Retrieved from http://www.census.gov/newsroom/releases/archives/population/cb12-90.html.

22.   Brodzinsky, D. M. (2011). Children's understanding of adoption: Developmental and clinical implications. *Professional Psychology: Research and Practice, 42,* 200–207.

23.   In a sample of over 1,200 families adopting children internationally to the Netherlands, 70–80% of adopting parents reported talking about adoption with the child since the time of placement. Juffer, F., & Tieman, W. (2009). Being adopted: Internationally adopted children's interest and feelings. *International Social Work, 52,* 635–637.

24.   Evan B. Donaldson Institute. (2009). *Beyond culture camp: Promoting healthy identity formation in adoption.* New York: Author.

25.   Howard, J. (2012). *Untangling the web: The Internet's transformative impact on adoption.* New York: Evan B. Donaldson Institute.

26.   Trenka, J. J., Oparah, J. C., & Shin, S. Y., Eds. (2006). *Outsiders within: Writing on transracial adoption.* Cambridge, MA: South End Press, p. 8.

27.   Trenka, J. J., Oparah, J. C., & Shin, S. Y., Eds. (2006). *Outsiders within: Writing on transracial adoption.* Cambridge, MA: South End Press, pp. 4–5.

28. For further critiques of existing research, see Mohanty, J., & Newhill, C. (2006). Adjustment of international adoptees: Implications for practice and a future research agenda. *Children and Youth Services Review, 28,* 384–395.

29. U.S. Census Bureau (2012, December 12). *U.S. Census Bureau projections show a slower growing, older, more diverse nation a half century from now.* Retrieved from http://www.census.gov/newsroom/ releases/archives/population/cb12-243.html.

30. U.S. Census Bureau. (2012, May 17). *Most children younger than age 1 are minorities, Census Bureau reports.* Retrieved from http:// www.census.gov/newsroom/releases/archives/population/ cb12-90.html.

31. U.S. Census Bureau. (2012, May 17). *Most children younger than age 1 are minorities, Census Bureau reports.* Retrieved from http:// www.census.gov/newsroom/releases/archives/population/ cb12-90.html.

32. U.S. Census Bureau (2012, September 27). *2010 Census shows multiple-race population grew faster than single-race population.* Retrieved from http://www.census.gov/newsroom/releases/ archives/race/cb12-182.html.

33. Welcome House, the agency that coordinated our adoption, was established by Pearl S. Buck in 1949, in part to facilitate international adoption of biracial children.

34. For deeper critique of the concept of exclusive belongingness, see Yngvesson, B. (2003). Going "home": Adoption, loss of bearings, and the mythology of roots. *Social Text, 21,* 7–27; Yngvesson, B., & Mahoney, M. A. (2000). 'As one should, ought and wants to be': Belonging and authenticity in identity narratives. *Theory, Culture & Society, 17,* 77–110.

35. Juffer, F., & Van IJzendoorn, M. H. (2007). Adoptees do not lack self-esteem: A meta-analysis of studies on self-esteem of transracial, international, and domestic adoptees. *Psychological Bulletin, 133,* 1067–1083.

36. Tan, T. X., & Jordan-Arthur, B. (2012). Adopted Chinese girls come of age: Feelings about adoption, ethnic identity, academic functioning, and global self-esteem. *Children and Youth Services Review, 34,* 1500–1508.

37. Lee, R. M., et al. (2010). Comparing the ethnic identity and well-being of adopted Korean Americans with immigrant/US-born Korean Americans and Korean international students. *Adoption Quarterly, 13,* 2–17.

38. For alternative measures of ethnic identity, see Mohanty, J. (2010). Development of the ethnic and racial socialization of transracial adoptee scale. *Research on Social Work Practice, 20,* 600–610.

39. Within each of the three groups, ethnic identification was correlated with positive emotion; however, as the authors acknowledge, this relationship could be due to the fact that both scales used positive emotion words, thus a person with a positively oriented personality would tend to score high on both measures. However, self-reported well-being was not correlated with ethnic identification. In sum, there is no evidence from this study that decreased ethnic identification causes decreased well-being. Lee, R. M., et al. (2010). Comparing the ethnic identity and well-being of adopted Korean Americans with immigrant/US-born Korean Americans and Korean international students. *Adoption Quarterly, 13,* 2–17.

40. Boivin, M., & Hassan, G. (2015). Ethnic identity and psychological adjustment in transracial adoptees: A review of the literature. *Ethnic and Racial Studies, 38,* 1084–1103; Castle, H., Knight, E., & Watters, C. (2011). Ethnic identity as a protective factor for looked after and adopted children from ethnic minority groups: A critical review of the literature. *Adoption Quarterly, 14,* 305–325.

41. See, for example, Benet-Martínez, V., & Haritatos, J. (2005). Bicultural identity integration (BII): Components and psychosocial antecedents. *Journal of Personality, 73,* 1015–1050; Chen, S. X., Benet-Martínez, V., Wu, W. C., Lam, B. C., & Bond, M. H. (2013). The role of dialectical self and bicultural identity integration in psychological adjustment. *Journal of Personality, 81,* 61–75; Downie, M., Koestner, R., ElGeledi, S., & Cree, K. (2004). The impact of cultural internalization and integration on well-being among tricultural individuals. *Personality and Social Psychology Bulletin, 30,* 305–314.

42. Manzi, C., Ferrari, L., Rosnati, R., & Benet-Martínez, V. (2014). Bicultural integration of transracial adolescent adoptees: Antecedents and outcomes. *Journal of Cross-Cultural Psychology, 45,* 888–904.

43. Evan B. Donaldson Institute. (2009). *Beyond culture camp: Promoting healthy identity formation in adoption.* New York: Author.

44. Evan B. Donaldson Institute. (2009). *Beyond culture camp: Promoting healthy identity formation in adoption.* New York: Author.

45. See also Juffer and Tieman (2009), who found that among Chinese and Indian adoptees to the Netherlands, approximately 30–50% of the adoptive parents indicated that the child had expressed a desire to be white. Juffer, F., & Tieman, W. (2009). Being adopted: Internationally adopted children's interest and feelings. *International Social Work, 52,* 635–637.

46. Reinoso, M., et al. (2013). Children's and parents' thoughts and feelings about adoption, birth culture identity and discrimination

in families with internationally adopted children. *Child & Family Social Work, 18,* 264–274.

47. See, for example, Brodzinsky, D. (2006). Family structural openness and communication openness as predictors in the adjustment of adopted children. *Adoption Quarterly, 9,* 1–18; Neil, E. (2009). Post-adoption contact and openness in adoptive parents' minds: Consequences for children's development. *British Journal of Social Work, 39,* 5–23; Rueter, M. A., & Koerner, A. F. (2008). The effect of family communication patterns on adopted adolescent adjustment. *Journal of Marriage and Family, 70,* 715–727; Le Mare, L., & Audet, K. (2011). Communicative openness in adoption, knowledge of culture of origin, and adoption identity in adolescents adopted from Romania. *Adoption Quarterly, 14,* 199–217; Wydra, M., O'Brien, K. M., & Merson, E. S. (2012). In their own words: Adopted persons' experiences of adoption disclosure and discussion in their families. *Journal of Family Social Work, 15,* 62–77.

48. Evan B. Donaldson Institute. (2009). *Beyond culture camp: Promoting healthy identity formation in adoption.* New York: Author.

49. See, for example, Basow, S. A., et al. (2008). Identity development and psychological well-being in Korean-born adoptees in the US. *American Journal of Orthopsychiatry, 78,* 473–480; Feigelman, W. (2007). A long-term follow-up of transracially adopted children in their young adult years. In K. J. S. Bergquist, M. E. Vonk, D. S. Kim, & M. D. Feit, Eds. *International Korean adoption: A fifty-year history of policy and practice.* New York: Routledge; Yoon, D. P. (2004). Intercountry adoption: The importance of ethnic socialization and subjective well-being for Korean-born adopted children. *Journal of Ethnic and Cultural Diversity in Social Work, 13,* 71–89; though, for somewhat conflicting results, see Adams, G., Tessler, R., & Gamache, G. (2005). Development of ethnic identity among Chinese adoptees: Paradoxical effects of school diversity. *Adoption Quarterly, 8,* 25–46. For diversity recommendations for transracial domestic adoptive families, see Roorda, R. M. (2007). Moving beyond the controversy of the transracial adoption of black and biracial children. In R. A. Javier (Ed.), *Handbook of adoption: Implications for researchers, practitioners, and families.* Thousand Oaks, CA: Sage Publications.

50. For data related to the role of perceived marginality in well-being among adoptees, see Mohanty, J., & Newhill, C. E. (2011). Asian adolescent and young adult adoptees' psychological well-being: Examining the mediating role of marginality. *Children and Youth Services Review, 33,* 1189–1195.

51. Evan B. Donaldson Institute. (2009). *Beyond culture camp: Promoting healthy identity formation in adoption.* New York: Author.

52. Docan-Morgan, S. (2011). "They don't know what it's like to be in my shoes": Topic avoidance about race in transracially adoptive families. *Journal of Social and Personal Relationships, 28*, 336–355. For perspectives of international adoptees in Sweden, see Hübinette, T. (2009). Post-racial utopianism, white colorblindness, and "the elephant in the room": Racial issues for transnational adoptees of color. In *Intercountry adoption: Policies, practices, and outcomes*. Surrey, UK: Ashgate. For perspectives from transracial adoptees in the United States, see Roorda, R. M. (2007). Moving beyond the controversy of the transracial adoption of black and biracial children. In R. A. Javier (Ed.), *Handbook of adoption: Implications for researchers, practitioners, and families*. Thousand Oaks, CA: Sage Publications.

53. Wright, J. C. (2006). Love is colorblind: Reflections of a mixed girl. In J. J. Trenka, J. C. Oparah, & S. Y. Shin (Eds.), *Outsiders within: Writing on transracial adoption*. Cambridge, MA: South End Press, p. 28.

54. Tuan, M., & Shiao, J. L. (2011). *Choosing ethnicity, negotiating race.* New York: Russell Sage Foundation; see also Berbery, M., & O'Brien, K. (2011). Predictors of white adoptive parents' cultural and racial socialization behaviors with their Asian adopted children. *Adoption Quarterly, 14*, 284–304.

55. Tuan, M., & Shiao, J. L. (2011). *Choosing ethnicity, negotiating race.* New York: Russell Sage Foundation. For research on the relationship between discrimination as perceived by adoptive parents and adopted children's behavior, see Lee, R. M. & Minnesota International Adoption Project Team (2010). Parental perceived discrimination as a postadoption risk factor for internationally adopted children and adolescents. *Cultural Diversity & Ethnic Minority Psychology, 16*, 493–500.

56. See, for example, Volkman, T. A. (2003). Embodying Chinese culture: Transnational adoption in North America. *Social Text, 21*, 29–55.

57. See, for example, Trenka, J. J. (2004). *The language of blood: A memoir*. St. Paul: Graywolf Press; Bishoff, T., & Rankin, J. (1997). *Seeds from a silent tree: An anthology by Korean adoptees*. San Diego: Pandal Press; Robinson, K. (2002). *A single square picture: A Korean adoptee's search for her roots*. New York: Berkley Books. For a different adoptee perspective, see Philps, A., & Lahutsky, J. (2009). *The boy from Baby House 10: From the nightmare of a Russian orphanage to a new life in America*. New York: St. Martin's.

58. Kim, E. J. (2010). *Adopted territory: Transnational Korean adoptees and the politics of belonging*. Durham, NC: Duke University Press.

59. Howard, J. (2012). *Untangling the web: The Internet's transformative impact on adoption*. New York: Evan B. Donaldson Institute.

60. Vonk, M. E. (2001). Cultural competence for transracial adoptive parents. *Social Work, 46,* 246–55; Vonk, M. E., & Angaran, R. (2003). Training for transracial adoptive parents by public and private adoption agencies. *Adoption Quarterly, 6,* 53–62. Note that both of these studies were published more than 10 years ago; anecdotal evidence suggests increases in agency training in issues of race and culture as prompted by the Hague Convention guidelines.

61. Volkman, T. A. (2003). Embodying Chinese culture: Transnational adoption in North America. *Social Text, 21,* 29–55; pp. 50–51.

62. Hellerstedt, W. L., Madsen, N. J., Gunnar, M. R., Grotevant, H. D., Lee, R. M., & Johnson, D. E. (2008). The International Adoption Project: Population-based surveillance of Minnesota parents who adopted children internationally. *Maternal and Child Health Journal, 12,* 162–171. See also Jacobsen, H. (2008). *Culture keeping: White mothers, international adoption, and the negotiation of family difference.* Nashville, TN: Vanderbilt University Press; Kim, O. M., et al. (2013). Cultural socialization in families with adopted Korean adolescents: A mixed-method, multi-informant study. *Journal of Adolescent Research, 28,* 69–95.

63. Müller, U., & Perry, B. (2001). Adopted persons' search for and contact with their birth parents I: Who searches and why? *Adoption Quarterly, 4,* 5–37.

64. Dukette, R. (1984). Value issues in present-day adoption. *Child Welfare, 63,* 233–243.

65. Modell, J. S. (2002). *A sealed and secret kinship: The culture of policies and practices in American adoption.* New York: Berghahn Books.

66. Pannor, R., & Baran, A. (1984). Open adoption as standard practice. *Child Welfare, 63*(3), 245–250; Siegel, D. H., & Smith, S. L. (2012). *Openness in adoption: From secrecy and stigma to knowledge and connections.* New York: Evan B. Donaldson Institute; Berge, J. M., et al. (2006). Adolescents' feelings about openness in adoption: Implications for adoption agencies. *Child Welfare–New York, 85,* 1011–1039.

67. Aumend, S. A., & Barrett, M. C. (1984). Self-concept and attitudes toward adoption: A comparison of searching and nonsearching adult adoptees. *Child Welfare, 63,* 251–259.

68. Note that Curtis and Pearson (2010) also report more psychological problems among those searchers who made contact with a birth family than searchers who had not, raising questions about whether birth parent contact necessarily has a beneficial outcome; though Howe and Feast (2001) report that the majority of those who made contact with a birth parent felt that it had been worthwhile to do so. Curtis, R., & Pearson, F. (2010). Contact with

birth parents: Differential psychological adjustment for adults adopted as infants. *Journal of Social Work, 10,* 347–367. Howe, D., & Feast, J. (2001). The long-term outcome of reunions between adult adopted people and their birth mothers. *British Journal of Social Work, 31,* 351–368.

69. Müller, U., & Perry, B. (2001). Adopted persons' search for and contact with their birth parents I: Who searches and why? *Adoption Quarterly, 4,* 5–37.

70. See, for example, Gailey, C. W. (2010). *Blue-ribbon babies and labors of love.* Austin: University of Texas Press. p. 111.

71. Tieman, W., et al. (2008). Young adult international adoptees' search for birth parents. *Journal of Family Psychology, 22,* 678–687. See also Wang, L. K., Ponte, I. C., & Ollen, E. W. (2015). Letting her go: Western adoptive families' search and reunion with Chinese birth parents. *Adoption Quarterly, 18,* 45–66.

72. Tieman, W., et al. (2008). Young adult international adoptees' search for birth parents. *Journal of Family Psychology, 22,* 678–687.

73. Adoptive Families: The Resource & Community for Adoption Parenting. http://www.adoptivefamilies.com/birthfamilysearch.

74. See, for example, Gailey, C. W. (2010). *Blue-ribbon babies and labors of love.* Austin: University of Texas Press. For the view articulating the importance of the "search" to adoptive parents, see Volkman, T. A. (2003). Embodying Chinese culture: Transnational adoption in North America. *Social Text, 21,* 29–55. See also Pinderhughes, E., Matthews, J., Deoudes, G., & Pertman, A. (2013). *A changing world: Shaping best practices through understanding of the new realities of intercountry adoption.* New York: Donaldson Adoption Institute.

75. Pinderhughes, E., Matthews, J., Deoudes, G., & Pertman, A. (2013). *A changing world: Shaping best practices through understanding of the new realities of international adoption.* New York: Donaldson Adoption Institute.

76. Beckett, C., et al. (2008). The importance of cultural identity in adoption: A study of young people adopted from Romania. *Adoption & Fostering, 32,* 9–22.

77. For critiques of essentialist thinking in the context of adoption, see Howell, S. (2009). Return journeys and the search for roots: Contradictory values concerning identity. In *International adoption: Global inequalities and the circulation of children.* New York: New York University Press; Lebner, A. (2000). Genetic "mysteries" and international adoption: The cultural impact of biomedical technologies on the adoptive family experience. *Family Relations, 49,* 371–377; Witt, C. (2004). Adoption, biological essentialism, and feminist theory. In N. R. Cahn & J. H. Hollinger (Eds.), *Families by law: An adoption reader.* New York: New York University Press; Yngvesson, B.

(2003). Going "home": Adoption, loss of bearings, and the mythology of roots. *Social Text*, *21*, 7–27. For an overview of genetic essentialism in psychology more generally, see Dar-Nimrod, I., & Heine, S. J. (2011). Genetic essentialism: On the deceptive determinism of DNA. *Psychological Bulletin*, *137*, 800–818.

78. Brodzinsky, D. (2006). Family structural openness and communication openness as predictors in the adjustmentof adopted children. *Adoption Quarterly*, *9*, 1–18.

79. See, for example, Colaner, C. W., & Soliz, J. (2015). A communication-based approach to adoptive identity: Theoretical and empirical support. *Communication Research*, 1–27; Farr, R. H., Grant-Marsney, H. A., & Grotevant, H. D. (2014). Adoptees' contact with birth parents in emerging adulthood: The role of adoption communication and attachment to adoptive parents. *Family Process*, *53*, 656–671; Grotevant, H. D., McRoy, R. G., Wrobel, G. M., & Ayers-Lopez, S. (2013). Contact between adoptive and birth families: Perspectives from the Minnesota/Texas Adoption Research Project. *Child Development Perspectives*, *7*, 193–198; Kirk, H. D. (1964). *Shared fate: A theory and method of adoptive relationships*. New York: Free Press; Rueter, M. A., & Koerner, A. F. (2008). The effect of family communication patterns on adopted adolescent adjustment. *Journal of Marriage and Family*, *70*, 715–727; Wrobel, G. M., Kohler, J. K., Grotevant, H. D., & McRoy, R. G. (2003). The family adoption communication model (FAC): Identifying pathways of adoption-related communication. *Adoption Quarterly*, *7*, 53–84. For somewhat contrasting results, see Neil, E. (2009). Post-adoption contact and openness in adoptive parents' minds: Consequences for children's development. *British Journal of Social Work*, *39*, 5–23.

80. For similar circumstances in India, see Mohanty, J., Ahn, J., & Chokkanathan, S. (2014). Adoption disclosure: Experiences of Indian domestic adoptive parents. *Child & Family Social Work*, doi:10.1111/cfs.12175. Regarding adoption taboos in Korea, see Evans, S. (2015, January 6). Taking on South Korea's adoption taboo. *BBC News*. Retrieved from http://www.bbc.com/news/world-asia-30692127.

81. Bartholet, E., & Smolin, D. (2012). The debate. In J. L. Gibbons & K. S. Rotabi (Eds.), *Intercountry adoption: Policies, practices, and outcomes*. Surrey, UK: Ashgate, p. 242

82. The Convention also seeks to protect political freedoms that are often not guaranteed in some countries of origin of adoptees. Specifically, the Convention argues that the child should have rights to "freedom of expression" (Article 13), "freedom of

thought, conscience and religion" (Article 14), and "freedom of association and . . . freedom of peaceful assembly" (Article 15). Such freedoms are not enjoyed in many countries of the former Soviet Union or China, for example.

CHAPTER 5

1. Bowie, F., Ed. (2004). *Cross-cultural approaches to adoption*. London: Routledge; Terrell, J., & Modell, J. (1994). Anthropology and adoption. *American Anthropologist, 96*, 155–161.

2. Alber, E. (2004). 'The real parents are the foster parents': Social parenthood among the Baatombu in Northern Benin. In F. Bowie (Ed.), *Cross-cultural approaches to adoption*. London: Routledge. Note that Alber uses the term "fosterage" rather than "adoption" because the child retains the family name of the biological father, but notes that the practice in all other ways resembles what we would call "adoption."

3. Alber, E. (2004). 'The real parents are the foster parents': Social parenthood among the Baatombu in Northern Benin. In F. Bowie (Ed.), *Cross-cultural approaches to adoption*. London: Routledge, p. 36

4. See, for example, Treide, D. (2004). Adoptions in Micronesia: Past and present. In F. Bowie (Ed.), *Cross-cultural approaches to adoption*. London: Routledge.

5. Betzig, L. L. (1988). Adoption by rank on Ifaluk. *American Anthropologist, 90*, 111–119.

6. Treide, D. (2004). Adoptions in Micronesia: Past and present. In F. Bowie (Ed.), *Cross-cultural approaches to adoption*. London: Routledge.

7. As cited in Terrell, J., & Modell, J. (1994). Anthropology and adoption. *American Anthropologist, 96*, 155–161.

8. Silk, J. B. (1987). Adoption among the Inuit. *Ethos, 15*, 320–330. See also data from the 2010 U.S. Census reporting that Alaska has the highest rate of adoption among U.S. states: Kreider, R. M., & Lofquist, D. A. (2014). Adopted children and stepchildren: 2010. *Current Population Reports*, P20–572. Washington, DC: U.S. Census Bureau.

9. Volk, A. A. (2011). Adoption: Forms, functions, and preferences. In C. Salmon & T. K. Shackelford (Eds.), *The Oxford handbook of evolutionary family psychology*. New York: Oxford University Press; see also Bowie, F., Ed. (2004). *Cross-cultural approaches to adoption*. London: Routledge.

10. Hamilton, W. D. (1964). The genetical evolution of social behaviour. II. *Journal of Theoretical Biology, 7*, 17–52. For application of kin selection theory to adoptive behavior, see Silk, J. B. (1987). Adoption and fosterage in human societies: Adaptations or enigmas? *Cultural Anthropology, 2*, 39–49.

11. Some researchers distinguish between animal "adoption" and "fostering," based on whether the relationships seem temporary or permanent, while other researchers use the terms interchangeably.

12. Hrdy, S. B. (1999). *Mother nature: A history of mothers, infants, and natural selection.* New York: Pantheon; Hrdy, S. B. (2009). *Mothers and others: The evolutionary origins of mutual understanding.* Cambridge, MA: Belknap Press.

13. Riedman, M. L. (1982). The evolution of alloparental care and adoption in mammals and birds. *Quarterly Review of Biology,* 405–435; Hrdy, S. B. (2009). *Mothers and others: The evolutionary origins of mutual understanding.* Cambridge, MA: Belknap Press.

14. Agoramoorthy, G., & Rudran, R. (1992). Adoption in free-ranging red howler monkeys, *Alouatta seniculus* of Venezuela. *Primates, 33,* 551–555; Cäsar, C., & Young, R. J. (2008). A case of adoption in a wild group of black-fronted titi monkeys (*Callicebus nigrifrons*). *Primates, 49,* 146–148; Ellsworth, J. A., & Andersen, C. (1997). Adoption by captive parturient rhesus macaques: Biological vs. adopted infants and the cost of being a "twin" and rearing "twins". *American Journal of Primatology, 43,* 259–264; Gould, L. (2000). Adoption of a wild orphaned ringtailed lemur infant by natal group members: Adaptive explanations. *Primates, 41,* 413–419; Hamilton III, W. J., Busse, C., & Smith, K. S. (1982). Adoption of infant orphan chacma baboons. *Animal Behaviour, 30,* 29–34; Izar, P., Verderane, M. P., Visalberghi, E., Ottoni, E. B., Gomes De Oliveira, M., Shirley, J., & Fragaszy, D. (2006). Cross-genus adoption of a marmoset (*Callithrix jacchus*) by wild capuchin monkeys (*Cebus libidinosus*): Case report. *American Journal of Primatology, 68,* 692–700; Lawrence, W. A. (1982). Bilateral infant transfer and adoption in olive baboons (*Papio cynocephalus*). *Journal of Human Evolution, 11,* 505–510; Nakamichi, M., Silldorff, A., Bingham, C., & Sexton, P. (2007). Spontaneously occurring mother–infant swapping and the relationships of infants with their biological and foster mothers in a captive group of lowland gorillas (*Gorilla gorilla gorilla*). *Infant Behavior and Development, 30,* 399–408; Thierry, B., & Anderson, J. R. (1986). Adoption in anthropoid primates. *International Journal of Primatology, 7,* 191–216; Wroblewski, E. E. (2008). An unusual incident of adoption in a wild chimpanzee (*Pan troglodytes*) population at Gombe National Park. *American Journal of Primatology, 70,* 995–998.

15. Hrdy, S. B. (2009). *Mothers and others: The evolutionary origins of mutual understanding.* Cambridge, MA: Belknap Press. p. 228

16. Izar, P., Verderane, M. P., Visalberghi, E., Ottoni, E. B., Gomes De Oliveira, M., Shirley, J., & Fragaszy, D. (2006). Cross-genus adoption of a marmoset (*Callithrix jacchus*) by wild capuchin

monkeys (*Cebus libidinosus*): Case report. *American Journal of Primatology, 68,* 692–700.

17. Boesch, C., Bole, C., Eckhardt, N., & Boesch, H. (2010). Altruism in forest chimpanzees: The case of adoption. *PLoS One, 5,* e8901.

18. For varied interpretations of adoption from an evolutionary perspective, see Avital, E., Jablonka, E., & Lachmann, M. (1998). Adopting adoption. *Animal Behaviour, 55,* 1451–1459; Hrdy, S. B. (2009). *Mothers and others: The evolutionary origins of mutual understanding.* Cambridge, MA: Belknap Press; Riedman, M. L. (1982). The evolution of alloparental care and adoption in mammals and birds. *Quarterly Review of Biology, 57,* 405–435; Silk, J. B. (1987). Adoption among the Inuit. *Ethos, 15,* 320–330; Volk, A. A. (2011). Adoption: Forms, functions, and preferences. In C. Salmon & T. K. Shackelford (Eds.), *The Oxford handbook of evolutionary family psychology.* New York: Oxford University Press.

19. De Waal, F. B. (2008). Putting the altruism back into altruism: The evolution of empathy. *Annual Review of Psychology, 59,* 279–300; Hrdy, S. B. (2009). *Mothers and others: The evolutionary origins of mutual understanding.* Cambridge, MA: Belknap Press.

20. Anderson, K. G. (2011). Stepparenting, divorce, and investment in children. In C. Salmon & T. K. Shackelford (Eds.), *The Oxford handbook of evolutionary family psychology.* New York: Oxford University Press.

21. Daly, M., & Wilson, M. (2008). Is the "Cinderella effect" controversial? A case study of evolution-minded research and critiques thereof. In C. Crawford & D. Krebs (Eds.), *Foundations of evolutionary psychology.* Mahwah, NJ: Lawrence Erlbaum.

22. For data on higher nurturing among adoptive fathers than among stepfathers, see Schwartz, S. J., & Finley, G. E. (2006). Father involvement, nurturant fathering, and young adult psychosocial functioning differences among adoptive, adoptive stepfather, and nonadoptive stepfamilies. *Journal of Family Issues, 27,* 712–731.

23. Hamilton, L., Cheng, S., & Powell, B. (2007). Adoptive parents, adaptive parents: Evaluating the importance of biological ties for parental investment. *American Sociological Review, 72,* 95–116.

24. Another study also found greater investment in adopted than in biological children within the same family, but attributes the difference to the greater neediness of adopted children. Gibson, K. (2009). Differential parental investment in families with both adopted and genetic children. *Evolution and Human Behavior, 30,* 184–189.

25. Golombok, S., Murray, C., Jadva, V., Lycett, E., MacCallum, F., & Rust, J. (2006). Non-genetic and non-gestational parenthood: Consequences for parent–child relationships and the psychological

well-being of mothers, fathers and children at age 3. *Human Reproduction, 21*, 1918–1924.

26. Though note that even in the rat, continued exposure of never-pregnant females to infants will eventually elicit aspects of normal maternal behavior; Numan, M., & Insel, T. R. (2003). *The neurobiology of parental behavior.* New York: Springer.

27. Fernandez-Duque, E., Valeggia, C. R., & Mendoza, S. P. (2009). The biology of paternal care in human and nonhuman primates. *Annual Review of Anthropology, 38*, 115–130.

28. For extensive discussion, see Numan, M., & Insel, T. R. (2003). *The neurobiology of parental behavior.* New York: Springer; Maestripieri, D. (2001). Is there mother–infant bonding in primates? *Developmental Review, 21*, 93–120.

29. See Wynne-Edwards, K. E. (2001). Hormonal changes in mammalian fathers. *Hormones and Behavior, 40*, 139–145.

30. For reviews, see Carter, C. S. (2014). Oxytocin pathways and the evolution of human behavior. *Annual Review of Psychology, 65*, 17–39; Carter, C. S., & Porges, S. W. (2012). The biochemistry of love: An oxytocin hypothesis. *EMBO Reports, 14*, 12–16; Feldman, R. (2012). Oxytocin and social affiliation in humans. *Hormones and Behavior, 61*, 380–391; Young, K. A., Gobrogge, K. L., Liu, Y., & Wang, Z. (2011). The neurobiology of pair bonding: Insights from a socially monogamous rodent. *Frontiers in Neuroendocrinology, 32*, 53–69.

31. See, for example, Pedersen, C. A., & Boccia, M. L. (2003). Oxytocin antagonism alters rat dams' oral grooming and upright posturing over pups. *Physiology & Behavior, 80*, 233–241; Pedersen, C. A., Vadlamudi, S. V., Boccia, M. L., & Amico, J. A. (2006). Maternal behavior deficits in nulliparous oxytocin knockout mice. *Genes, Brain and Behavior, 5*, 274–281.

32. Cho, M. M., DeVries, A. C., Williams, J. R., & Carter, C. S. (1999). The effects of oxytocin and vasopressin on partner preferences in male and female prairie voles (*Microtus ochrogaster*). *Behavioral Neuroscience, 113*, 1071–1079; for evidence associating oxytocin with affiliative behavior in primates, see also Crockford, C., Wittig, R. M., Langergraber, K., Ziegler, T. E., Zuberbühler, K., & Deschner, T. (2013). Urinary oxytocin and social bonding in related and unrelated wild chimpanzees. *Proceedings of the Royal Society B: Biological Sciences, 280*, 20122765; Snowdon, C. T., Pieper, B. A., Boe, C. Y., Cronin, K. A., Kurian, A. V., & Ziegler, T. E. (2010). Variation in oxytocin is related to variation in affiliative behavior in monogamous, pairbonded tamarins. *Hormones and Behavior, 58*, 614–618.

33. Kenkel, W. M., Paredes, J., Yee, J. R., Pournajafi-Nazarloo, H., Bales, K. L., & Carter, C. S. (2012). Neuroendocrine and

behavioural responses to exposure to an infant in male prairie voles. *Journal of Neuroendocrinology, 24*, 874–886; for other physiological responses to infants among adult males, see Kenkel, W. M., et al. (2013). Autonomic substrates of the response to pups in male prairie voles. *PLoS One, 8*, e69965.

34. For review of the variety of mechanisms of parental behavior across species, see Olazábal, D., et al. (2013). Flexibility and adaptation of the neural substrate that supports maternal behavior in mammals. *Neuroscience and Biobehavioral Reviews, 37,* 1875–1892.

35. For review, see Galbally, M., Lewis, A. J., IJzendoorn, M. V., & Permezel, M. (2011). The role of oxytocin in mother–infant relations: A systematic review of human studies. *Harvard Review of Psychiatry, 19*, 1–14.

36. For evidence of the role of oxytocin in promoting parental behavior in primates, see Saito, A., & Nakamura, K. (2011). Oxytocin changes primate paternal tolerance to offspring in food transfer. *Journal of Comparative Physiology A, 197*, 329–337; Woller, M. J., Sosa, M. E., Chiang, Y., Prudom, S. L., Keelty, P., Moore, J. E., & Ziegler, T. E. (2012). Differential hypothalamic secretion of neurocrines in male common marmosets: Parental experience effects? *Journal of Neuroendocrinology, 24,* 413–421.

37. Feldman, R., Gordon, I., Schneiderman, I., Weisman, O., & Zagoory-Sharon, O. (2010). Natural variations in maternal and paternal care are associated with systematic changes in oxytocin following parent–infant contact. *Psychoneuroendocrinology, 35*, 1133–1141; for similar results, see Gordon, I., Zagoory-Sharon, O., Leckman, J. F., & Feldman, R. (2010). Oxytocin and the development of parenting in humans. *Biological Psychiatry, 68*, 377–382; Strathearn, L., Fonagy, P., Amico, J., & Montague, P. R. (2009). Adult attachment predicts maternal brain and oxytocin response to infant cues. *Neuropsychopharmacology, 34*, 2655–2666; Feldman, R., et al. (2012). Sensitive parenting is associated with plasma oxytocin and polymorphisms in the *OXTR* and *CD38* genes. *Biological Psychiatry, 72*, 175–181.

38. Bick, J., Dozier, M., Bernard, K., Grasso, D., & Simons, R. (2013). Foster mother–infant bonding: Associations between foster mothers' oxytocin production, electrophysiological brain activity, feelings of commitment, and caregiving quality. *Child Development, 84*, 826–840.

39. Grasso, D. J., Moser, J. S., Dozier, M., & Simons, R. (2009). ERP correlates of attention allocation in mothers processing faces of their children. *Biological Psychology, 81*, 95–102.

40. See, for example, Numan, M., & Insel, T. R. (2003). *The neurobiology of parental behavior.* New York: Springer.

41. Rozin, P., Fischler, C., & Shields-Argelès, C. (2012). European and American perspectives on the meaning of natural. *Appetite, 59,* 448–455.

42. Howell, S. (2003). Kinning: The creation of life trajectories in transnational adoptive families. *Journal of the Royal Anthropological Institute, 9,* 465–484; Howell, S. (2007). *The kinning of foreigners: Transnational adoption in a global perspective.* New York: Berghahn Books; Howell, S. (2009). Adoption of the unrelated child: Some challenges to the anthropological study of kinship. *Annual Review of Anthropology, 38,* 149–166; Howell, S., & Marre, D. (2006). To kin a transnationally adopted child in Norway and Spain: The achievement of resemblances and belonging. *Ethnos, 71,* 293–316.

43. For related research on perceived "family resemblance" as it relates to the issue of paternity uncertainty among birth parents, see Bressan, P., & Kramer, P. (2015). Human kin detection. *Wiley Interdisciplinary Reviews: Cognitive Science, 6,* 299–311.

44. See Witt, C. (2014). A critique of the bionormative concept of the family. In F. Baylis & C. McLeod (Eds.), *Family-making: Contemporary ethical challenges.* Oxford, UK: Oxford University Press; Witt, C. (2005). Family resemblances: Adoption, personal identity, and genetic essentialism. In S. Haslanger & C. Witt (Eds.), *Adoption matters: Philosophical and feminist essays.* Ithaca, NY: Cornell University Press.

45. Hrdy, S. B. (1999). *Mother nature: A history of mothers, infants, and natural selection.* New York: Pantheon.

Chapter 6

1. Weir, F. (2013, March 4). As emotions over US-Russia adoptions intensify, a rift widens into a chasm. *Christian Science Monitor.*

2. Weir, F. (2013, February 19). Adopted toddler's alleged death-by-abuse in Texas inflames Russia. *Christian Science Monitor.*

3. Weir, F. (2013, February 19). Adopted toddler's alleged death-by-abuse in Texas inflames Russia. *Christian Science Monitor.* Note that the case that triggered the 2013 Russian protests was ruled an accidental death by the judicial system in Texas. For more on the difficulty in ascertaining death and abuse rates among adopted and foster children, see Barth, R., & Hodorowicz, M. (2011). Foster and adopted children who die from filicide: What can we learn and what can we do? *Adoption Quarterly, 14,* 85–106; Miller, L. C., Chan, W., Reece, R. A., Tirella, L. G., & Pertman, A. (2007). Child abuse fatalities among internationally adopted children. *Child Maltreatment, 12,* 378–380.

4. See, for example, Batty, D. (2010, April 10). U.S. mother sparks outrage after sending adopted child back to Russia alone. *The Guardian*; Associated Press (2010, April 16). Russia suspends U.S. adoptions after 7-year-old boy returned. *Moscow Times*.

5. Babich, D. (2010, April 30). International adoption: Everyone wants the best for children. *RIA Novosti*.

6. Twohey, M. (2013, September 9). Americans use the Internet to abandon children adopted from overseas. *Reuters*.

7. Vandivere, S., Malm, K., & Radel, L. (2009). *Adoption USA: A chartbook based on the 2007 National Survey of Adoptive Parents*. Washington, DC: U.S. Department of Health and Human Services. The number of internationally adopted children who are rehomed cannot be exactly zero, because investigative journalists did discover some evident cases. Furthermore, the parents of a child who was rehomed might not be likely NSAP survey respondents. Nevertheless, the survey data indicate that virtually 100% of parents with adopted children in their homes have not even considered dissolving the adoption.

8. Van IJzendoorn, M. H., Euser, E. M., Prinzie, P., Juffer, F., & Bakermans-Kranenburg, M. J. (2009). Elevated risk of child maltreatment in families with stepparents but not with adoptive parents. *Child Maltreatment, 14*, 369–375.

9. Pertman, A. (2006). Adoption in the media: In need of editing. In K. Wegar (Ed.), *Adoptive families in a diverse society*. New Brunswick, NJ: Rutgers University Press. See also Waggenspack, B. M. (1998). The symbolic crises of adoption: Popular media's agenda setting. *Adoption Quarterly, 1*, 57–82; Wegar, K. (1997). In search of bad mothers: Social constructions of birth and adoptive motherhood. *Women's Studies International Forum, 20*, 77–86.

10. Potter, J. E. (2013). Adopting commodities: A Burkean cluster analysis of adoption rhetoric. *Adoption Quarterly, 16*, 108–127; see also Kline, S. L., Chatterjee, K., & Karel, A. I. (2009). Healthy depictions? Depicting adoption and adoption news events on broadcast news. *Journal of Health Communication, 14*, 56–69.

11. Pertman, A. (2006). Adoption in the media: In need of editing. In K. Wegar (Ed.), *Adoptive families in a diverse society*. New Brunswick, NJ: Rutgers University Press; see also Gailey, C. W. (2006). Urchins, orphans, monsters, and victims: Images of adoptive families in U.S. commercial films, 1950–2000. In K. Wegar (Ed.), *Adoptive families in a diverse society*. New Brunswick, NJ: Rutgers University Press; Creedy, K. B. (2000). Movies, celebrity specials, late night talk shows, commercials, stamps, and tabloid journalism send mixed messages about adoption. *Adoption Quarterly, 4*, 119–124.

12. Jacobson, H. (2014). Framing adoption: The media and parental decision making. *Journal of Family Issues, 35,* 654–676.
13. Kline, S. L., Karel, A. I., & Chatterjee, K. (2006). Covering adoption: General depictions in broadcast news. *Family Relations, 55,* 487–498.
14. Fisher, A. P. (2003). A critique of the portrayal of adoption in college textbooks and readers on families, 1998–2001. *Family Relations, 52,* 154–160.
15. Harris Interactive. (2002). *National Adoption Attitudes Survey: A research report.* Evan B. Donaldson Adoption Institute and Dave Thomas Foundation for Adoption.
16. Princeton Survey Research Associates. (1997). *Benchmark adoption survey: Report on the findings.* Evan B. Donaldson Adoption Institute.
17. For more on adoption as a "second-best" or deviant choice, see Fisher, A. P. (2003). Still "not quite as good as having your own"? Toward a sociology of adoption. *Annual Review of Sociology, 29,* 335–361; Wegar, K. (2000). Adoption, family ideology, and social stigma: Bias in community attitudes, adoption research, and practice. *Family Relations, 49,* 363–369; Kressierer, D. K., & Bryant, C. D. (1996). Adoption as deviance: Socially constructed parent–child kinship as a stigmatized and legally burdened relationship. *Deviant Behavior, 17,* 391–415.
18. Hellerstedt, W. L., Madsen, N. J., Gunnar, M. R., Grotevant, H. D., Lee, R. M., & Johnson, D. E. (2008). The international adoption project: Population-based surveillance of Minnesota parents who adopted children internationally. *Maternal and Child Health Journal, 12,* 162–171.
19. It is possible that sampling bias could inflate the estimated socioeconomic levels of the adoptive parents, as might be the case if more educated parents were more likely to complete long surveys. However, the researchers were able to rule out such sampling bias using data available from the state of Minnesota's Department of Human Services, which collected basic demographic information at the time the adoptions were finalized.
20. Vandivere, S., Malm, K., & Radel, L. (2009). *Adoption USA: A chartbook based on the 2007 National Survey of Adoptive Parents.* Washington, DC: U.S. Department of Health and Human Services; Bramlett, M. D. (2011). *The National Survey of Adoptive Parents: Benchmark estimates of school performance and family relationship quality for adopted children.* Washington, DC: U.S. Department of Health and Human Services. For an overview, see Bramlett, M. D., & Radel, L. F. (2010). The National Survey of Adoptive Parents: An introduction to the special issue of adoption quarterly. *Adoption Quarterly, 13,* 147–156.

21. See, for example, Briggs, L., & Marre, D. (2009). Introduction: The circulation of children. In D. Marre & L. Briggs (Eds.), *International adoption: Global inequalities and the circulation of children*. New York: New York University Press.

22. Joyce, K. (2013). *The child catchers: Rescue, trafficking, and the new gospel of adoption*. New York: PublicAffairs.

23. Bausch, R. S. (2006). Predicting willingness to adopt a child: A consideration of demographic and attitudinal factors. *Sociological Perspectives*. 49, 47–65.

24. See, for example, Brian, K. (2007). Choosing Korea: Marketing "multiculturalism" to choosy adopters. In K. J. S. Bergquist, M. E. Vonk, D. S. Kim, & M. D. Feit (Eds.), *International Korean adoption: A fifty-year history of policy and practice*. New York: Routledge; Perry, T. L. (1998). Transracial and international adoption: Mothers, hierarchy, race, and feminist legal theory. *Yale Journal of Law & Feminism*, 10, 101; Ortiz, A. T., & Briggs, L. (2003). The culture of poverty, crack babies, and welfare cheats: The making of the "healthy white baby crisis". *Social Text*, 21, 39–57; Quiroz, P. A. (2008). Transnational adoption: Reflections of the "diaper diaspora": On reconfiguring race in the USA. *International Journal of Sociology and Social Policy*, 28, 440–457.

25. According to the U.S. Department of State, Ethiopia was second only to China in the number of children adopted by Americans in each of the years 2009 through 2013. U.S. Department of State, Bureau of Consular Affairs. (n.d). *Intercountry adoption: Statistics*. Retrieved from http://adoption.state.gov/about_us/statistics.php.

26. For additional data suggesting that race is not the primary reason that Americans are hesitant to adopt from foster care, see also Harris Interactive. (2002). *National Adoption Attitudes Survey: A research report*. Evan B. Donaldson Adoption Institute and Dave Thomas Foundation for Adoption; see also Zhang, Y., & Lee, G. R. (2011). Intercountry versus transracial adoption: Analysis of adoptive parents' motivations and preferences in adoption. *Journal of Family Issues*, 32, 75–98.

27. Davis, M. A. (2011). *Children for families or families for children: The demography of adoption behavior in the US* (Vol. 29). New York: Springer, p. 158.

28. Kubo, K. (2010). Desirable differences: The shadow of racial stereotypes in creating transracial families through transnational adoption. *Sociology Compass*, 4, 263–282; Klevan, M. (2012). Resolving race: How adoptive parents discuss choosing the race of their child. *Adoption Quarterly*, 15, 88–115.

29. Ishizawa, H., & Kubo, K. (2013). Factors affecting adoption decisions: Child and parental characteristics. *Journal of Family Issues*,

35, 627–653. Although it is possible that parents are reluctant to admit racial preferences on a survey simply because they want to appear unbiased, it's unclear why that would be more the case for internationally than domestically adopting parents.

30. Ishizawa, H., Kenney, C. T., Kubo, K., & Stevens, G. (2006). Constructing interracial families through intercountry adoption. *Social Science Quarterly, 87,* 1207–1224.

31. Vandivere, S., Malm, K., & Radel, L. (2009). *Adoption USA: A chartbook based on the 2007 National Survey of Adoptive Parents.* Washington, DC: U.S. Department of Health and Human Services.

32. Ceballo, R., Lansford, J. E., Abbey, A., & Stewart, A. J. (2004). Gaining a child: Comparing the experiences of biological parents, adoptive parents, and stepparents. *Family Relations, 53,* 38–48.

33. Rosnati, R., Ranieri, S., & Barni, D. (2013). Family and social relationships and psychosocial well-being in Italian families with internationally adopted and non-adopted children. *Adoption Quarterly, 16,* 1–16; see also McKay, K., Ross, L. E., & Goldberg, A. E. (2010). Adaptation to parenthood during the post-adoption period: A review of the literature. *Adoption Quarterly, 13,* 125–144.

34. Smit, E. M., Delpier, T., Tarantino, S. L., & Anderson, M. L. (2005). Caring for adoptive families: Lessons in communication. *Pediatric Nursing, 32,* 136–143.

35. Rueter, M. A., Keyes, M. A., Iacono, W. G., & McGue, M. (2009). Family interactions in adoptive compared to nonadoptive families. *Journal of Family Psychology, 23,* 58–66; see also Loehlin, J. C., Horn, J. M., & Ernst, J. L. (2010). Parent–child closeness studied in adoptive families. *Personality and Individual Differences, 48,* 149–154.

36. Vandivere, S., Malm, K., & Radel, L. (2009). *Adoption USA: A chartbook based on the 2007 National Survey of Adoptive Parents.* Washington, DC: U.S. Department of Health and Human Services. For other findings of high levels of satisfaction among internationally adopting parents, see Castle, J., et al. (2009). Parents' evaluation of adoption success: A follow-up study of intercountry and domestic adoptions. *American Journal of Orthopsychiatry, 79,* 522–531; Younes, M. N., & Klein, S. A. (2014). The international adoption experience: Do they live happily ever after? *Adoption Quarterly, 17,* 65–83.

37. Palacios, J., Román, M., Moreno, C., & León, E. (2009). Family context for emotional recovery in internationally adopted children. *International Social Work, 52,* 609–620.

38. Vandivere, S., Malm, K., & Radel, L. (2009). *Adoption USA: A chartbook based on the 2007 National Survey of Adoptive Parents.* Washington, DC: U.S. Department of Health and Human Services.

39.   For additional evidence of no difference between adoptive and birth mothers in responsiveness to infants, see also Suwalsky, J. T., Cote, L. R., Bornstein, M. H., Hendricks, C., Haynes, O. M., & Bakeman, R. (2012). Mother–infant socioemotional contingent responding in families by adoption and birth. *Infant Behavior and Development, 35*, 499–508.

40.   Vandivere, S., Malm, K., & Radel, L. (2009). *Adoption USA: A chartbook based on the 2007 National Survey of Adoptive Parents*. Washington, DC: U.S. Department of Health and Human Services. In this survey, "married" referred to opposite-sex marriages, though since that time same-sex marriage has been legalized in all U.S. states.

41.   Tan, T. X. (2005). Child adjustment of single-parent adoption from China: A comparative study. *Adoption Quarterly, 8*, 1–20; see also Tan, T. X., & Baggerly, J. (2009). Behavioral adjustment of adopted Chinese girls in single-mother, lesbian-couple, and heterosexual-couple households. *Adoption Quarterly, 12*, 171–186.

42.   For overview of research issues related to single-parent adoption, see Pakizegi, B. (2007). Single-parent adoptions and clinical implications. In J. A. Javier, A. L. Baden, F. A. Biafora, & A. Camacho-Gingerich (Eds.), *Handbook of adoption: Implications for researchers, practitioners, and families*. Thousand Oaks, CA: Sage Publications.

43.   Spencer, N. (2005). Does material disadvantage explain the increased risk of adverse health, educational, and behavioural outcomes among children in lone parent households in Britain? A cross sectional study. *Journal of Epidemiology and Community Health, 59*, 152–157. For similar studies in other samples in the U.S., U.K., New Zealand, and Sweden, see Fergusson, D. M., Boden, J. M., & Horwood, L. J. (2007). Exposure to single parenthood in childhood and later mental health, educational, economic, and criminal behavior outcomes. *Archives of General Psychiatry, 64*, 1089–1095; Joshi, H., Cooksey, E. C., Wiggins, R. D., McCulloch, A., Verropoulou, G., & Clarke, L. (1999). Diverse family living situations and child development: A multi-level analysis comparing longitudinal evidence from Britain and the United States. *International Journal of Law, Policy and the Family, 13*, 292–314; Weitoft, G. R., Hjern, A., Haglund, B., & Rosén, M. (2003). Mortality, severe morbidity, and injury in children living with single parents in Sweden: A population-based study. *Lancet, 361*, 289–295.

44.   Gates, G. J., Badgett, M. V., Macomber, J. E., & Chambers, K. (2007). *Adoption and foster care by gay and lesbian parents in the United States*. The Williams Institute.

45.   *Obergefell v. Hodges*, 135 S.Ct. 2584 (2015); Appell, A. R. (2014).
        Legal issues in lesbian and gay adoption. In D. M. Brodzinsky &
        A. Pertman (Eds.), *Adoption by lesbians and gay men: A new dimen-
        sion in family diversity.* New York: Oxford University Press; Hol-
        linger, J. B. (2004). Second parent adoptions protect children
        with two mothers or two fathers. In N. R. Cahn & J. H. Hol-
        linger (Eds.), *Families by law: An adoption reader.*
        New York: New York University Press. See also Brodzinsky,
        D. M., & the Evan B. Donaldson Adoption Institute. (2011).
        *Expanding resources for children III: Research-based best practices in
        adoption by gays and lesbians.* Evan B. Donaldson Adoption Insti-
        tute; Brodzinsky, D. M. (2014). Adoption by lesbians and gay
        men: A national survey of adoption agency policies and prac-
        tices. In D. M. Brodzinsky & A. Pertman (Eds.), *Adoption by lesbi-
        ans and gay men: A new dimension in family diversity.*
        New York: Oxford University Press.
46.   For reviews, see Anderssen, N., Amlie, C., & Ytterøy, E. A. (2002).
        Outcomes for children with lesbian or gay parents. A review
        of studies from 1978 to 2000. *Scandinavian Journal of Psychology,
        43*, 335–351; Biblarz, T. J., & Stacey, J. (2010). How does the gen-
        der of parents matter? *Journal of Marriage and Family, 72*, 3–22;
        Patterson, C. J. (2006). Children of lesbian and gay parents.
        Current Directions in Psychological Science, 15, 241–244; Perrin,
        E. C. (2002). Technical report: Coparent or second-parent
        adoption by same-sex parents. *Pediatrics, 109*, 341–344. For
        studies specifically comparing children adopted by same-sex
        versus opposite-sex partners, see Averett, P., Nalavany, B., &
        Ryan, S. (2009). An evaluation of gay/lesbian and heterosexual
        adoption. *Adoption Quarterly, 12*, 129–151; Lavner, J. A., Water-
        man, J., & Peplau, L. A. (2012). Can gay and lesbian parents
        promote healthy development in high-risk children adopted
        from foster care? *American Journal of Orthopsychiatry, 82*, 465;
        Leung, P., Erich, S., & Kanenberg, H. (2005). A comparison of
        family functioning in gay/lesbian, heterosexual and special
        needs adoptions. *Children and Youth Services Review, 27*, 1031–
        1044; Tan, T. X., & Baggerly, J. (2009). Behavioral adjustment of
        adopted Chinese girls in single-mother, lesbian-couple, and
        heterosexual-couple households. *Adoption Quarterly, 12*, 171–
        186. See also Crouch, S. R., Waters, E., McNair, R., Power, J., &
        Davis, E. (2014). Parent-reported measures of child health and
        wellbeing in same-sex parent families: A cross-sectional sur-
        vey. *BMC Public Health, 14*, 635.
47.   Paige, R. U. (2005). Proceedings of the American Psychological
        Association, Incorporated, for the legislative year 2004. Minutes
        of the meeting of the Council of Representatives July 28 & 30,

2004, Honolulu, HI. Retrieved from http://www.apa.org/
governance/. Some have argued that the APA position is over-
stated due to methodological limitations in the supporting evidence; for discussion, see Amato, P. R. (2012). The well-being of
children with gay and lesbian parents. *Social Science Research, 41,*
771–774; Marks, L. (2012). Same-sex parenting and children's
outcomes: A closer examination of the American Psychological
Association's brief on lesbian and gay parenting. *Social Science
Research, 41,* 735–751.

48. Paige, R. U. (2005). Proceedings of the American Psychological
Association, Incorporated, for the legislative year 2004. Minutes
of the meeting of the Council of Representatives July 28 & 30,
2004, Honolulu, HI. Retrieved from http://www.apa.org/
governance/.

49. Gates, G. J., Badgett, M. V., Macomber, J. E., & Chambers, K.
(2007). *Adoption and foster care by gay and lesbian parents in the
United States.* The Williams Institute.

50. Farr, R. H., & Patterson, C. J. (2009). Transracial adoption by
lesbian, gay, and heterosexual couples: Who completes transracial adoptions and with what results? *Adoption Quarterly, 12,*
187–204; Goldberg, A. E., Kinkler, L. A., & Hines, D. A. (2011).
Perception and internalization of adoption stigma among gay,
lesbian, and heterosexual adoptive parents. *Journal of GLBT
Family Studies, 7,* 132–154; Jennings, S., Mellish, L., Tasker, F.,
Lamb, M., & Golombok, S. (2014). Why adoption? Gay, lesbian,
and heterosexual adoptive parents' reproductive experiences
and reasons for adoption. *Adoption Quarterly, 17,* 205–226;
Raleigh, E. (2012). Are same-sex and single adoptive parents
more likely to adopt transracially? A national analysis of race,
family structure, and the adoption marketplace. *Sociological
Perspectives, 55,* 449–471; see review in Farr, R. H., & Patterson,
C. J. (2013). Lesbian and gay adoptive parents and their children. In A. E. Goldberg & K. R. Allen (Eds.), *LGBT-parent families: Innovations in research and implications for practice.*
New York: Springer. Though for evidence of high similarity in
the kinds of children adopted by same-sex and opposite-sex
partners, see Brooks, D., Kim, H., & Wind, L. H. (2014). Supporting gay and lesbian adoptive families before and after
adoption. In D. M. Brodzinsky & A. Pertman (Eds.), *Adoption
by lesbians and gay men: A new dimension in family diversity.*
New York: Oxford University Press.

51. Farr, R. H., & Patterson, C. J. (2013). Lesbian and gay adoptive
parents and their children. In A. E. Goldberg & K. R. Allen
(Eds.), *LGBT-parent families: Innovations in research and implications for practice.* New York: Springer.

52. Farr, R. H., & Patterson, C. J. (2013). Coparenting among lesbian, gay, and heterosexual couples: Associations with adopted children's outcomes. *Child Development, 84,* 1226–1240.

53. Farr, R. H., Forssell, S. L., & Patterson, C. J. (2010). Parenting and child development in adoptive families: Does parental sexual orientation matter? *Applied Developmental Science, 14,* 164–178; Golombok, S., Mellish, L., Jennings, S., Casey, P., Tasker, F., & Lamb, M. E. (2014). Adoptive gay father families: Parent–child relationships and children's psychological adjustment. *Child Development, 85,* 456–468; Lamb, M. E. (2012). Mothers, fathers, families, and circumstances: Factors affecting children's adjustment. *Applied Developmental Science, 16,* 98–111; Lansford, J. E., Ceballo, R., Abbey, A., & Stewart, A. J. (2001). Does family structure matter? A comparison of adoptive, two-parent biological, single-mother, stepfather, and stepmother households. *Journal of Marriage and Family, 63,* 840–851; Patterson, C. J., & Wainwright, J. L. (2014). Adolescents with same-sex parents: Findings from the National Longitudinal Study of Adolescent Health. In D. M. Brodzinsky & A. Pertman (Eds.), *Adoption by lesbians and gay men: A new dimension in family diversity.* New York: Oxford University Press.

54. For more detailed discussion about various definitions of "family," see Bernardes, J. (1999). We must not define "the family"! *Marriage & Family Review, 28,* 21–41; Holstein, J. A., & Gubrium, J. (1999). What is family? Further thoughts on a social constructionist approach. *Marriage & Family Review, 28,* 3–20; Trost, J. (1990). Do we mean the same by the concept of family? *Communication Research, 17,* 431–443; Turner, L. H., & West. R. (2015). The challenge of defining "family". In *SAGE Handbook of Family Communication.* Thousand Oaks, CA: Sage Publications.

55. See, for example, Lofquist, D., Lugaila, T., O'Connell, M., & Feliz, S. (2012). *Households and families: 2010.* United States Census Bureau.

56. Weigel, D. J. (2008). The concept of family: An analysis of laypeople's views of family. *Journal of Family Issues, 29,* 1426–1447.

57. For additional evidence that laypeople value emotional factors more than blood relations or legal ties in defining a family, see also Anyan, S. E., & Pryor, J. (2002). What is in a family? Adolescent perceptions. *Children & Society, 16,* 306–317.

58. Weigel, D. J. (2008). The concept of family: An analysis of laypeople's views of family. *Journal of Family Issues, 29,* 1426–1447.

59. See also Anyan, S. E., & Pryor, J. (2002). What is in a family? Adolescent perceptions. *Children & Society, 16,* 306–317; Baxter, L. A., Henauw, C., Huisman, D., Livesay, C. B., Norwood, K., Su, H., Wolf, B., & Young, B. (2009). Lay conceptions of

"family": A replication and extension. *Journal of Family Communication, 9*, 170–189; Rigg, A., & Pryor, J. (2007). Children's perceptions of families: What do they really think? *Children & Society, 21*, 17–30.

60. Smith, B., Surrey, J. L., & Watkins, M. (2006). "Real" mothers: Adoptive mothers resisting marginalization and recreating motherhood. In K. Wegar (Ed.), *Adoptive families in a diverse society*. New Brunswick, NJ: Rutgers University Press; Suter, E. A., & Ballard, R. L. (2009). "How much did you pay for her?" Decision-making criteria underlying adoptive parents' responses to inappropriate remarks. *Journal of Family Communication, 9*, 107–125; Suter, E. A., Baxter, L. A., Seurer, L. M., & Thomas, L. J. (2014). Discursive constructions of the meaning of "family" in online narratives of foster adoptive parents. *Communication Monographs, 81*, 59–78; Suter, E. A., Reyes, K. L., & Ballard, R. L. (2011). Adoptive parents' framing of laypersons' conceptions of family. *Qualitative Research Reports in Communication, 12*, 43–50.

61. Krusiewicz, E. S., & Wood, J. T. (2001). 'He was our child from the moment we walked in that room': Entrance stories of adoptive parents. *Journal of Social and Personal Relationships, 18*, 785–803.

Chapter 7

1. Reynolds, J., & Medina, S. (2008). Challenges and resiliency factors of families with internationally adopted children. In G. R. Walz, J. C. Bleuer, & R. K. Yep (Eds.), *Compelling counseling interventions*. Ann Arbor, MI: Counseling Outfitters, p. 85.

2. Reynolds, J., & Medina, S. (2008). Challenges and resiliency factors of families with internationally adopted children. In G. R. Walz, J. C. Bleuer, & R. K. Yep (Eds.), *Compelling counseling interventions*. Ann Arbor, MI: Counseling Outfitters, p. 85.

3. Albers, L. H., Johnson, D. E., Hostetter, M. K., Iverson, S., & Miller, L. C. (1997). Health of children adopted from the former Soviet Union and Eastern Europe: comparison with preadoptive medical records. *JAMA, 278*, 922–924; Pinderhughes, E., Matthews, J., Deoudes, G., & Pertman, A. (2013). *A changing world: Shaping best practices through understanding of the new realities of international adoption*. New York: Donaldson Adoption Institute.

4. Countries of the former Soviet Union have among the highest alcohol consumption rates in the world. See World Health Organization. (2014). *World Health Statistics 2014: Part III Global Health Indicators*, pp. 119–125.

5. Kristjanson, A. F., Wilsnack, S. C., Zvartau, E., Tsoy, M., & Novikov, B. (2007). Alcohol use in pregnant and nonpregnant Russian women. *Alcoholism: Clinical and Experimental Research, 31*, 299–307; Miller, L. C., Chan, W., Litvinova, A., Rubin, A., Comfort, K., Tirella, L., et al. (2006). Fetal alcohol spectrum disorders in children residing in Russian orphanages: A phenotypic survey. *Alcoholism: Clinical and Experimental Research, 30*, 531–538; see also Balachova, T., et al. (2014). Women's receptivity to fetal alcohol spectrum disorders prevention approaches: A case study of two regions in Russia. *International Journal of Alcohol and Drug Research, 3*, 5–15; Popova, S., et al. (2014). What research is being done on prenatal alcohol exposure and fetal alcohol spectrum disorders in the Russian research community? *Alcohol and Alcoholism, 49*, 84–95.

6. Note that there are systematic differences in the amount and quality of pre-adoptive health and family history information depending on the country of origin. For example, see Welsh, J. A., Viana, A. G., Petrill, S. A., & Mathias, M. D. (2008). Ready to adopt: Characteristics and expectations of preadoptive families pursuing international adoptions. *Adoption Quarterly, 11*, 176–203.

7. Hague Convention on Protection of Children and Co-operation in Respect of Intercountry Adoption, Article 16(1)(a); see also elaboration in Hague Conference on Private International Law. (2008). *The implementation and operation of the 1993 Hague Intercountry Adoption Convention: Guide to good practice*, pp. 85–86.

8. See Hague Conference on Private International Law. (2008). *The implementation and operation of the 1993 Hague Intercountry Adoption Convention: Guide to good practice*, pp. 91ff

9. Kreider, R. M., & Cohen, P. N. (2009). Disability among internationally adopted children in the United States. *Pediatrics, 124*, 1311–1318.

10. Kreider, R. M., & Cohen, P. N. (2009). Disability among internationally adopted children in the United States. *Pediatrics, 124*, 1311–1318.

11. Selman, P. (2012). The global decline of intercountry adoption: What lies ahead? *Social Policy and Society, 11*, 381–397.

12. Vandivere, S., Malm, K., & Radel, L. (2009). *Adoption USA: A chartbook based on the 2007 National Survey of Adoptive Parents*. Washington, DC: U.S. Department of Health and Human Services.

13. Pinderhughes, E., Matthews, J., Deoudes, G., & Pertman, A. (2013). *A changing world: Shaping best practices through understanding of the new realities of international adoption*. New York: Donaldson Adoption Institute.

14. For discussion of the potentially different issues that may arise in families who did versus did not anticipate special needs, see Lindstrom, S. E., Voynow, S., & Boyer, B. A. (2013). Adoption of children with special health care needs. In V. M. Brabender & A. E. Fallon (Eds.), *Working with adoptive parents: Research, theory, and therapeutic interventions*. Hoboken, NJ: Wiley.

15. Pinderhughes, E., Matthews, J., Deoudes, G., & Pertman, A. (2013). *A changing world: Shaping best practices through understanding of the new realities of international adoption*. New York: Donaldson Adoption Institute.

16. For a global perspective on disability in children worldwide, see UNICEF. (2013). *The state of the world's children 2013: Children with disabilities*. Retrieved from http://www.unicef.org/sowc2013/files/SWCR2013_ENG_Lo_res_24_Apr_2013.pdf.

17. Human Rights Watch. (2013, September 11). *Barriers everywhere: Lack of accessibility for people with disabilities in Russia*. Retrieved from https://www.hrw.org/report/2013/09/11/barriers-everywhere/lack-accessibility-people-disabilities-russia.

18. See, for example, see Kikkas, K. (2001). Lifting the iron curtain. In M. Priestly (Ed.), *Disability and the life cycle: Global perspectives*. Cambridge, UK: Cambridge University Press.

19. Iarskaia-Smirnova, E. (1999). "What the future will bring I do not know": Mothering children with disabilities in Russia and the politics of exclusion. *Frontiers: A Journal of Women Studies, 20*, 68–86.

20. For harrowing reports of such institutions, see Philps, A., & Lahutsky, J. (2009). *The boy from Baby House 10: From the nightmare of a Russian orphanage to a new life in America*. New York: St. Martin's Press; Human Rights Watch (1998). *Abandoned to the state: Cruelty and neglect in Russian orphanages*. New York: Author; Human Rights Watch (2014, September 15). *Abandoned by the state: Violence, neglect, and isolation for children with disabilities in Russian orphanages*. Retrieved from https://www.hrw.org/report/2014/09/15/abandoned-state/violence-neglect-and-isolation-children-disabilities-russian.

21. Human Rights Watch (1998). *Abandoned to the state: Cruelty and neglect in Russian orphanages*. New York: Author. Human Rights Watch (2014). *Abandoned by the state: Violence, neglect, and isolation for children with disabilities in Russian orphanages*.

22. Shakespeare, T. (2012). Disability in developing countries. In N. Watson, A. Roulstone, & C. Thomas (Eds.), *Routledge handbook of disability studies*. London: Routledge.

23. Human Rights Watch. (2013, July 15). *"As long as they let us stay in class": Barriers to education for persons with disabilities in China*.

Retrieved from https://www.hrw.org/report/2013/07/15/long-they-let-us-stay-class/barriers-education-persons-disabilities-china.

24. Human Rights Watch. (2011, August 24). *Futures stolen: Barriers to education for children with disabilities in Nepal.* Retrieved from https://www.hrw.org/report/2011/08/24/futures-stolen/barriers-education-children-disabilities-nepal. For discussion of interaction between poverty and disability in India, see also Ghai, A. (2001). Marginalisation and disability: Experiences from the Third World. In M. Priestly (Ed.), *Disability and the life cycle: Global perspectives.* Cambridge, UK: Cambridge University Press. For discussion of disability in Ethiopia, see Beyene, G., & Tizazu, Y. (2011). Attitudes of teachers towards inclusive education in Ethiopia. *Ethiopian Journal of Education and Sciences, 6*, 89–96; Fitaw, Y., & Boersma, J. M. (2006). Prevalence and impact of disability in northwestern Ethiopia. *Disability & Rehabilitation, 28*, 949–953.

25. Rosenthal, E., & Mental Disability Rights International. (2009). *The rights of children with disabilities in Viet Nam*; Ahern, L., & Rosenthal, E. (2006). *Hidden suffering: Romania's segregation and abuse of infants and children with disability.* Washington, DC: Mental Disability Rights International; Mental Disability Rights International. (2004). *Human rights and mental health in Peru*; Disability Rights International. (2013). *Left behind: The exclusion of children and adults with disabilities from reform and rights protection in the Republic of Georgia*; see also Muiznieks, M. (2014). *Report following his visit to Romania.* Commissioner for Human Rights, Council of Europe; Hartley, S., & Newton, C. R. (2009). Children with developmental disabilities in the majority of the world. In M. Shevell (Ed.), *Neurodevelopmental disabilities: Clinical and scientific foundations.* London: Mac Keith Press.

26. Cho, S. J., Singer, G. H., & Brenner, M. (2000). Adaptation and accommodation to young children with disabilities: A comparison of Korean and Korean American parents. *Topics in Early Childhood Special Education, 20*, 236–249; Cho, S. J., Singer, G. H., & Brenner, B. (2003). A comparison of adaptation to childhood disability in Korean immigrant and Korean mothers. *Focus on Autism and Other Developmental Disabilities, 18*, 9–19; see also Shin, J. Y. (2002). Social support for families of children with mental retardation: Comparison between Korea and the United States. *Mental Retardation, 40*, 103–118.

27. See, for example, Dubinsky, K. (2010). *Babies without borders: Adoption and migration across the Americas.* New York: New York University Press; Joyce, K. (2013). *The child catchers: Rescue, trafficking, and the new gospel of adoption.*

New York: Public Affairs. For an alternative view, see Rulli, T. (2014). The unique value of adoption. In F. Baylis & C. McLeod (Eds.), *Family-making: Contemporary ethical challenges*. Oxford, UK: Oxford University Press.

28. Vandivere, S., Malm, K., & Radel, L. (2009). *Adoption USA: A chartbook based on the 2007 National Survey of Adoptive Parents*. Washington, DC: U.S. Department of Health and Human Services.

29. Tan, T. X., Marfo, K., & Dedrick, R. F. (2007). Special needs adoption from China: Exploring child-level indicators, adoptive family characteristics, and correlates of behavioral adjustment. *Children and Youth Services Review, 29*, 1269–1285.

30. Judge, S. (2003). Determinants of parental stress in families adopting children from Eastern Europe. *Family Relations, 52*, 241–248; Palacios, J., & Sánchez-Sandoval, Y. (2006). Stress in parents of adopted children. *International Journal of Behavioral Development, 30*, 481–487; see also Ceballo, R., Lansford, J. E., Abbey, A., & Stewart, A. J. (2004). Gaining a child: Comparing the experiences of biological parents, adoptive parents, and stepparents. *Family Relations, 53*, 38–48; Sánchez-Sandoval, Y., & Palacios, J. (2012). Stress in adoptive parents of adolescents. *Children and Youth Services Review, 34*, 1283–1289.

31. Judge, S. (2003). Determinants of parental stress in families adopting children from Eastern Europe. *Family Relations, 52*, 241–248; Mainemer, H., Gilman, L. C., & Ames, E. W. (1998). Parenting stress in families adopting children from Romanian orphanages. *Journal of Family Issues, 19*, 164–180; Viana, A. G., & Welsh, J. A. (2010). Correlates and predictors of parenting stress among internationally adopting mothers: A longitudinal investigation. *International Journal of Behavioral Development, 34*, 363–373.; see also Hoksbergen, R., Rijk, K., Van Dijkum, C. O. R., & Ter Laak, J. A. N. (2004). Adoption of Romanian children in the Netherlands: Behavior problems and parenting burden of upbringing for adoptive parents. *Journal of Developmental & Behavioral Pediatrics, 25*, 175–180; Reilly, T., & Platz, L. (2003). Characteristics and challenges of families who adopt children with special needs: An empirical study. *Children and Youth Services Review, 25*, 781–803.

32. Rushton, A. (2007). Outcomes of adoption from public care: Research and practice issues. *Advances in Psychiatric Treatment, 13*, 305–311; Rushton, A., & Dance, C. (2006). The adoption of children from public care: A prospective study of outcome in adolescence. *Journal of the American Academy of Child & Adolescent Psychiatry, 45*, 877–883. For a book-length treatment of adoption disruption focused on older children adopted from the

U.S. child welfare system, see Barth, R. P., & Berry, M. (1988). *Adoption and disruption.* New York: Aldine De Gruyter.

33. Rushton, A., & Monck, E. (2009). Adopters' experiences of preparation to parent children with serious difficulties. *Adoption & Fostering, 33,* 4–12; Wind, L. H., Brooks, D., & Barth, R. P. (2006). Adoption preparation: Differences between adoptive families of children with and without special needs. *Adoption Quarterly, 8,* 45–74.

34. Welsh, J. A., Viana, A. G., Petrill, S. A., & Mathias, M. D. (2008). Ready to adopt: Characteristics and expectations of preadoptive families pursuing international adoptions. *Adoption Quarterly, 11,* 176–203.

35. Viana, A. G., & Welsh, J. A. (2010). Correlates and predictors of parenting stress among internationally adopting mothers: A longitudinal investigation. *International Journal of Behavioral Development, 34,* 363–373.

36. Ji, J., Brooks, D., Barth, R. P., & Kim, H. (2010). Beyond preadoptive risk: The impact of adoptive family environment on adopted youth's psychosocial adjustment. *American Journal of Orthopsychiatry, 80,* 432–442.

37. Kriebel, D. K., & Wentzel, K. (2011). Parenting as a moderator of cumulative risk for behavioral competence in adopted children. *Adoption Quarterly, 14,* 37–60.

38. Whitten, K. L., & Weaver, S. R. (2010.). Adoptive family relationships and healthy adolescent development: A risk and resilience analysis. *Adoption Quarterly, 13,* 209–226. For additional studies examining the role of parenting styles, see also Levy-Shiff, R. (2001). Psychological adjustment of adoptees in adulthood: Family environment and adoption-related correlates. *International Journal of Behavioral Development, 25,* 97–104; Palacios, J., & Sánchez-Sandoval, Y. (2006). Stress in parents of adopted children. *International Journal of Behavioral Development, 30,* 481–487; Rueter, M. A., & Koerner, A. F. (2008). The effect of family communication patterns on adopted adolescent adjustment. *Journal of Marriage and Family, 70,* 715–727; Simmel, C. (2007). Risk and protective factors contributing to the longitudinal psychosocial well-being of adopted foster children. *Journal of Emotional and Behavioral Disorders, 15,* 237–249.

39. Harwood, R., Feng, X., & Yu, S. (2013). Preadoption adversities and postadoption mediators of mental health and school outcomes among international, foster, and private adoptees in the United States. *Journal of Family Psychology, 27,* 409–420.

40. Asok, A., Bernard, K., Roth, T. L., Rosen, J. B., & Dozier, M. (2013). Parental responsiveness moderates the association between

early-life stress and reduced telomere length. *Development and Psychopathology, 25*, 577–585.

41. Dozier, M., Peloso, E., Lindhiem, O., Gordon, M. K., Manni, M., Sepulveda, S., Ackerman, J., & Levine, S. (2006). Developing evidence-based interventions for foster children: An example of a randomized clinical trial with infants and toddlers. *Journal of Social Issues, 62*, 767–785; Dozier, M., Peloso, E., Lewis, E., Laurenceau, J. P., & Levine, S. (2008). Effects of an attachment-based intervention on the cortisol production of infants and toddlers in foster care. *Development and Psychopathology, 20*, 845–859; Lewis-Morrarty, E., Dozier, M., Bernard, K., Terracciano, S. M., & Moore, S. V. (2012). Cognitive flexibility and theory of mind outcomes among foster children: Preschool follow-up results of a randomized clinical trial. *Journal of Adolescent Health, 51*, S17–S22.

42. Mary Dozier, personal communication, June 16, 2015.

43. Cicchetti, D., Rogosch, F. A., Toth, S. L., & Sturge-Apple, M. L. (2011). Normalizing the development of cortisol regulation in maltreated infants through preventive interventions. *Development and Psychopathology, 23*, 789–800; Fisher, P. A., Gunnar, M. R., Dozier, M., Bruce, J., & Pears, K. C. (2006). Effects of therapeutic interventions for foster children on behavioral problems, caregiver attachment, and stress regulatory neural systems. *Annals of the New York Academy of Sciences, 1094*, 215–225; Fisher, P. A., Stoolmiller, M., Gunnar, M. R., & Burraston, B. O. (2007). Effects of a therapeutic intervention for foster preschoolers on diurnal cortisol activity. *Psychoneuroendocrinology, 32*, 892–905; Fisher, P. A., Van Ryzin, M. J., & Gunnar, M. R. (2011). Mitigating HPA axis dysregulation associated with placement changes in foster care. *Psychoneuroendocrinology, 36*, 531–539.

44. Juffer, F., Bakermans-Kranenburg, M. J., & IJzendoorn, M. H. (2005). The importance of parenting in the development of disorganized attachment: Evidence from a preventive intervention study in adoptive families. *Journal of Child Psychology and Psychiatry, 46*, 263–274; see also Bakermans-Kranenburg, M. J., Van Ijzendoorn, M. H., & Juffer, F. (2003). Less is more: Meta-analyses of sensitivity and attachment interventions in early childhood. *Psychological Bulletin, 129*, 195–215; Juffer, F., Bakermans-Kranenburg, M. J., & van IJzendoorn, M. H. (2008). *Promoting positive parenting: An attachment-based intervention.* Mahwah, NJ: Lawrence Erlbaum. For another intervention approach focused on attachment, see also Colonnesi, C., et al. (2012). Basic trust: An attachment-oriented intervention based on mind-mindedness in adoptive families. *Research on Social Work Practice, 23*, 179–188.

45. For review, see Dozier, M., Albus, K., Fisher, P. A., & Sepulveda, S. (2002). Interventions for foster parents: Implications for developmental theory. *Development and Psychopathology, 14,* 843–860.

46. Vandivere, S., Malm, K., & Radel, L. (2009). *Adoption USA: A chartbook based on the 2007 National Survey of Adoptive Parents.* Washington, DC: U.S. Department of Health and Human Services.

47. For more on the training of "adoption-competent" mental health professionals, see Brodzinsky, D. M. (2013). *A need to know: Enhancing adoption competence among mental health professionals.* New York: Donaldson Adoption Institute.

48. For example, see Federici, R. S. (2003). *Help for the hopeless child: A guide for families.* Alexandria, VA: Dr. Ronald S. Federici and Associates; see also Barth, R. P., & Miller, J. M. (2000). Building effective post-adoption services: What is the empirical foundation? *Family Relations, 49,* 447–455; Welsh, J. A., Viana, A. G., Petrill, S. A., & Mathias, M. D. (2007). Interventions for internationally adopted children and families: A review of the literature. *Child and Adolescent Social Work Journal, 24,* 285–311; Brodzinsky, D. M. (2013). *A need to know: Enhancing adoption competence among mental health professionals.* New York: Donaldson Adoption Institute.

49. Purvis, K. B., Cross, D. R., & Pennings, J. S. (2009). Trust-Based Relational Intervention™: Interactive principles for adopted children with special social-emotional needs. *Journal of Humanistic Counseling, Education and Development, 48,* 3–22; Purvis, K. B., Cross, D. R., Dansereau, D. F., & Parris, S. R. (2013). Trust-based relational intervention (TBRI): A systemic approach to complex developmental trauma. *Child & Youth Services, 34,* 360–386.

50. Purvis, K. B., Cross, D. R., Federici, R., Johnson, D., & McKenzie, L. B. (2007). The Hope Connection: A therapeutic summer day camp for adopted and at-risk children with special socioemotional needs. *Adoption & Fostering, 31,* 38–48; see also Purvis, K. B., McKenzie, L. B., Cross, D. R., & Razuri, E. B. (2013). A spontaneous emergence of attachment behavior in at-risk children and a correlation with sensory deficits. *Journal of Child and Adolescent Psychiatric Nursing, 26,* 165–172.

51. Purvis, K. B., & Cross, D. R. (2007). Improvements in salivary cortisol, depression, and representations of family relationships in at-risk adopted children utilizing a short-term therapeutic intervention. *Adoption Quarterly, 10,* 25–43.

52. McKenzie, L. B., Purvis, K. B., & Cross, D. R. (2014). A trust-based home intervention for special-needs adopted children: A case study. *Journal of Aggression, Maltreatment & Trauma,*

23, 633–651; Purvis, K. B., McKenzie, L. B., Razuri, E. B., Cross, D. R., & Buckwalter, K. (2014). A trust-based intervention for complex developmental trauma: A case study from a residential treatment center. *Child and Adolescent Social Work Journal*, 31, 355–368.

53. For diversity of viewpoints, see Barth, R. P., Crea, T. M., John, K., Thoburn, J., & Quinton, D. (2005). Beyond attachment theory and therapy: Towards sensitive and evidence-based interventions with foster and adoptive families in distress. *Child & Family Social Work*, 10, 257–268; DeJong, M. (2010). Some reflections on the use of psychiatric diagnosis in the looked after or "in care" child population. *Clinical Child Psychology and Psychiatry*, 15, 589–599; Gleason, M. M., et al. (2011). Validity of evidence-derived criteria for reactive attachment disorder: Indiscriminately social/disinhibited and emotionally withdrawn/inhibited types. *Journal of the American Academy of Child & Adolescent Psychiatry*, 50, 216–231; Glowinski, A. L. (2011). Reactive attachment disorder: An evolving entity. *Journal of the American Academy of Child & Adolescent Psychiatry*, 50, 210–212; O'Connor, T. G., & Zeanah, C. H. (2003). Attachment disorders: Assessment strategies and treatment approaches. *Attachment & Human Development*, 5, 223–244; O'Connor, T. G., Spagnola, M., & Byrne, J. G. (2012). Reactive attachment disorder and severe attachment disturbances. In M. Hersen & P. Sturmey (Eds.), *Handbook of evidence-based practice in clinical psychology, Vol 1: Child and adolescent disorders*. Hoboken, NJ: Wiley; Rutter, M., Kreppner, J., & Sonuga-Barke, E. (2009). Emanuel Miller Lecture: Attachment insecurity, disinhibited attachment, and attachment disorders: Where do research findings leave the concepts? *Journal of Child Psychology and Psychiatry*, 50, 529–543.

54. Barth, R. P., Crea, T. M., John, K., Thoburn, J., & Quinton, D. (2005). Beyond attachment theory and therapy: Towards sensitive and evidence-based interventions with foster and adoptive families in distress. *Child & Family Social Work*, 10, 257–268; DeJong, M. (2010). Some reflections on the use of psychiatric diagnosis in the looked after or "in care" child population. *Clinical Child Psychology and Psychiatry*, 15, 589–599.

55. O'Connor, T. G., Spagnola, M., & Byrne, J. G. (2012). Reactive attachment disorder and severe attachment disturbances. In M. Hersen & P. Sturmey (Eds.), *Handbook of evidence-based practice in clinical psychology, Vol. 1: Child and adolescent disorders*. Hoboken, NJ: Wiley.

56. For critiques of holding therapy, see Boris, N. W. (2003). Attachment, aggression and holding: A cautionary tale. *Attachment & Human Development*, 5, 245–247; Dozier, M. (2003). Attachment-

based treatment for vulnerable children. *Attachment & Human Development*, *5*, 253–257; Mercer, J. (2002). Attachment therapy: A treatment without empirical support. *Scientific Review of Mental Health Practice*, *1*, 105–112; Mercer, J. (2001). Attachment therapy using deliberate restraint: An object lesson on the identification of unvalidated treatments. *Journal of Child and Adolescent Psychiatric Nursing*, *14*, 105–114; O'Connor, T. G., & Zeanah, C. H. (2003). Attachment disorders: Assessment strategies and treatment approaches. *Attachment & Human Development*, *5*, 223–244.

57. For book-length treatment of the Candace Newmaker case in the context of "attachment therapy," see Mercer, J., Sarner, L., & Rosa, L. (2003). *Attachment therapy on trial: The torture and death of Candace Newmaker*. Westport, CT: Praeger.

58. Some evidence suggests increasing use of services as children get older. See Wind, L. H., Brooks, D., & Barth, R. P. (2007). Influences of risk history and adoption preparation on post-adoption services use in US adoptions. *Family Relations*, *56*, 378–389.

59. Tan, T. X., & Marn, T. (2013). Mental health service utilization in children adopted from US foster care, US private agencies and foreign countries: Data from the 2007 National Survey of Adoption Parents (NSAP). *Children and Youth Services Review*, *35*, 1050–1054; see also Hartinger-Saunders, R. M., Trouteaud, A., & Matos-Johnson, J. (2014). Post adoption service need and use as predictors of adoption dissolution: Findings from the 2012 National Adoptive Families Study. *Adoption Quarterly*, DOI:10.1080/10926755.2014.895469; Reilly, T., & Platz, L. (2004). Post-adoption service needs of families with special needs children: Use, helpfulness, and unmet needs. *Journal of Social Service Research*, *30*, 51–67.

60. Hartinger-Saunders, R. M., Trouteaud, A., & Matos-Johnson, J. (2014). Post adoption service need and use as predictors of adoption dissolution: Findings from the 2012 National Adoptive Families Study. *Adoption Quarterly*, DOI:10.1080/10926755.2014.895469.

61. Pinderhughes, E., Matthews, J., Deoudes, G., & Pertman, A. (2013). *A changing world: Shaping best practices through understanding of the new realities of international adoption*. New York: Donaldson Adoption Institute.

62. Vandivere, S., Malm, K., & Radel, L. (2009). *Adoption USA: A chartbook based on the 2007 National Survey of Adoptive Parents*. Washington, DC: U.S. Department of Health and Human Services.

63. Vandivere, S., Malm, K., & Radel, L. (2009). *Adoption USA: A chartbook based on the 2007 National Survey of Adoptive Parents*.

Washington, DC: U.S. Department of Health and Human Services.

64. Hawk, B. N., & McCall, R. B. (2011). Specific extreme behaviors of postinstitutionalized Russian adoptees. *Developmental Psychology, 47*, 732–738.

CHAPTER 8

1. Groark, C. J., & Mccall, R. B. (2011). Implementing changes in institutions to improve young children's development. *Infant Mental Health Journal, 32*, 509–525; McCall, R. B. (2013). The consequences of early institutionalization: Can institutions be improved? Should they? *Child and Adolescent Mental Health, 18*, 193–201. See also work in China by the non-profit Half the Sky, detailed in Bowen, J. (2014). *Wish you happy forever: What China's orphans taught me about moving mountains*. New York: Harper Collins.

2. Nelson, C., Fox, N., & Zeanah, C. (2014). *Romania's abandoned children: Deprivation, brain development, and the struggle for recovery*. Cambridge, MA: Harvard University Press.

3. See, for example, Tan, T. X. (2005). Child adjustment of single-parent adoption from China: A comparative study. *Adoption Quarterly, 8*, 1–20; see also Tan, T. X., & Baggerly, J. (2009). Behavioral adjustment of adopted Chinese girls in single-mother, lesbian-couple, and heterosexual-couple households. *Adoption Quarterly, 12*, 171–186; Anderssen, N., Amlie, C., & Ytterøy, E. A. (2002). Outcomes for children with lesbian or gay parents. A review of studies from 1978 to 2000. *Scandinavian Journal of Psychology, 43*, 335–351; Biblarz, T. J., & Stacey, J. (2010). How does the gender of parents matter? *Journal of Marriage and Family, 72*, 3–22; Patterson, C. J. (2006). Children of lesbian and gay parents. *Current Directions in Psychological Science, 15*, 241–244.

4. Walton, J. (2012). Supporting the interests of intercountry adoptees beyond childhood: Access to adoption information and identity. *Social Policy and Society, 11*, 443–454. See also Brodzinsky, D. M. (2011). Children's understanding of adoption: Developmental and clinical implications. *Professional Psychology: Research and Practice, 42*, 200–207; Evan B. Donaldson Institute. (2009). *Beyond culture camp: Promoting healthy identity formation in adoption*. New York: Author.

5. Wall, S. (2012). Ethics and the socio-political context of international adoption: Speaking from the eye of the storm. *Ethics and Social Welfare, 6*, 318–332.

6. One of the only studies to date comparing outcomes between currently institutionalized and internationally adopted children

from the same country of origin is Lee, R. M., Seol, K. O., Sung, M., & Miller, M. J. (2010). The behavioral development of Korean children in institutional care and international adoptive families. *Developmental Psychology, 46,* 468–478.

7. Carter, R. (2005). *Family matters: A study of institutional childcare in Central and Eastern Europe and the former Soviet Union.* London: EveryChild; Rudnicki, A. A. (2012). The development of Russia's child protection and welfare system. *Demokratizatsiya: Journal of Post-Soviet Democratization, 20,* 29–46; Tobis, D. (2000). *Moving from residential institutions to community-based social services in Central and Eastern Europe and the former Soviet Union.* Washington, DC: World Bank. See also Astoiants, M. S. (2007). Orphaned children: An analysis of life and practices in a residential institution. *Russian Education & Society, 49,* 23–42; Stein, M., & Verweijen-Slamnescu, R. (2012). *When care ends: Lessons from peer research. Insights from young people on leaving care in Albania, the Czech Republic, Finland and Poland.* SOS Children's Villages International; Stepanova, E., & Hackett, S. (2014). Understanding care leavers in Russia: Young people's experiences of institutionalisation. *Australian Social Work, 67,* 118–134. For more systematic studies of those who age out of care in Western countries, see Stein, M. (2006). Young people aging out of care: The poverty of theory. *Children and Youth Services Review, 28,* 422–434; Stein, M. (2006). Research review: Young people leaving care. *Child & Family Social Work, 11,* 273–279; Richter, D., & Lemola, S. (2014). Institutional rearing is associated with lower general life satisfaction in adulthood. *Journal of Research in Personality, 48,* 93–97.

8. Tengrinews. (2013, June 24). *Most of children raised in Kazakhstan orphanages turn to prostitution or crime.* Retrieved from http://m.tengrinews.kz/en/people/Most-of-children-raised-in-Kazakhstan-orphanages-turn-to-prostitution-or-crime-20299.

9. See, for example, Save the Children (2012). *International adoption: Policy brief, June 2012;* EveryChild (2012). *Adopting better care: Improving adoption services around the world.* London: EveryChild.

10. Herszenhorn, D., & Eckholm, E. (2012, December 28). Russia's plan to bar adoptions upends families. *New York Times,* A1.

11. High, A. J. (2014). Pondering the politicization of intercountry adoption: Russia's ban on American "forever families." *Cardozo Journal of International and Comparative Law, 22,* 497–737; Youde, J. (2014). Shame, ontological insecurity and intercountry adoption. *Cambridge Review of International Affairs, 27,* 424–441.

12. See, for example, Briggs, L. (2012). *Somebody's children.* Durham, NC: Duke University Press.

13. Dubinsky, K. (2010). *Babies without borders: Adoption and migration across the Americas*. New York: New York University Press.

14. Groza, V., & Bunkers, K. M. (2014). Adoption policy and evidence-based domestic adoption practice: A comparison of Romania, Ukraine, India, Guatemala, and Ethiopia. *Infant Mental Health Journal, 35*, 160–171.

15. Groza, V., & Bunkers, K. M. (2014). Adoption policy and evidence-based domestic adoption practice: A comparison of Romania, Ukraine, India, Guatemala, and Ethiopia. *Infant Mental Health Journal, 35*, 160–171, p. 163. For other studies of domestic adoption and child welfare within Romania, see also Bejenaru, A., & Roth, M. (2012). Romanian adoptive families: Stressors, coping strategies and resources. *Children and Youth Services Review, 34*, 1317–1324; Groza, V., Muntean, A., & Ungureanu, R. (2012). The adoptive family within the Romanian cultural context: An exploratory study. *Adoption Quarterly, 15*, 1–17; Leon, J. (2011). The shift towards family reunification in Romanian child welfare policy: An analysis of changing forms of governmental intervention in Romania. *Children & Society, 25*, 228–238; Nedelcu, C., & Groza, V. (2012). Child welfare in Romania: Contexts and processes. In J. L. Gibbons & K. S. Rotabi (Eds.), *Intercountry adoption: Policies, practices, and outcomes*. Surrey, UK: Ashgate.

16. Groza, V., & Bunkers, K. M. (2014). Adoption policy and evidence-based domestic adoption practice: A comparison of Romania, Ukraine, India, Guatemala, and Ethiopia. *Infant Mental Health Journal, 35*, 160–171; see also Mohanty, J., Ahn, J., & Chokkanathan, S. (2014). Adoption disclosure: Experiences of Indian domestic adoptive parents. *Child & Family Social Work*, doi:10.1111/cfs.12175.

17. Evans, S. (2015, January 6). Taking on South Korea's adoption taboo. *BBC News*. Retrieved from http://www.bbc.com/news/world-asia-30692127.

18. Brown, S., & Groza, V. (2012). A comparison of adoptive parents' perceptions of their child's behavior among Indian children adopted to Norway, the United States, and within country: Implications for adoption policy. *Child Welfare, 92*, 119–143.

19. Human Rights Watch. (2014). *Abandoned by the state: Violence, neglect, and isolation for children with disabilities in Russian orphanages*. New York: Author.

20. Human Rights Watch (2014). *Abandoned by the state: Violence, neglect, and isolation for children with disabilities in Russian orphanages*. New York: Author.

21. Groza, V., & Bunkers, K. M. (2014). Adoption policy and evidence-based domestic adoption practice: A comparison of

Romania, Ukraine, India, Guatemala, and Ethiopia. *Infant Mental Health Journal, 35,* 160–171.

22. Nelson, C., Fox, N., & Zeanah, C. (2014). *Romania's abandoned children: Deprivation, brain development, and the struggle for recovery.* Cambridge, MA: Harvard University Press; Julian, M. M., & McCall, R. B. (2011). The development of children within alternative residential care environments. *International Journal of Child and Family Welfare, 14,* 119–147; Miller, L., Chan, W., Comfort, K., & Tirella, L. (2005). Health of children adopted from Guatemala: Comparison of orphanage and foster care. *Pediatrics, 115,* e710–e717.

23. Vinnerljung, B., & Hjern, A. (2011). Cognitive, educational and self-support outcomes of long-term foster care versus adoption. A Swedish national cohort study. *Children and Youth Services Review, 33,* 1902–1910; Lloyd, E. C., & Barth, R. P. (2011). Developmental outcomes after five years for foster children returned home, remaining in care, or adopted. *Children and Youth Services Review, 33,* 1383–1391. For evidence that adoption disruption is correlated with length of time in pre-adoptive foster care and number of moves within a foster care system, see Wijedasa, D., & Selwyn, J. (2014). *Beyond the adoption order: An investigation of adoption disruption in Wales.* Hadley Centre for Adoption and Foster Care Studies School for Policy Studies, University of Bristol.

24. See the numerous books about the broken child welfare system in the United States, such as Beam, C. (2013). *To the end of June: The intimate life of American foster care.* Boston: Houghton Mifflin Harcourt; Berrick, J. D. (2009). *Take me home: Protecting America's vulnerable children and families.* New York: Oxford University Press; Shirk, M., & Stangler, G. (2004). *On their own: What happens to kids when they age out of the foster care system?* Boulder, CO: Westview Press.

25. There is little empirical evidence on outcomes among children raised in small-group residential-care settings. For somewhat equivocal findings comparing outcomes for children in SOS villages versus orphanage care, see Lassi, Z. S., Mahmud, S., Syed, E. U., & Janjua, N. Z. (2011). Behavioral problems among children living in orphanage facilities of Karachi, Pakistan: Comparison of children in an SOS Village with those in conventional orphanages. *Social Psychiatry and Psychiatric Epidemiology, 46,* 787–796. Other sources, such as reports from the SOS organization, provide descriptive findings of SOS populations but do not directly compare them to other care alternatives; see, for example, Lill-Rastem, B., & Babic, B. (2010). *Tracking footprints: Global report 2010.* SOS Children's Villages International; Exenberger,

S., & Moremi, M. (2012). *Families first—Research final report*. SOS Children's Villages International.

26. See, for example, Graff, E. J. (2008). The lie we love. *Foreign Policy, 169*, 58–66.

27. Smolin, D. M. (2004). Intercountry adoption as child trafficking. *Valparaiso Law Review, 39*, 281–325; Smolin, D. M. (2006). Child laundering: How the intercountry adoption system legitimizes and incentivizes the practices of buying, trafficking, kidnaping, and stealing children. *Wayne Law Review, 52*, 113–200; Williams, P. (December 20, 2010). Save the children? Adoption has become a form of trafficking in and of itself. *The Nation*.

28. See, for example, Article 4c of the Hague Convention on Protection of Children and Co-operation in Respect of Intercountry Adoption, which requires that "consents [for adoption, by birth parents or relevant authorities] have not been induced by payment or compensation of any kind." It is, of course, much simpler to state such a general principle than to detail standards for ensuring its implementation in practice. See also Hague Conference on Private International Law. (2008). *The implementation and operation of the 1993 Hague Intercountry Adoption Convention: Guide to good practice*, pp. 32–37.

29. Dempsey, K. T. (2014). *Paper chains: Report on U.S. government actions and the impact of these actions on Nepal's abandoned children, 2010–present*. Both Ends Burning. Retrieved from https://bothendsburning.org/wp-content/uploads/2014/06/Paper-Chains-Full-Report.pdf.

30. See, for example, Gingerich, D. W. (2013). *Political institutions and party-directed corruption in South America: Stealing for the team*. Cambridge, UK: Cambridge University Press; Johnston, M. (2013). *Corruption, contention and reform: The power of deep democratization*. Cambridge, UK: Cambridge University Press; Klitgaard, R. (1988). *Controlling corruption*. Berkeley: University of California Press; McMann, K. M. (2014). *Corruption as a last resort: Adapting to the market in Central Asia*. Ithaca, NY: Cornell University Press.

31. Oka, N. (2013). Everyday corruption in Kazakhstan: An ethnographic analysis of informal practices. In *Exploring informal networks in Kazakhstan: A multidimensional approach*. Institute of Developing Economies–Japan External Trade Organization; Werner, C. (2000). Gifts, bribes, and development in post-Soviet Kazakstan. *Human Organization, 59*(1), 11–22.

32. For discussion of corruption in Kazakhstani domestic adoption, see Kamalova, G. (n.d.). $1.5 million database for orphans and potential parents: Dealing with orphanage corruption. *Tengri News*. Retrieved from http://en.tengrinews.kz/people/

15-million-database-for-orphans-and-potential-parents-259079/. For corruption in Chinese domestic adoption, see Tatlow, D. K. (2014, February 28). Crackdown on baby trafficking zeroes in on websites. *New York Times*.

33. Engle, P. L., Groza, V. K., Groark, C. J., Greenberg, A., Bunkers, K. M., & Muhamedrahimov, R. J. (2011). VIII. The situation for children without parental care and strategies for policy change. *Monographs of the Society for Research in Child Development, 76,* 190–222; Tobis, D. (2000). *Moving from residential institutions to community-based social services in Central and Eastern Europe and the former Soviet Union.* Washington, DC: World Bank; Whewell, T. (2013, April 2). Russia: Are efforts to help thousands of 'abandoned' children being resisted? *BBC News.*

34. Graff, E. J. (2008). The lie we love. *Foreign Policy, 169,* 58–66.

35. Graff, E. J. (2008). The lie we love. *Foreign Policy, 169,* 58–66.

36. Graff, E. J. (2008). The lie we love. *Foreign Policy, 169,* 58–66; Graff, E. J. (2009, January 11). The adoption underworld. *Washington Post,* B2; Oreskovic, J., & Maskew, T. (2008). Red thread or slender reed: Deconstructing Prof. Bartholet's mythology of international adoption. *Buffalo Human Rights Law Review, 14,* 71–128.

37. Graff, E. J. (2008). The lie we love. *Foreign Policy, 169,* 58–66; Siegal, E. (2011). *Finding Fernanda: Two mothers, one child, and a cross-border search for the truth.* Oakland: Cathexis Press, pp. 86–88; Rotabi, K. S. (2012). Fraud in intercountry adoption: Child sales and abduction in Vietnam, Cambodia, and Guatemala. In J. L. Gibbons & K. S. Rotabi (Eds.), *Intercountry adoption: Policies, practices, and outcomes.* Surrey, UK: Ashgate.

38. Bartholet, E., & Smolin, D. (2012). The debate. In J. L. Gibbons & K. S. Rotabi (Eds.), *Intercountry adoption: Policies, practices, and outcomes.* Surrey, UK: Ashgate; Oreskovic, J., & Maskew, T. (2008). Red thread or slender reed: Deconstructing Prof. Bartholet's mythology of international adoption. *Buffalo Human Rights Law Review, 14,* 71–128.

39. Chou, S., & Browne, K. (2008). The relationship between institutional care and the international adoption of children in Europe. *Adoption & Fostering, 32,* 40–48. For critique, see Gay y Blasco, P., Macrae, S., Selman, P., & Wardle, H. (2008). 'The relationship between institutional care and the international adoption of children in Europe': A rejoinder to Chou and Browne (2008). *Adoption & Fostering, 32,* 63–67; Sacco, K. C., & Sacco, P. (2008). Institutional care and international adoption: Letter to the editor. *Adoption & Fostering, 32,* 68–69.

40. Chou, S., & Browne, K. (2008). The relationship between institutional care and the international adoption of children in Europe. *Adoption & Fostering, 32,* 40–48, p. 40

41. Bartholet, E., & Smolin, D. (2012). The debate. In J. L. Gibbons & K. S. Rotabi (Eds.), *Intercountry adoption: Policies, practices, and outcomes*. Surrey, UK: Ashgate, p. 243. Elsewhere Smolin has echoed similar sentiments, for example, saying about adoptive families that "There is no fool like the one who wants to be fooled." Graff, E. J. (2008). The lie we love. *Foreign Policy, 169,* 58–66, p. 66

42. Transparency International. (2013). *Corruption Perceptions Index 2013.* Retrived from https://www.transparency.org/cpi2013/results

43. See, for example, United Nations Office on Drugs and Crime. (n.d.). *Human trafficking.* Retrieved from http://www.unodc.org/unodc/en/human-trafficking/what-is-human-trafficking.html; U.S. Department of Homeland Security. (n.d.). *Definition of human trafficking.* Retrieved from https://www.dhs.gov/definition-human-trafficking.

44. See Tverdova, Y.V. (2011). Human trafficking in Russia and other post-Soviet states. *Human Rights Review, 12,* 329–344; Orlova, A. V. (2004). From social dislocation to human trafficking: The Russian case. *Problems of Post-Communism, 51,* 14–22; McKinney, J. R. (2009). Russian babies, Russian babes: Economic and demographic implications of international adoption and international trafficking for Russia. *Demokratizatsiya: Journal of Post-Soviet Democratization, 17,* 19–40.

45. See, for example, Briggs, L. (2012). *Somebody's children.* Durham, NC: Duke University Press; Riggs, D. W. (2012). Intercountry adoption and the inappropriate/d other: Refusing the disappearance of birth families. *Social Policy and Society, 11,* 455–464.

46. Xinran. (2011). *Messages from an unknown Chinese mother: Stories of loss and love.* New York: Random House.

47. Johnson, K. (2012). Challenging the discourse of intercountry adoption: Perspectives from rural China. In J. L. Gibbons & K. S. Rotabi (Eds.), *Intercountry adoption: Policies, practices, and outcomes.* Surrey, UK: Ashgate.

48. Siegal, E. (2011). *Finding Fernanda: Two mothers, one child, and a cross-border search for the truth.* Oakland: Cathexis Press, pp. 86–88.

49. Agence France-Presse (2013, February 28). Russian orphan's tragedy starts with poverty and alcohol. *Global Post;* Herszenhorn, D. (2013, February 22). Russians demand return of brother of adopted boy who died in Texas. *New York Times;* Vasilyeva, N. (2013, February 22). Max Shatto dead: U.S. Ambassador speaks out against "exploitations" of adopted Russian boy's death. *Associated Press/The World Post.*

50. See, for example, Kelly, R. (2009). Emerging voices—reflections on adoption from the birth mother's perspective. In G. M. Wrobel &

E. Neil (Eds.), *International advances in adoption research for practice*. West Sussex: Wiley; Neil, E. (2007). Coming to terms with the loss of a child: The feelings of birth parents and grandparents about adoption and post-adoption contact. *Adoption Quarterly, 10,* 1–23; Smeeton, J., & Boxall, K. (2011). Birth parents' perceptions of professional practice in child care and adoption proceedings: Implications for practice. *Child & Family Social Work, 16,* 444–453; Wiley, M. O. L., & Baden, A. L. (2005). Birth parents in adoption research, practice, and counseling psychology. *Counseling Psychologist, 33,* 13–50.

51. Grotevant, H. D., McRoy, R. G., Wrobel, G. M., & Ayers-Lopez, S. (2013). Contact between adoptive and birth families: Perspectives from the Minnesota/Texas Adoption Research Project. *Child Development Perspectives, 7,* 193–198; see also Henney, S. M., Ayers-Lopez, S., McRoy, R. G., & Grotevant, H. D. (2007). Evolution and resolution: Birthmothers' experience of grief and loss at different levels of adoption openness. *Journal of Social and Personal Relationships, 24,* 875–889; Ge, X., Natsuaki, M. N., Martin, D. M., Leve, L. D., Neiderhiser, J. M., Shaw, D. S., et al. (2008). Bridging the divide: Openness in adoption and postadoption psychosocial adjustment among birth and adoptive parents. *Journal of Family Psychology, 22,* 529–540.

52. Neil, E. (2013). The mental distress of the birth relatives of adopted children: 'disease'or 'unease'? Findings from a UK study. *Health & Social Care in the Community, 21,* 191–199.

53. Clapton, G. (2007). The experiences and needs of birth fathers in adoption: What we know now and some practice implications. *Practice, 19,* 61–71; Ge, X., Natsuaki, M. N., Martin, D. M., Leve, L. D., Neiderhiser, J. M., Shaw, D. S., et al. (2008). Bridging the divide: Openness in adoption and postadoption psychosocial adjustment among birth and adoptive parents. *Journal of Family Psychology, 22,* 529–540.

54. See, for example, Smolin, D. M. (2007). Intercountry adoption and poverty: A human rights analysis. *Capital University Law Review, 36,* 413–453; see critique in Dwyer, J. G. (2014). Intercountry adoption and the special rights fallacy. *University of Pennsylvania Journal of International Law, 35,* 189–267. For a nuanced review of the challenges of deinstitutionalization in the former Soviet sphere, see Ismayilova, L., Ssewamala, F., & Huseynli, A. (2014). Reforming child institutional care in the Post-Soviet bloc: The potential role of family-based empowerment strategies. *Children and Youth Services Review, 47,* 136–148.

55. Julian, M. M., & McCall, R. B. (2011). The development of children within alternative residential care environments. *International Journal of Child and Family Welfare, 14,* 119–147; see also

McCall, R. B., Groark, C. J., Fish, L., Muhamedrahimov, R. J., Palmov, O. I., & Nikiforova, N. V. (2014). Characteristics of children transitioned to intercountry adoption, domestic adoption, foster care, and biological families from institutions in St. Petersburg, Russian Federation. *International Social Work*, doi: 10.1177/0020872814531302.

INDEX ■

foster care (*Cont.*)
  preference for, 153
  race and culture, 60, 203*n*26
  research, 151, 155–57
  responsive parenting, 139–40, 145
  reunification with birth
    families, 157
  sexual orientation, 118
  temporary, 14
  United States, 109–11, 139–40,
    145, 218*n*59

Guatemala, 10, 15, 153, 154

Hague Convention, 58, 127, 135, 157,
    168*n*10, 168*n*6, 172*n*40, 185*n*5,
    192*n*60, 210*n*7–8, 223*n*28
holding therapy, 143–44, 217*n*56
hormones, 23–24
  biology of parenting, 95–100
  cognitive development, 23–24
  cortisol and stress response, 47–49
  estrogen, 96, 97
  oxytocin, 97–100
  progesterone, 96, 97
Human Rights Watch, 131–32, 155–56,
    211*n*17, 211*n*20–21, 211–12*n*23,
    212*n*24, 221*n*19–20

identity
  nationality and culture, 57–59
  race and culture, 60–63
  search for birth families, 75–80
India, 154, 155, 189*n*45, 194*n*80,
    212*n*24, 221*n*14–16,
    221*n*18, 222*n*21
Indian Child Welfare Act, 60
indiscriminate friendliness, 42–43,
    179*n*11, 179*n*14–15
industry, adoption as, 160–62
institutionalization
  behavior control of institutional-
    ized children, 32–33
  causing international
    adoption, 161–63
  children in former Soviet
    Union, 13
  executive functions, 33–34
internats (state-run institutions), 131
IQ (intelligence quotient)

adopted and nonadopted children,
    174*n*14, 174*n*19
cognitive outcome, 26–29, 34, 66

Kazakhstan, 13
  adoption, 5–7
  adoption procedures, 38–39
  age of eligibility for adoption, 37
  baby house, 21
  corruption, 163
  direct experience in, 16–17, 37–39,
    85–87, 101, 166
  domestic adoptions, 79–80
  government funding of
    orphanages, 127
  Ministry of Education, 85, 86
  opposition to foreign adoption, 153
  separations, 37–38
  "travel-blind" country, 125
Kazakhstan Academy of Nutrition, 23
kidnapping, 15, 158, 161, 164, 185*n*6
Korean adoptees
  disabled child, 132
  ethnic identification, 66,
    68–69, 70–74
  foster rearing, 35
Kyrgyzstan, 4–5, 5

language
  acquisition, 29–31, 34, 136
  adoption agencies, 101
  barriers, 76
  birth culture, 75
  English as a second, 62
  human rights conventions, 58
  international adoption, 29–31, 34,
    175*n*25–28, 176*n*29–32, 177*n*41
  Kazakh, 166
  medical terminology, 127
  positive benefits of adoption, 11
Latin Americans, ethnic
  identity, 69–70

maltreatment
  child welfare system, 138
  infants, 215*n*43
  resilience, 184*n*54
  risk for adoptees, 81, 115, 201*n*8
media reports
  adoption, 103–7

CPSIA information can be obtained
at www.ICGtesting.com
Printed in the USA
BVHW04s1207170518
515959BV00003B/12/P